"What the soul is to the body,
Christians are to the world."

Letter to Diognetus, 6.1

GEORGE WEIGEL is the president of the Ethics and Public Policy Center, Washington, D.C. He is the author of nine other books, including *Idealism Without Illusions: U.S. Foreign Policy in the 1990s* (1994), *The Final Revolution: The Resistance Church and the Collapse of Communism* (1992), and *Catholicism and the Renewal of American Democracy* (1989). In addition to contributing essays and reviews to scholarly and opinion journals, he frequently appears on the op-ed pages of leading newspapers and writes a nationally syndicated weekly column for the Catholic press. His work has been translated into several languages, including Spanish, Italian, and Polish.

SOUL OF THE WORLD

Notes on the Future of Public Catholicism

GEORGE WEIGEL

ETHICS AND PUBLIC POLICY CENTER
WASHINGTON, D.C.

WILLIAM B. EERDMANS PUBLISHING COMPANY
GRAND RAPIDS, MICHIGAN

Gracewing.

Copyright © 1996 by the Ethics and Public Policy Center
1015 Fifteenth St. N.W., Washington, D.C. 20005

Published jointly 1996 in the United States by
the Ethics and Public Policy Center and
Wm. B. Eerdmans Publishing Co.
255 Jefferson Ave. S.E., Grand Rapids, Michigan 49503
and in the U.K. by Gracewing
2 Southern Avenue, Leominster HR6 0QF

Printed in the United States of America

01 00 99 98 97 96   7 6 5 4 3 2 1

Library of Congress Cataloging-in-Publication Data

Weigel, George.
Soul of the world: notes on the future of public Catholicism/
George Weigel.
p.   cm.
Includes bibliographical references and index.
ISBN 0-8028-4207-0 (pbk.)
1. Sociology, Christian (Catholic) 2. Christianity and politics —
Catholic Church. 3. Church and state — Catholic Church.
4. Catholic Church — Doctrines. 5. Sociology, Christian (Catholic) —
Forecasting. 6. Christianity and politics — Catholic Church — Forecasting.
7. Church and state — Catholic Church — Forecasting.
8. Catholic Church — Doctrines — Forecasting. 9. Catholic Church —
United States — History — 20th century. 10. Catholic Church —
United States — History — Forecasting. I. Title.
BX1753.W387   1996
261.8′08′822 — dc20   96-2483
                                             CIP

Gracewing ISBN 0 85244 376 5

For
James M. Harvey

Coraggio!

Contents

Acknowledgments

Many friends and colleagues helped to make this book possible.

Chapter One reflects themes developed in conversation with colleagues at the Institute on Religion and Democracy.

Carl Braaten, Robert Jenson, and the Center for Catholic and Evangelical Theology in Northfield, Minnesota, caused me to revisit *Diognetus* (and my ancestral roots in Lancaster County, Pennsylvania) and thus produce an earlier form of Chapter Two. I thank them for the invitation, and salute the ecumenical importance of their work.

Leon Kass and Nathan Tarcoff invited me to lecture at the University of Chicago, and the results were an earlier draft of Chapter Three. The hospitality of the university community, and particularly the members of the John M. Olin Center for Inquiry into the Theory and Practice of Democracy, was very much appreciated, as were the sharp and probing questions. When *cognoscenti* of the Chicago White Sox are so genial in the presence of a veteran Baltimore Orioles fan, we may know that there is hope for civil society in America yet.

Chapter Four grew out of a conference led by my colleague Michael Cromartie, head of the Ethics and Public Policy Center's Evangelical Studies Project. My thanks go to Mike, to his project's many generous supporters, and to the participants in the conference, especially Michael Farris, Richard Land, and Ralph Reed.

An earlier version of Chapter Five appeared in *The Weekly Standard;* I appreciate the invitation of William Kristol, Fred Barnes, and John Podhoretz to write about Pope John Paul II for their readers.

Chapter Six has gone through several redactions, in English and in Polish. I have taken the occasion of this book to re-re-revise and update an essay that first appeared in 1989, thanks to Brad Roberts of *The Washington Quarterly*. My students and faculty colleagues in the 1991-95 summer seminars in Liechtenstein and Poland on *"Centesimus Annus* and the Free Society" helped me refine the argument; here I should pay a special tribute to Rocco Buttiglione for his distinctive reading of the relation of *Centesimus Annus* to the history of Catholic social doctrine and church-state theory. The summer seminar has also given me the opportunity to deepen my long-standing friendship and collaboration with Richard John Neuhaus and Michael Novak, whose influence on my thinking will be obvious in what follows.

Chapter Seven similarly benefited from the summer *Centesimus Annus* seminars, as well as from the opportunity given me to deliver one of the Andrew R. Cecil Lectures on Moral Values in a Free Society at the University of Texas at Dallas in 1993. My thanks, then, to Dr. Cecil and his associate, Dr. W. Lawson Taitte, for making my visit to "Big D" so pleasant.

The argument of Chapter Eight was influenced by conversation with my colleagues in the Ramsey Colloquium and Dulles Colloquium, both of which are sponsored by the Institute on Religion and Public Life in New York. A finer group of theologians, and a merrier band of friends, one does not find it easy to imagine.

Center senior editor Carol Griffith, one of the last dedicated practitioners of a dying craft, did a superb job of editing. Ann Derstine prepared the manuscript with considerable skill.

The travel schedule hinted at above has put special demands on my family. So my fond thanks go to Joan, Gwyneth, Monica, and Stephen for their patience when I'm away, and their welcome when I return.

This book is dedicated to Monsignor James M. Harvey, a priest of the Archdiocese of Milwaukee now serving in the Secretariat of State of the Holy See. Our conversation and collaboration in recent years bear witness to the truth of Cicero's suggestion in the *De amicitia,* that friendships flourish "where men harmonize in their views of things human and divine."

GEORGE WEIGEL
Washington, D.C.
Thanksgiving 1995

PROLOGUE

Thoughts on Some Mid-Course Corrections

Much has changed during the nearly twenty years in which I have been writing about Catholicism and public life. The world is a dramatically different place. The social doctrine of the Church has evolved in ways that I could not have imagined when I began this work in the mid-1970s. And the Church's recent public witness, especially as exemplified by Pope John Paul II, has left a marked imprint on the lives of nations and peoples. These three dynamics of change—in world history, in Catholic social doctrine, and in the tenor of the Church's activism in the world—have decisively refuted the charge that Catholicism is a defender of privilege, the last authoritarian bastion of the *ancien régime*. More importantly, they have put Catholicism in a singular position to help make the twenty-first century a far more humane epoch than its bloody predecessor, now drawing to a close.

"How my mind has changed" is a topic frequently indulged in by writers, for whom introspection is an occupational disease. Such an examination of intellectual conscience is probably of more interest to the author than to his audience (with two possible exceptions: his critics, and other scribes in the galleries). But the genre occasionally helps to clarify, even correct, misunderstandings, and so I ask the reader's indulgence for the autobiographical musings that follow. They reflect four developments—all right, call them "changes"—in my thinking during the years I have been involved in public debate.

1

Lengthening the Horizon

When I wrote *Tranquillitas Ordinis: The Present Failure and Future Promise of American Catholic Thought on War and Peace* in the mid-1980s, I argued that the Church's "incarnational humanism" was the necessary antidote to the apocalyptic despair that marked (and marred) much of the nuclear-weapons debate during the last decade of the Cold War. By "incarnational humanism" I did not mean a naïve optimism about the human prospect; rather, I meant that Christian faith ought to inspire a calm and measured confidence that reason and courage, married in the prudence of wise statecraft, could meet the twin challenges posed by Communist totalitarianism and nuclear deterrence. That judgment has, I believe, been vindicated by the non-violent Revolution of 1989, in which commitments to the truth about the human person and his inalienable rights proved stronger than the politics of propaganda, lies, and coercion. Viewed from a Catholic perspective, the moral revolution that preceded and made possible the non-violent political revolutions of 1989 was a powerful example of incarnational humanism at work, challenging and ultimately defeating the false humanism of Marxism-Leninism.

And yet a decade after *Tranquillitas Ordinis* I find that the eschatological dimension of Christian faith is impressing itself far more assertively into my thinking and writing, tempering and in some instances redirecting my "incarnational" thinking about the public Church. This change surely has something to do with the impending Great Jubilee of 2000. That extraordinary anniversary ought to prompt Christians to take more seriously the ways in which the Incarnation of the Word of God has sanctified all of time and history. It should also remind us that God's redemptive purposes will be completed only when the Kingdom has come in its fullness, in the time beyond time when we have truly arrived at "the end of history."

What the Church most urgently needs to teach the world is that the world's fulfillment lies beyond history, and that the nature of that fulfillment has been disclosed in the resurrection of Jesus Christ, the "first-born among many brethren" (Rom. 8:29, RSV). That Gospel, that good news, puts all our worldly efforts under judgment, even as it invests them with their proper dignity. For the Risen Lord of history, having been incarnate in history, has given human striving, under grace, a new nobility, even as he has freed that striving from hubris by locating it within its proper, trans-historical horizon.

This heightened eschatological perspective has caused me to think that the Church has less of an agenda "for the world" than I might once have thought; but thinking within that horizon has also led me to conclude that the Church can distinctively, perhaps even uniquely, say to the world the things the world most needs to hear. The agenda is both narrower (at least as Washington understands "agendas") and deeper.

History Is Cruciform

A second change in my thinking, closely related to the first, has to do with the omnipresence of the Cross, the instrument of our re-demption, in all of Christian life—including the Church's public witness in and to the world. One prominent current in post–Vatican II Catholic theology has tended to underplay the Cross as the "form" of the Christian life; another current, usually found in the various theologies of liberation, has reduced the Cross to a political statement. Neither seems adequate to the fullness of Christian orthodoxy, nor to the exigencies of the world situation at the end of the twentieth century.

There is no moment in its history when the world does not have to be reminded of its need for redemption: and not "redemption" understood as self-fulfillment, but redemption effected through self-emptying love, *kenosis,* the utter abandonment of self to the will of the Father. A Christ without a cross may be an inspiring teacher or moral exemplar; but a Christ without a cross is no redeemer. Thus the Cross must be central in any Christian humanism.[1]

It is true that Christ died out of love, and that "love is the most living thing there is."[2] But the new life of love made possible by the Risen Lord necessarily passed through Calvary. And the confrontation with Calvary is no easy business. Here is Hans Urs von Balthasar, reflecting on the fifth sorrowful mystery of the rosary, the Crucifixion:

Every word is silenced before this last station, when God's living Word is nailed by men into deathly immobility. It is the Father's hour, when the eternal triune plan is executed to clear out all the refuse of the world's sin by burning it in the fire of suffering love. This fire has burned eternally in God as the blazing passion that is always intent on the eternal good, in which God's counsel has decided that the world should participate. This good is the resolute commitment of the divine Persons to one another, the triune radicalism which here reaches out to include the world.[3]

If the "triune radicalism" made manifest in Christ crucified is the "scandal" that the Church must preach to the world, then a cruciform Christology must have a decisive influence on the ways in which the Church thinks about the world of affairs. The Church that is born from the pierced side of its crucified Lord must mirror that origin in its address to "the world." Some would argue that this singular origin of the Church means that the Church has nothing to say to the world of affairs—"the world" conquered by the death and resurrection of Christ, "the world" that is passing away (I Cor. 13:10). I disagree, as the pages that follow will illustrate. But I am only too aware that I have just begun to work through some of the implications of a Cross-centered Catholic social ethic.

I owe whatever insight I may have gained into this central mystery of Christian faith to Balthasar; and while I would in no way suggest that I have become a specialist in his thought in recent years, the work of this great Swiss theologian has done much to change the ways in which I think about Christian discipleship in the world.

John Paul the Great

The teaching and pastoral initiative of Pope John Paul II are responsible, in the third place, for much of how my mind has changed —or, in this case, developed—over the past two decades.

The evolution of Catholic social doctrine referred to at the outset has been in essential continuity with the principal themes of Catholic social thought throughout the twentieth century—personalism, the common good, subsidiarity. And recent Catholic activism centered on the defense of basic human rights has been an application, in the world of affairs, of themes that entered the Catholic discussion decades ago. Yet how different, how astonishingly different, it has all been since October 16, 1978. The Pope who preached, "Be not afraid! Open the doors to Christ!" at his inauguration has given the social doctrine of the Church a distinctive new direction, even as he has made a public witness to human rights a leitmotif of the pastoral journeys that have taken him into almost every corner of the globe.

The pontificate of John Paul II bridges, of course, the Cold War and post–Cold War worlds (indeed, the pontificate of John Paul II is one of the reasons why we are living in a post–Cold War world). Prior to the Revolution of 1989, the social magisterium of John Paul placed great stress on religious freedom as the first of human rights and the foundation of any meaningful scheme of "rights." As a son of Poland who had worked on the Second Vatican Council's path-breaking Declaration on Religious Freedom in 1964-65, John Paul was passionately committed to religious freedom in its own right. But as time and events would show, the Pope had also intuited that religious freedom was the key to pluralism, that pluralism was the key to the reconstruction (or renovation) of civil society, and that civil society was the key to the replacement of authoritarian or totalitarian politics with democratic and participatory politics. The rest, as they say, is history.

In the 1990s (after the revolution, so to speak), John Paul has continued to focus his attention on the moral-cultural dimension of society, although he has not ignored the political and economic sectors. The Pope seems convinced that the free society will contribute to genuine human flourishing only if democracy and the market are disciplined by a vibrant public moral culture grounded in shared public convictions about moral truth. Thus John Paul has taken the social doctrine of the Church in what some might call a "postmodern" direction.

The Holy Father's emphasis on religious freedom has long had a pronounced impact on my own thinking. When I first began to write and agitate on behalf of religious freedom in the latter half of the 1970s, I suppose I thought that reform was possible in Communist societies: that, given enough pressure, Communist regimes could evolve into social-democratic regimes that respected the civil liberties of their people. But when I began to probe more seriously into the nature of religious freedom and the nature of Communism, it quickly became apparent that strategic compromise was an illusion and a self-reforming Communist system an oxymoron (as Mr. Gorbachev eventually discovered). Committed as I was to religious freedom, I was, therefore, soon committed to a vigorous, rather than merely abstract, anti-Communism.

In the midst of the fevered politics of peace in the 1980s, that stance, and the emphasis I placed on human rights in U.S.-Soviet relations, soon got me branded a dangerous fellow by other Catholic social ethicists who had become, in my judgment, mesmerized by the nuclear genie. But no matter how nasty those polemics got, there was John Paul II, vigorously and persistently making the case for religious freedom in the face of far more ugliness than was conceivable in the tong-wars of the American intellectuals. His calm courage confirmed me in my convictions, even as his magisterium was giving those convictions a deeper theological foundation.

The Pope's post-1989 stress on culture—better, on the revitalization of moral culture as the key to democratic renewal—has also had a marked influence on my thinking and writing. To put it simply, I am less interested in politics, the quest for power and the administrative and legislative exercise of power, than I used to be. Conversely, I find myself far more interested in the "software" side of the democratic experiment: the pre-political institutions and the habits of the mind and heart that make democracy possible. In this I am hardly alone, of course, and no doubt the current condition of American democracy has tempered my interest in the political game (narrowly construed) and helped to push my thinking down this moral-cultural path. But John Paul II has given a sophisticated theological and philosophical rationale for this focus on the culture of freedom as the key to the Church's public witness, and his arguments on that front, which will be explored in considerable detail in the chapters that follow, have made a deep impression on me.

The Holy Father's influence has been personal as well as intellectual. To experience human greatness is a grand thing; to be in the presence of a great man of extraordinary humility who takes an interest in your life, family, and work, who encourages your efforts and invites you into his conversation, a hero with whom you can both pray and tell jokes—that is a marvelous thing. I have been immeasurably blessed by my encounter with the mind, heart, and spirit of Pope John Paul II, and if he looms large in the reflections that follow, that is how it should be.

The American Possibility

The fourth change of mind that I discern in my work over the past two decades has to do with my general "take" on the American prospect.

When I first began writing about these things, the fashion among American Catholic intellectuals was to adopt a "prophetic" stance over against a racist, militarist, imperialist, and, latterly, sexist America. This seemed to me overwrought, ungrateful, and intellectually unsatisfying, not least because the primary reference points for this critique in the mid-1970s were various Latin American liberation theologians whose work I found neither theologically impressive nor politically serious. My instinctive doubts about faculty-club radicalism soon got a more secure intellectual foundation through my encounter with the work of the late John Courtney Murray, S.J.

Murray's critical analysis of, yet appreciation for, the American democratic experiment seemed to me to strike precisely the right balance for a Catholic thinking about the history and future prospects of American democracy. Here was an intellectual who was deeply Catholic and authentically American, although his Catholicism would be held suspect by lesser minds and his patriotism demeaned by an ill-bred successor generation. And so I began to write about the "Murray Project" in the days when the men and women who should have been Murray's intellectual legatees were either ignoring him or dismissing him as impossibly old hat.

Murray was no uncritical apologist for America. Indeed, neither paleo-conservatives nor leftists have ever managed so stinging and serious a critique of the modern American circumstance as did Murray when he argued that this uniquely "proposition country" lacked a public philosophy capable of sustaining its structures of democratic self-governance over the long haul. In this, Murray anticipated something of the "postmodern" thrust of John Paul II's social doctrine and its emphasis on the role of public moral culture in sustaining democracy.

So where does this leave me today, in the mid-1990s? Still bullish on the American possibility, but deeply concerned about the near-term future of the United States. The breakdown of civility in American life—"defining deviancy down," as it has come to be called—cannot continue indefinitely. Neither can America long endure a situation in which its cultural elites exhibit all the characteristics of what Ernest Fortin has called "debonair nihilism": a studied insouciance about moral truth and a deep cynicism about public life, married to a commitment to the pleasure principle as the be-all and end-all of human experience. Nor can America long survive the phenomenon described by the columnist Charles Krauthammer in these frightening terms:

> Never in history have the purveyors of a degraded, almost totally uncensored, culture had direct, unmediated access to the mind of a society's young. An adolescent plugged into a Walkman playing "gangsta rap" represents a revolutionary social phenomenon: youthful consciousness almost literally hardwired to the most extreme and corrupting cultural influences.[4]

Some observers see, looming on the horizon, a fourth Great Awakening that augurs a great national moral renewal. Irving Kristol, in an essay that appeared side by side with Krauthammer's in the thirtieth-anniversary issue of *The Public Interest* (Fall 1995), argues that it is precisely the influences Krauthammer deplores that make such a counter-revolution inevitable. Whatever the political fortunes of the religious new right, Kristol is convinced that, "in a century of ever more extreme hedonism, antinomianism, personal and sexual individualism [and] licentiousness (as it used to be called)," no one who has bothered to "read a bit of history should be surprised if [all of this] culminates in some kind of aggressive religious awakening."[5]

That may well be true, although Kristol would be the first to caution that assertions of historical inevitability can mask wishful thinking. But if it *is* true, it's going to be a different kind of Great Awakening this time around. It will, for one thing, be ecumenical, involving Catholics as well as evangelical Protestants; indeed, the intense evangelical interest in the teaching of John Paul II on life issues and on the moral structure of democracy is part of the foundation of a new ecumenism that will, I suspect, come to overshadow the classic ecumenism of the post-conciliar period during the next decades. Any fourth Great Awakening will also be inter-religious, involving Christians and Jews, perhaps some Muslims, and, one suspects, a few people of a decidedly secular cast of mind.

There are no guarantees about any of this. One does not order up national moral and spiritual revivals like mail-order goods, and after two millennia of Christian history, believers should have long ago learned that the Spirit blows where and when he will. But I have become ever more convinced in recent years that, if American democracy is to be in moral-cultural continuity with its Founding when it celebrates its tricentenary in 2076, it will be because such a Great Awakening has renovated the country and its culture.

A Brief Guide to What Follows

Enough of autobiography and the rear-view mirror. Since this book is about the future of an argument, it is time to look ahead.

The "notes" that follow probe into various aspects of public Catholicism on the threshold of a new millennium. The first two chapters advance explicitly theological arguments about the nature of the Church as a communion of believers on pilgrimage through history. Here I take up several of the great issues explored by the Second Vatican Council in its Dogmatic Constitution on the Church *(Lumen Gentium)* and its Pastoral Constitution on the Church in the Modern World *(Gaudium et Spes)*. What is distinctive about this community? What does it ask of the world—and what should the world expect of the Church? These are the initial, framework-setting questions to be explored. In the third chapter, I note the "danger" that Christians have always posed to the world, and ask what it is that this distinctive *communio* of Christians brings to the debate over worldly governance at a time when the democratic ideal inspires peoples around the globe. While particular attention is paid here to the American situation, the arguments about the desacralization of politics, the cultural conditions necessary for "making" democrats, and the legitimation of the democratic enterprise will have, I think, implications and applications beyond the borders of the United States. The fourth chapter is about manners, which are no small thing. There is a lot of "public Christianity" in the United States these days, and the question of how Christians ought to comport themselves on the various Mars Hills of this republic is surely one that bears reflection. In this, I believe, Roman Catholics have some things to teach our evangelical Protestant brethren (even as they, of course, have some things to teach Catholics in America).

I then turn to the modern transformation of Roman Catholic thinking about the "public Church," with special reference to the social magisterium of John Paul II. I begin with an overview of the Holy Father's "public project," review some of the history that made the pontificate of Karol Wojtyła possible, and then examine the evolution of the Pope's distinctive proposal for the future of the democratic experiment. That proposal is informed by a profound critique of the inadequacies of certain contemporary philosophical constructions of democracy: inadequacies that illustrate, in the pain and suffering of real human lives, the verity contained in Richard Weaver's famous aphorism that ideas have consequences. Here the "*t* word"—namely, "truth," the truth about the human person known by reason and revelation—looms large on the analytic horizon. Much misunderstanding has greeted the Pope's relentless pressing of the question about the relation between moral truth and the democratic experiment; I hope that chapters seven and eight identify the issues at stake and clarify the basic terms of the bold proposal John Paul II is making.

In his address to the United Nations General Assembly on October 5, 1995, the Holy Father remarked on a certain bitter irony present on the threshold of the new millennium. Modernity, which began with humanity's proud assertion of its "coming of age" and its "autonomy," is ending in fear: fear of the future, fear of man himself, fear of what humanity might be capable of. The antidote to fear, the Holy Father suggested, is to be found in a renewal of hope, a virtue "nurtured in that inner sanctuary of conscience where 'man is alone with God, whose voice echoes in his depths.'"[6]

Hope might not seem to be the business of an international political organization. Yet, as John Paul continued, "the politics of nations can never ignore the transcendent, spiritual dimension of the human experience without harming the cause of man and the cause of human freedom."[7] Christian hope is, of course, centered on Christ. But because Christ is a part of the history of humanity, John Paul concluded, "Christian hope for the world and its future extends to every human person."[8] And thus the Church that confesses Jesus Christ as the answer to the question that is every human life is, necessarily, a public Church, confessing a truth with great public consequences.

1

The Sovereignty of Christ and the Public Church

"Jesus Christ is Lord." That brief Christological confession in Philippians 2:11 is the most important thing Christians say about everything, including public life. Christians believe that what we now proclaim through grace by faith—that Jesus is indeed Lord—will be revealed to everyone in the fullness of time. And in the revelation of the Lordship of Christ, it will be made clear to all (as it should be clear to Christians now) that every earthly power and every earthly sovereignty is subordinate to the power and the sovereignty of Christ.

That affirmation, "Jesus Christ is Lord," certainly tells us something about Jesus, the incarnate Word of God. But the Christian confession of the Lordship of Christ also tells us something crucially important (the adverb is etymologically deliberate) about ourselves, and about our societies. For as Christian orthodoxy has insisted from apostolic times onward, Jesus Christ reveals, not only the love of God and the glory of God, but also the full meaning of humanness and the ultimate destiny of human beings. What we see in the risen and glorified Christ is the destiny that a God of infinite mercy and compassion has intended for human beings from the first moment of creation. What we see and love in Christ is what we are empowered by the Holy Spirit to hope we shall become: "They shall see his face, and his name shall be on their foreheads. And night shall be no more; they need no light of lamp or sun, for the Lord God will be their light, and they shall reign for ever and ever" (Rev. 22:4-5).

11

On a certain secular reading of its message, Christianity is alienating, off-putting, incapable of giving a satisfactory account of the heights, depths, and quotidian plains of the human experience. Yet that is to get the matter precisely backwards. For the problem with the Christian claim is not that it demeans human freedom or diminishes the struggles and the glories of the human condition; the problem, rather, is that the Christian claim can seem too good to be true. No less an exponent of Christian orthodoxy than Pope John Paul II articulated that claim, and its radical implications for human self-understanding, with unambiguous boldness in his inaugural encyclical, *Redemptor Hominis* ("The Redeemer of Man"). In that personal letter to the Church, in which he laid out the basic themes of his papal ministry, John Paul wrote as follows:

> Through the Incarnation, God gave human life the dimension that he intended man to have from his first beginning; he has granted that dimension definitively . . . and he has granted it also with the bounty that enables us, in considering the original sin and the whole history of the sins of humanity, and in considering the errors of the human intellect, will, and heart, to repeat with amazement the words of the Sacred Liturgy: "O happy fault . . . which gained us so great a Redeemer!" . . .
>
> The Redeemer of the world! In him has been revealed in a new and more wonderful way the fundamental truth concerning creation to which the Book of Genesis gives witness when it repeats several times: "God saw that it was good" (Genesis 1, *passim*).[1]

To put it in a slightly different way, the Christian confession of the Lordship of Christ is a proclamation that, in Jesus Christ, God finally and definitively achieved what he had intended for human beings from the beginning: glorification as companions of God in the inner life of the Trinity. Thus Christianity exalts the human person and the human race almost beyond the point of human comprehension, for the Christian claim is that the divinely willed destiny of every human being is, in the startling term of the eastern fathers of the Church, nothing less than Θέωσις, "theosis," or "deification."[2] "God was made man so that man might become God" is the characteristic patristic formulation of this dramatic assertion.

Incorporation into Christ is thus the very opposite of "alienation."

For, on the orthodox Christian understanding of these things, the closer we come to God and the more dependent we are upon him, the freer we are as human beings. As Dorothy L. Sayers once put it, God's "love is anxiously directed to confirm each individual soul in its own identity, so that the nearer it draws to Him, the more truly it becomes its unique and personal self."[3] Jesus of Nazareth, the man most radically and unsurpassably open to the God he called "Father," was, in his complete human dependence on the Father and his total abandonment of self to the Father's will, the incarnate Son of God. Thus the *Logos,* the Word of God, comes into history, not to fetch us out of our humanity, but to redeem us *in* and *through* our humanness, and by doing so, to transform us into the glorified condition that God has intended for us from the beginning. "God is not beggarly," writes Hippolytus, "and for the sake of his own glory he has given us a share in his divinity."[4]

The gospel episode that most dramatically captures this central truth of Christianity is the story of the Transfiguration of Jesus.[5] There, on Mt. Tabor, Peter, James, and John were given, not only a vision of the glorified Christ, but also a glimpse of their own future glorification. And as it was for them, so it is for us. Although we see only with the eyes of faith, we have Christ's pledge that "blessed are those who have not seen and yet believe" (John 20:29). Seeing Christ, one like us, transfigured, we can know our own destiny. Or, as the Apostle Paul put it to the early Christians of Corinth, we can understand that in Christ we are being transformed "from one degree of glory to another" (II Cor. 3:18). All of this is, to repeat, the furthest possible thing from "alienation."

This is emphatically *not* to say that Christianity is simply a religious variant on the secular myth of progress. For at the heart of the Christian claim is the Cross: *the* great confrontation with the alternative claims of the principalities and powers of this world. In the eyes of the world, of course, Jesus is the ultimate victim, and perhaps even the ultimate fool. But to the eyes of faith, the way of the Cross—the mystery of the redemptive death of Jesus Christ—is the necessary path to the Resurrection, and thus to eternal life in the light and love of the Trinity.

From the Christian point of view, then, all of reality is "cruciform" in its basic configuration, its "form," its *Gestalt.* As the Swiss theologian Hans Urs von Balthasar put it, the "historical event of Christ's redemption of mankind" cuts through the entire cosmos "in longitudinal section," leaving no person, and indeed no aspect of creation, untouched.[6] Thus the cross of Christ, and God's triumphant vindication of Christ's sacrifice on the cross, is the ultimate Christian answer to the claims of the world and all its sovereignties.

Witnesses Past and Present

Christians (and those of their persecutors who defend an ultimate earthly sovereignty—which is to say, a false god) have always understood that the Christian claim engages issues of ultimate consequence. Thus, as we shall have occasion to recall several times in what follows, the prototype of the Christian witness is the martyr. Indeed, the original Greek word simply meant "witness." Its usage was not confined to those who had died for the faith; rather, all who had suffered persecution "for the sake of the Name" (Acts 5:41) were witnesses, "martyrs." And their witness was not simply to their own convictions, powerful as they were, but to the demands of living in the truth as these witnesses had been grasped by that truth in the person of the Risen Christ.

We may find it hard to imagine, these days, the conviction of being "grasped by the truth" that animated the martyrs of the Roman arena. They lived not merely in a different time and place but in a dramatically different intellectual and imaginative environment, one in which the border between the transcendent and the mundane was far more permeable than it has been in the post-Enlightenment world.[7] But "martyrdom" is not something confined to the Christian past. Among our own contemporaries we have Christian witnesses whose decision to "live in the truth," as they put it, cost them dearly and yet finally proved its transformative power: the brave men and women of the resistance Church in central and eastern Europe, China, and Vietnam. Hundreds of thousands of Christians died "for the sake of the Name" under the Communist persecution, the greatest since Diocletian. And among the living "confessors" of the faith must also be counted those further tens of thousands of Christians whose participation in the human-rights movements in central and eastern Europe during the 1980s helped overthrow European Communism in the non-violent Revolution of 1989.[8]

Christians in the West should not have been surprised that these contemporary "martyr-confessors" based their resistance to an evil political system on a theory of the "power of the powerless," a power derived from the individual conscientious decision to "live in the truth," to live "as if" one were a free person.[9] That, after all, is what Christian witnesses had been doing for two thousand years. And that is what Christians are destined to do, in the face of the dehumanizing claims of those who would absolutize worldly sovereignties, until the end of time.

The Body

The Church is the community of believers, gathered and sustained in the power of the Holy Spirit, who proclaim to all the world's peoples and cultures the truth of the Lordship of Christ in history. Thus the community (the *communio* or "communion") of the Church continues to preach the Good News of God's redeeming love first enunciated by Jesus of Nazareth some two millennia ago. The Lord's promise to his disciples that he would not leave them orphans but would beseech the Father to "give you another Counselor, to be with you forever, even the Spirit of truth . . . [who] will teach you all things, and bring to your remembrance all that I have said to you" (John 14:16-17, 26) is fulfilled in the *communio* of the Church, the communion formed by the Spirit at Pentecost[10] and sustained by the same Spirit until the end of time (Rev. 22:17).

The Church is not accidental or peripheral to the saving event that is the life, death, resurrection, and glorification of Jesus Christ. To affirm, as Christians do in the ancient Roman baptismal formula we know as the "Apostles' Creed," one's belief in "the holy catholic Church" is to affirm that the Church is no mere human invention.[11] Rather, the Church is of the will of Christ. The Church is a dominically ordered community, and incorporation into the Church is part of one's incorporation into Christ. Indeed, we are incorporated into, or grafted onto, Christ by being incorporated into and grafted onto the Church: through the Church's proclamation of the Word and the action of the Church's ministry in baptism. Thus the Church is, in another ancient image, the "body of Christ" (Eph. 4:12), and we "put on the Lord Jesus Christ" (Rom. 13:14) by putting on the Church:

by living in the *communio* of the faithful, in whose prayer and praise of God we experience a foretaste of the glory that is to be ours in the fullness of time.

Christians have long debated the specific doctrinal weight to be given to the Church, and two thousand years of Christian history have not resolved the divisions on many questions of ecclesiology. It may be that some will remain unresolved until the Lord returns in glory. But all orthodox Christians, whether "high church" or "low church" in their ecclesial sensibility, affirm that there is only one Church of Christ, because there is only one Christ and the Church is his Body.[12] Moreover, one of the more intriguing signs of these times is a new consciousness among traditionally "low church" evangelical Protestants of the importance of the Church in God's plan for the salvation of the world. Thus Charles Colson has recently argued that "the Body" is no mere sociological phenomenon, but rather a *communio sanctorum,* a "communion of saints" that makes manifest God's saving work to the world "by gathering into confessing communities to fulfill His mission—that is, to administer the sacraments, preach the Word, and make disciples."[13]

The Church is not incidental to the Gospel. Rather, the Church is the *scola sanctorum,* the "school" in which we "saints" learn our true nature and destiny, as revealed by Christ. Some Christians believe that the Church is an integral part of the Gospel; others believe that it is a communal consequence of the Gospel. But all Christians believe that the Gospel and the Church are inextricably related.

For any Christian, then, the Church is the first community of commitment, the *privileged* community of identity and allegiance. Because our first allegiance is to the Christ who has saved us, our first institutional or corporate commitment is to his Body, the Church. For it is in the Church that we "live to the Lord"; it is in the Church that we "die to the Lord"; and it is in the Church, the "Bride . . . of the Lamb," that we shall reign with Christ forever (Rom. 14:8; Rev. 21:9).

Christians assert the priority of the Church, not to demean other human commitments, but to place those commitments in their proper context, within the cruciform configuration of all reality. Or, to vary the imagery, Christians believe that through the cruciform grammar of the Christian claim, all the other stories of our lives—the covenantal commitments of husband and wife, the deep bonds between parents and children, the civic friendships within a democratic political community, the various obligations we assume in our work—find their true meaning and value. To put it most simply, Christians believe that they are better husbands, wives, children, parents, friends, colleagues, and citizens precisely because their commitments to wives, husbands, parents, children, friends, co-workers, and fellow citizens reflect their fundamental commitment to live in imitation of Christ, within the Body of Christ that is the Church.

The *priority* of the Church requires that Christians maintain a certain critical distance from all other earthly sovereignties. Jesus himself put the matter dramatically when he said that "if anyone comes to me and does not hate his own father and mother and wife and children and brothers and sisters, yes, and even his own life, he cannot be my disciple" (Luke 14:26). The point is not, of course, that the love of Christ obliges us to loathe our closest relatives. But the radical demands of the Gospel require that we subordinate even our most intimate and cherished human relationships to the cruciform pattern of the Christian life, such that every aspect of our lives is lived within the grammar of the cross; for, as Jesus continues, "whoever does not bear his own cross and come after me, cannot be my disciple" (Luke 14:27). No human commitment, not the most solemn covenantal bond of marriage nor the self-giving love of parent for child, can take precedence over the Christian's commitment to Christ. But in that prior commitment, Christians believe, we find the ultimate affirmation and true "location" of every other commitment, relationship, and obligation of our lives. Thus in the Gospel of Luke, the Lord's first articulation of the demands of discipleship—"If any man would come after me, let him deny himself and take up his cross daily and follow me. For whoever would save his life will lose it; and whoever loses his life for my sake, he will save it" (Luke 9:23-24)—is immediately followed by the Transfiguration, the revelation of future glory (Luke 9:28-36).

Citizens and Aliens

All this gives "Christian citizenship" a distinctive character. To introduce an image that will recur throughout these reflections, the

Christian is always a "resident alien" in the world, because the Christian insists on the singular priority of his commitment to Christ and to the Church. At times, when the surrounding culture is more compatible with the way of life that Christians are obliged to embody, the stress can be on "resident." Then the Church is truly a "leaven" in society, as the Second Vatican Council taught in 1965.[14] At other times, the stress will be on the Christian as "alien."[15] In such circumstances (recall the Confessing Church in Germany during the Nazi period), what is often dismissed as "sectarianism" is exactly what is required of the Church: for in cultures that deny the basic truths about the human person that Christians must affirm, to be "sectarian" is simply to be faithful. As Richard John Neuhaus has written,

> Any discussion of Church and society that is not marked by a sympathetic awareness of the sectarian option is not to be fully trusted. In Catholicism, the monastic tradition keeps alive the awareness that there is a radically "other way," and that, in some circumstances of cultural disintegration and hostility to the Gospel, it may be the best way, indeed the normative way. No matter how impressive its institutions or how large its numbers or how palpable its cultural influence, the Church must never forget that it is, in the final analysis, the "little flock" completely dependent upon the promise of its Lord.[16]

Most Christians in established and new democracies today do not seem to feel obliged to take a radically "over-against" or sectarian stance. But the possibility remains that they might, as the experience of Christians who have lived under totalitarianism should remind us. In moments of extreme cultural decadence, for example, Christians will be obliged to speak and act as a distinctively countercultural community. In any event, Christian public life will always be lived in the tension between being "residents" and being "aliens." That this unavoidable tension can be creative is a lesson to be drawn from the history of Christian political thought.

In sum, the Body of Christ is a *communio* of people who are obliged to live ahead of time. Because we have seen, in the resurrection of the Church's Lord, the "grace of God [which] has appeared for the salvation of all men" (Titus 2:11), and because we have seen the "glory of God" shining on "the face of Christ" (II Cor. 4:6), we believe, with

Paul, that in the fullness of time God will "unite all things in him" (Eph. 1:10). Thus the end of the story, to be finally accomplished in God's good time, in the time beyond time, will be the fulfillment of the vision of Isaiah: "Every valley shall be lifted up, and every mountain and hill made low; the uneven ground shall become level, and the rough places a plain. And the glory of the Lord shall be revealed, and all flesh shall see it together" (Isa. 40:4-5).

It is precisely as a people "ahead of time" that Christians live their public lives as "resident aliens," without insouciance (for whatever is in the world is, in the final analysis, an object of God's salvific purposes), but also without *Angst*. Because Christians know how the story is going to turn out, and because they know that the worst that could happen in history has already happened, on Good Friday, Christians can live within the unfolding of the world and its story at a critical distance. That critical distance allows Christians both to affirm the world as the arena of God's saving acts and to challenge the temptation of the world's sovereignties to assume an ultimacy that is not theirs.

Public Truth, Public Consequences

From the world's point of view, Christians have always been a maddeningly public people. On the birthday of the Church, Pentecost, Peter simply couldn't contain himself. Not for him a quiet, private celebration of the gift of the Spirit with his fellow Christians; no, Peter had to go charging out into the middle of one of the great festivals of the Jewish year and start proclaiming all manner of things, such that some of his hearers at first thought he was drunk.[17] And ever since, Christians have declined to shut up, so to speak. The people who are ahead of time can't stop talking about the good news that has been entrusted to them. The Gospel they preach is inescapably public in character.

That preaching has had worldly (indeed, political), as well as ecclesial, consequences. The first object of the Church's preaching is, of course, the missionary proclamation of "Jesus Christ our Lord, through whom we have received grace and apostleship to bring about the obedience of faith for the sake of his name among all the nations" (Rom. 1:5). But the nations themselves have not been unaffected by the Church's insistent preaching of "Christ crucified . . . the power of God and the wisdom of God" (I Cor. 1:23-24). Indeed, as we shall see, that preaching has had a profoundly formative effect on the political history of the West—and through that, upon the political history of the world.

For the Christian proclamation of the Lordship of Christ and the Fatherhood of God is, at the same time, a tacit refutation of the claims to godliness, to ultimacy, that might be made by any other power. Because God is God, Caesar is not God. And because Caesar is not God, Caesar's "reach" into our lives is limited. Indeed, because God is God and Caesar is not God, Caesar cannot reach into that part of us that is most deeply and definingly human, the part in which we encounter our Creator, of whom we say, "I believe in God, the Father Almighty, Creator of heaven and earth. . . ." According to the classic teaching of the Church, it is only in the Spirit that we are empowered to say, "Abba, Father!" (Rom. 8:15). But that affirmation and that acclamation imply that within every human person there is a privileged sanctuary of conscience (of personhood, if you will) into which the state's writ does not reach.[18]

Because God is God, no other power is God, and no other commitment of the Christian's life can be so life-forming as the confession of the Fatherhood of God and the Lordship of Christ. At the same time, commitment to Christ empowers Christians to fulfill the obligations implicit in the other loyalties of their lives in a way that locates those loyalties within a horizon of ultimate consequence, yet avoids absolutizing (and thus distorting, and possibly destroying) the goods of this world.

Christianity, then, is fundamentally anti-totalitarian: which is to say, Christianity implies pluralism. The matter of pluralism will engage us (at some length) later. For now, suffice it to note that the radical demands of the Christian claim disclose a world in which our absolute obligation to one final sovereignty, and the communal expression of that obligation in the Body that is the-Church-in-the-world, create the personal and social space in which we can fulfill our duties to the many other lesser sovereignties (family, profession, voluntary association, the state) with legitimate claims upon us—and without absolutizing any of them. Thus the Church's commitment to a God beyond history helps make pluralism possible in history. And pluralism is a condition for the possibility of civil society, the tensile strength of which is a barrier to the temptation of all states to enlarge the scope of their power.

This anti-totalitarian—or, put positively, *pluralistic*—public trajectory of Christianity's basic claim is a truth with serious consequences, not least under the conditions of modernity (and given the technological means of coercive social control that modernity has made possible). We live in an age in which worldly sovereignties have frequently demanded incense, and have tried to enforce that demand at the cost of unspeakable human suffering. Nazi racial ideology and the class idol of Marxism-Leninism are the two most murderous examples of Caesars-who-would-be-gods in the twentieth century. But other, lesser idols abound: radical claims of nationalism and ethnicity continue to wreak havoc in Europe, the heartland of Western civilization; racial and tribal hatreds—idols—continue to make social progress difficult, if not in some cases impossible, in Africa.

Americans should not think themselves immune to the temptation to make Caesar into God. When the Supreme Court of the United States suggests that the aggrandizement of the imperial autonomous Self is the be-all and end-all of the American democratic experiment (as it did in deciding *Casey v. Planned Parenthood of Southeastern Pennsylvania* in 1992), the principalities and powers are demanding that incense be offered to what is unworthy of our worship. Various campaigns for gender- or race-based "political correctness" are additional evidence of the American susceptibility to the veneration of idols. Given the fantastic imagination that the human race has exhibited throughout recorded history, the words "never" and "every" should be deployed with great circumspection. Yet it does seem that every human society is tempted to absolutize itself, or some aspect of itself, so that we can speak of a perennial human temptation to idolatry. And idolatry enforced by the coercive power of the state is very bad news for human freedom.

Thus the dual Christian insistence that God is God and that Caesar is not God has had, is having, and will continue to have great *public* consequences. It influenced the fate of the Roman Empire (if not quite the way Edward Gibbon imagined). It profoundly shaped one of the great civilizations of the world, that of the Christian Middle Ages, whose prototypical "civil society" would serve as a kind of pre-school for democracy. It contributed to the evolution of modern

democratic political theory, not least through the influence of Cal-
vinism on the Scottish Enlightenment (and thence on the American
Founding).[19] And in our own time, as we have seen, the Christian
refusal to burn incense to a modern idol helped to bring about the
collapse of European Communism and the demise of the most far-
flung continental empire since the days of the Romans.

Christians are, in this sense, dangerous people. But the threat they
pose is to those who would make for themselves (or of themselves)
a molten calf and demand that others worship it. Thus the public
"danger" of Christianity is its most basic contribution to the preser-
vation of human freedom and to the structuring of a public life
conducive to the exercise of that freedom. The fact that their commitment *to* the world is mediated through their eschatological distance
from the world makes Christians good citizens of any state that does
not fancy itself God.

The Temptation of the Church

The Church has not, of course, always lived up to the majesty of
its mission. The Church is a gathering of sinners. It is through the
"earthen vessels" of our humanity (II Cor. 4:7) that the *communio* of
the Church proclaims the Good News of Jesus Christ and attempts
to discern the public implications of that Gospel in different cultures
and circumstances. Sometimes the Church fails in its discernment.

The classic literary meditation on this failure is Dostoevsky's
"Legend of the Grand Inquisitor" in *The Brothers Karamazov*. The chief
inquisitor, a prince of the Church, interrogates Christ, who has suddenly returned to earth. And the cardinal inquisitor berates Christ . . .
for what? For his proclamation of human freedom:

> I tell you that man has no more tormenting care than to find
> someone to whom he can hand over as quickly as possible that gift
> of freedom with which the miserable creature is born. But he alone
> can take over the freedom of men who appeases their con-
> science. . . . Instead of taking over men's freedom, you increased
> it still more for them! Did you forget that peace and even death are
> dearer to man than free choice in the knowledge of good and evil?
> There is nothing more seductive for man than the freedom of his
> conscience, but there is nothing more tormenting, either. And so,

instead of a firm foundation for appeasing human conscience once and for all, you chose everything that was unusual, enigmatic, and indefinite, you chose everything that was beyond men's strength, and thereby acted as if you did not love them at all—and who did this? He who came to give his life for them! Instead of taking over men's freedom, you increased it and forever burdened the kingdom of the human soul with its torments. . . .

Is it the fault of the weak soul that it is unable to contain such terrible gifts? Can it be that you indeed came only to the chosen ones and for the chosen ones? But if so, there is a mystery here, and we cannot understand it. And if it is a mystery then we, too, had the right to preach mystery and to teach them that it is not the free choice of the heart that matters, and not love, but the mystery, which they must blindly obey, even setting aside their own conscience. And so we did. We corrected your deed. . . . And mankind rejoiced that they were once more led like sheep, and that at least such a terrible gift, which had brought them so much suffering, had been taken from their hearts. Tell me, were we right in teaching and doing this? Have we not, indeed, loved mankind, in so humbly recognizing their impotence, in so lovingly alleviating their burden and allowing their feeble nature to sin, even with our permission? Why have you come to interfere with us now? And why are you looking at me so silently and understandingly with your meek eyes?[20]

The enduring temptation of the Church is to substitute itself and its authority for the freedom of human beings. As Dostoevsky suggests, the Church can do this out of misplaced compassion as well as for institutional self-aggrandizement; indeed, the Grand Inquisitor's whole defense of ecclesiastical and political authoritarianism is that it lifts from men the burden of freedom. And freedom is indeed a fearsome thing.

But it is in overcoming our fear of freedom, and in bending freedom to ends worthy of human beings made in the image of God, that we live out our vocation as creatures endowed with intelligence and free will. Thus the Church violates human dignity, as well as the explicit mandate of its Lord, when it denies men and women the freedom that is their birthright as sons and daughters of God. "For freedom Christ has set us free; stand fast therefore, and do not submit again to a yoke of slavery" (Gal. 5:1).

The typical way in which the Church has succumbed to the temptation embodied in the legend of the Grand Inquisitor is by forging inappropriate alliances between altar and throne, so that the coercive power of the state is put behind the truth claims of the Church. This is bad for both the Church and the state.

It is bad for the Church because coerced faith is no faith. In 1774, in his *Summary View of the Rights of British America,* Thomas Jefferson wrote that "the God who gave us life gave us liberty, at the same time."[21] Two centuries later, in 1986, Cardinal Joseph Ratzinger and the Congregation for the Doctrine of the Faith affirmed that "God wishes to be adored by people who are free."[22] These two striking declarations, born of very different philosophical positions, nonetheless touch on a single great truth: that God created us for freedom, the freedom to assent freely to the truth about ourselves (which includes the truth about the right ordering of our communities). Christians believe that the core of that truth—that we come from God and are destined for God—is definitively revealed in Jesus Christ. The Christian claim that God takes our lives seriously is embodied in the Christian affirmation that the assent of faith, to be genuine, must be freely given.

Coercion is bad for individuals within the Church or contemplating entry into the Church. It also bad for the public witness of the Church. A community gathered or maintained by coercive state power cannot give full and effective witness to the liberating love of God in Christ. A Church dependent (or even heavily reliant) on the sword of the state has misplaced the trust it ought to place in God alone. Americans, in particular, are wary about the excessive "entanglement" of Church and state because of what that "entanglement" can do to the state and to civil society. But for Christians the first reason for the Church to eschew any excessive reliance on the state is our overriding concern for the integrity of the Church. The Gospel has its own power, and the Church must bear witness to that. Moreover, a Church dependent on the authority of the state is open to forms of manipulation that are incongruent with the Gospel and that dangerously narrow the Church's necessary critical distance from all worldly sovereignties.

As we noted before, God has not ordained any single pattern of relationship between Church and state, between the *communio* of the Body of Christ and the *civitas* of public life. Nor need we think that the right ordering of the relationship between the Church and civil public authority requires what Richard John Neuhaus has termed the "naked public square."[23] Neither Christian orthodoxy nor democratic theory demands that public life be denuded of a people's religious convictions. Indeed, both would seem to require that the public discourse engage the citizenry's deepest convictions as they bear on determining and advancing the common good. And those convictions, in the American democracy and in many of the new democracies of central and eastern Europe, are religious convictions. (Perhaps more precisely, and in terms of public policy, they are religiously grounded moral convictions.) But how the relationship between the Church and the polity is ordered will necessarily vary according to historical circumstances and differences among cultures. The two extremes to be avoided are the sacralization of the state and the consequent subordination of the Church, and the politicization of the Church with a consequent deterioration of the state's (and the citizenry's) legitimate prerogatives. Between these extremes there is considerable room for both Christian orthodoxy and political science to maneuver.

Adopting the World's Agenda

The dramatically coercive authoritarianism of the Grand Inquisitor is not the only mode in which the Church betrays its evangelical birthright and corrupts its distinctive integrity. The Church can succumb to worldly temptation in more subtle ways that also diminish both Christian witness and human freedom. Take, for example, one of the slogans of the World Council of Churches: "The World Sets the Agenda for the Church." The best possible construction of this aphorism is that it seeks to capture in a catchy phrase the Church's enduring commitment to be a servant of humankind. Yet in principle, and, as things worked out, in practice, the slogan meant that the Church abandoned its critical distance; in the name of being "prophetic," it lost its prophetic edge. As expressed in the programs of the WCC, "the world sets the agenda for the Church" meant that the Church adopted a certain politics and economics as the index of Christian orthodoxy. (The politics and economics were, in this case, leftist, but that is not what really mattered; the problem had arisen earlier in untoward Christian alliances with political forces on the right.) Christians who could not, in conscience, agree that the politics and economics in question best contributed to human flourishing were excommunicate, *de facto* if not *de iure*. This is to subordinate the sovereignty of Christ to a worldly sovereignty, to subordinate the mission of the Church to a political agenda, and to subordinate the unity of the Church to a partisan definition of *communio*. Such subordinations cannot fail to corrupt the Church and to diminish its evangelical witness.

The temptation to subordinate the Gospel to politics has not, evidently, abated. Thus the Rev. Joan Brown Campbell, the general secretary of the National Council of Churches of Christ in the U.S.A., proposed in early 1993 that President Bill Clinton occupied "the ultimate pulpit in this country." This was a curious affirmation for a minister of the Gospel to make. The freely elected president of the world's leading democracy surely occupies a powerful position, and the presidency can indeed be a powerful instrument for moral, and even religious, persuasion. As Robert Bellah and others have noted, the American presidency, by combining the offices of chief of state and head of government in one person, has inevitably acquired a certain sacerdotal dimension in terms of the nation's "civil religion": no other public official can "speak for America" (and speak to America) as the president can.[24]

But to suggest that the bully pulpit of the presidency is the country's "ultimate" pulpit is to demean the power of the Gospel and to reverence the presidency in ways that can damage both Church and state. It is also to suggest that the most important decisions Americans make are political decisions, and that society's gravest problems are susceptible to a political solution. Neither of these suggestions sits easily with Christian orthodoxy or with sound democratic theory.

That the Church is the prior community of Christian commitment is, to repeat, a fundamental Christian doctrine. But that prior community has not received detailed instructions from its Lord on a myriad of questions about the right ordering of social and political life. To suggest that it has cheapens revelation and demeans the legitimate autonomy and authority of the civil community. The Church, in other words, has limited competence; but because its competence engages the most urgent questions of human life, it can help to orient the public discussion of less urgent issues toward ends worthy of human beings.

In other words, it is by being the evangelist of the Gospel that the Church is most truthfully and effectively the servant of the world. This is increasingly understood throughout the Christian communion, and it would seem to be no accident that the churches that are vigorously advancing the Church's primary mission of evangelization are those showing the greatest vitality on the edge of the third Christian millennium. Further, the highest teaching authority of the Catholic Church (Dostoevsky's model of coercive authoritarianism) has flatly rejected any coercion, ecclesiastical or political, in its missionary and public activity. As Pope John Paul II put it in his 1990 encyclical *Redemptoris Missio* ("The Mission of the Redeemer"), "the Church proposes; she imposes nothing."[25] The days of altar-and-throne seem to be a thing of the past. That arrangement is now understood to be an inadequate model of the Church, as well as of a rightly ordered state.

The Public Church Today: "Defensor Hominis"

The world at the end of the twentieth century badly needs a vital Christianity that proclaims the sovereignty of God and bears witness to human freedom. Totalitarianism—the radical subordination of the individual and his personhood to the claims of the worldly sovereignty of the state, legitimated by ideology and enforced by draconian means of social control—may not be implied by the logic of modernity, as some conservatives suggest. But totalitarianism in either its Fascist or Communist form is quite probably implied by some accounts of modernity (not least, by those dependent for their ideological impetus on the Jacobin radicalism of the French Revolution); and in any case, totalitarianism is a distinctively modern form of political organization. The scars of the century's totalitarian experiments run deep, and not only in countries that have lived under the totalitarian jackboot.

It would be the height of folly to think that totalitarianism can happen only to "other people," indeed to inferior "other people." The Nazi horror took place in what was arguably the most cultured nation in Europe. Recall also the approbation that far, far too many men and women of intellectual and artistic accomplishment gave, serially, to Lenin, Stalin, and Mao. For totalitarianism is, on one reading, the modern, technological solution to the ancient human problem of freedom. As the thirst for freedom is universal, so is the fear of freedom. And the fear of freedom can lead a nation to reach for chains.

Nor should we think that only people addicted to ideology are vulnerable to the totalitarian temptation. Totalitarianism—or some variant that involves extremely unpleasant forms of social control—can arise as a response to chaos and the breakdown of social order. And that precipitating breakdown need not happen only under conditions of general economic disaster, as in Weimar Germany during the great depression. It could happen under conditions of relative prosperity.

For if freedom is decisively severed from the truth about the human person (not that difficult to imagine in a cultural climate in which the very notion of such a "truth" is regarded as impossibly *outré*—which is to say, a cultural climate like that of North America and western Europe) we will soon be reminded of a hard fact of public life: that a free-standing and merely instrumental freedom inevitably degenerates into license. License, the distorted diminishment of freedom, then becomes freedom's undoing. For as Nietzsche discerned a century ago, social life in which freedom is not tethered to moral truth reduces down to the assertion of power, and power understood as my capacity to impose my will on yours.[26] The contest between conflicting wills-to-power then yields social chaos. And as the Grand Inquisitor knew so well, men cannot live without order. They may fear freedom, but they absolutely abhor chaos; rather than endure chaos, they will ask, even demand, to be chained.

During the great struggle against totalitarianism that occupied fifty-five years in the middle of the twentieth century, Christianity played a crucial public role (sometimes more adequately, sometimes less) as a lobe of humanity's conscience on questions fundamental to the dignity of the human person. As the Second Vatican Council put it in the midst of that struggle, the Church is "the sign and the safeguard of the transcendence of the human person."[27] And the Church is that sign and safeguard precisely because it discerns in every person the God-given capacity for final communion with the Creator. The Church is the *defensor hominis,* the defender of man, because the Church is the Bride of the Lamb who "redeemed us to God by his blood" (Rev. 5:9).

At the end of a century pockmarked by the scars of tyranny, at a time when the human capacity for self-governance is justifiably regarded with a measure of skepticism even among free peoples, one crucial public task of the Church is to bear witness to the enduring truths about the human person that we learn from the biblical tradition. These truths about humanity are what make free government possible. The first, which reaches back to Genesis 1–3, is that we are creatures of intelligence and free will, capable of rational reflection and decision-making. The second, a specification of the first (and a truth in which Christian tradition is complemented by classical philosophy), is that we are capable of discerning the truth of things by reflecting on the structure of the world and discovering the moral logic hard-wired into the human person and the human condition. And the third truth is the public implication of the first two: that we are creatures capable of ordering social and political life so that they serve the ends of human flourishing.

The Church best witnesses to these truths, and thereby serves the cause of human freedom, when it *is* the Church: a universal, inclusive *communio* of faith, hope, and love with a special care for the marginal and the dispossessed. To put it another way, the first public task of the Church is neither policy analysis nor policy prescription; it is to be the Church. In so doing, the Church reminds society of the destiny for which God created the world. And by reminding society of that destiny, the Church best helps society resist the totalitarian temptation, which is another form of the temptation to idolatry.

First Things First

This is not to say that all the Church has to offer to the debate over the right ordering of our freedom is a general doctrine of humanity's origin and goal. For well over fifteen hundred years, Christians have drawn out the implications of the gospel vision of the dignity and end of the human person in a second-order reflection on freedom and justice in society. In other words, Christians have engaged, as Christians, in political philosophy. More recently, Christian social ethicists and political theorists have focused on specific matters of public policy, from issues of war and peace to highly complex questions of medical research. At all these levels of public engagement, though, the Church is giving witness to the self-understanding of its public mission proclaimed by the Second Vatican Council in 1965:

The joy and hope, the grief and anguish of the men of our time, especially of those who are poor or afflicted in any way, are the joy and hope, the grief and anguish of the followers of Christ as well. Nothing that is genuinely human fails to find an echo in their hearts. For theirs is a community composed of men who, united in Christ and guided by the Holy Spirit, press on towards the kingdom of the Father and are bearers of a message of salvation intended for all men. That is why Christians cherish a feeling of deep solidarity with the human race and its history.[28]

The question, finally, comes down to putting first things first. There are three of these "first things": the Lordship of Christ; the *communio* of the Body of Christ, the Church; and the Church's proclamation, through the power of the Holy Spirit, of the saving action of God in Christ, in which the world learns its destiny and all men and women discover their true dignity as human beings.

When these priorities shape the Church's witness to the world, the Church's evangelical mission and its sacramental celebration of the mystery of God's redemptive love disclose certain basic truths about the right ordering of society. The Church's self-understanding as a *communio* both in and beyond time also clarifies the distinctive auton-omy and dignity of the institutions of governance in the world. The Church must have no desire to be Caesar, and Caesar must not pretend to be God. The cause of human freedom and dignity is best served when Church and state acknowledge, freely and respectfully, each other's spheres of competence. While the Church knows that its competence is in matters of ultimate consequence, this is no barrier to its acknowledgment of the state's authority in those things that pertain "to Caesar" (Luke 20:25).

The implications of all this? No partisan Church, but rather a *public* Church. No sacred state, but a limited state at the service of human dignity and the common good. In short: a *public Church* in a *civil society* served by a *limited state*. Or, in the American shorthand, a free people under a limited government.

This is not, to be sure, the Kingdom of God, which is a reality of God's making. But it is a form of governance that has shown itself compatible with the truth about the human person that is at the heart of the gospel message. And that compatibility is the basic point of tangency between Christianity and democracy.

2

What the Church Asks of the World, Or, Diognetus Revisited

In the summer of 1994 I was invited to address a retreat attended by most of the Roman Catholic bishops of the United States. The retreat's theme was "Shepherding a Future of Hope," and my assigned topic was "Hope in Society." Some of the bishops were, I expect, anticipating a bit of "social justice" shoptalk, leavened with a few lurid political tales from the Potomac fever swamps, where I have my office. But I began then as I begin now in thinking through the Church's hopes for the world: not with our late twentieth century, or with the impending twenty-first, but with the second century, the time of "the churches the apostles left behind."[1]

My text is the *Epistula ad Diognetum,* the *Letter to Diognetus,* which has become an important patristic reference point for contemporary Roman Catholic social thought.[2]

We don't know who Diognetus was, nor do we know who wrote him this letter. But that anonymous Christian apologist created an image of the-Church-in-the-world that has had a powerful influence on Christian reflection ever since, when he suggested that "what the soul is to the body, Christians are to the world."[3] To be the *soul* of the world: the image carries with it paradoxical (some would say, dialectical) connotations of distance and intimacy, the present and the future, the mundane and the transcendent.

Those implications were further spelled out when the *Letter to Diognetus* described Christians-in-the-world in these terms:

. . . Christians are not distinguished from the rest of humanity by country, language, or custom. For nowhere do they live in cities of their own, nor do they speak some unusual dialect, nor do they practice an eccentric life-style. . . . But while they live in both Greek and barbarian cities, as each one's lot was cast, and follow the local customs in dress and food and other aspects of life, at the same time they demonstrate the remarkable and admittedly unusual character of their own citizenship. They live in their own countries, but only as aliens; they participate in everything as citizens, and endure everything as foreigners. Every foreign country is their fatherland, and every fatherland is foreign. They marry like everyone else, and have children, but they do not expose their offspring. They share their food but not their wives. They are "in the flesh," but they do not live "according to the flesh." They live on earth but their citizenship is in heaven. They obey the established laws; indeed in their private lives they transcend the laws.[4]

RESIDENT ALIENS

This image of the "resident alien" nicely captures the worldly position of Christians, which is distinctive because it is always in the mode of an experiment. There is one Christian orthodoxy, but there is no single way of Christian being-in-the-world. Sometimes Christians will be more comfortably "resident" there; at other times, the wickedness of the principalities and powers will require them to be more defiantly "alien," even "sectarian" (which, as we have seen, can be a synonym for "faithful"). At all times, though, Christians live in the world in a somewhat unsettled condition. For the world, in Christian perspective, is both the arena of God's action in history and an antechamber to our true home, which is "the city of the living God" (Heb. 12:22).

Through the "resident alien" image, *Diognetus* also reminds us that the Church's basic Christological confession—"Jesus Christ is Lord" (Phil. 2:11)—is the only secure ground for our hope. Anything else is simply optimism, and optimism is a fragile commodity, especially in that part of "the world" that is politics. In contrast, Christian hope, built on the transformative conviction that Jesus is Lord, is the sturdy, enduring theological virtue that, as the recently issued Catechism of the Catholic Church teaches, "responds to the aspiration to happiness which God has placed in the heart of every man," an aspiration Christians pursue by "placing our trust in Christ's promises and relying not on our own strength, but on the help of the grace of the Holy Spirit."[5] Hope is built on faith, not on any utilitarian calculus of probabilities.

Ahead of Time

Lived out in the world amidst the agitations of the politics of the world, Christian hope should reflect the temporal paradox of Christian life: that Christians are a people both *in* and *ahead of* time. Christians are the people who know, and who ought to live as if they knew, that the Lord of history is, in the final analysis, in charge of history. Christians are the people who know how the story is going to turn out, and that puts Christians in a unique position vis-à-vis the flow of history. As Hans Urs von Balthasar has put it, Christians are the ones who, amidst the world's accelerating development, "can confront [that development] with a divine plan of salvation that is coextensive with it, indeed that always runs ahead of it because it is eschatological."[6]

Christians know how the story is going to turn out. It is in this sense of "making sense" of the world that the *Letter to Diognetus* develops the image of Christians as the "soul of the world," claiming that, while "Christians are detained in the world as if in a prison, they in fact hold the world together."[7] Christians know and bear witness to the fact that, in the power of the Spirit, God and his Christ will be vindicated. Or, to recall a phrase that caused a stir in 1989, Christians know all about "the end of history."[8] Christians know that at the end of history, the world's story, which is anticipated in the Church's story, will be consummated in the Supper of the Lamb, in the New Jerusalem whose "temple is the Lord God the Almighty and the Lamb" (Rev. 21:22). Christians know that the world's story will be fulfilled beyond the world, in that true city, the "dwelling of God . . . with men," where God will "wipe away every tear from their eyes, and death shall be no more, neither shall there be mourning nor crying nor pain any more, for the former things have passed away" (Rev. 21:3a, 4).

Now if *that* is what you know—if *that* is the conviction on which your life is built, the perception that orients reality for you—well, that gives you a rather distinctive "take" on the world and its politics. The further paradox, noted in the previous chapter, is that it is the *eschatological* dimension of Christian hope that creates the moral and cultural conditions in which it is possible to build a pluralist democracy whose public life contributes to genuine human flourishing. More will be said about this in a moment. For now, suffice it to say that our Christian hope as lived in the world must be a reflection of our conviction that the end of the story—the end of our story, and the end of the world's story—has already been disclosed in the resurrection of Jesus Christ and his ascension to the right hand of the Father in glory.

Eschatological Hope and Worldly Courage

Formed by that truth (which is the central truth of history), and within those aforementioned dialectics of intimacy and distance, present and future, the mundane and the transcendent, Christian "resident aliens" can tackle their tasks as citizens without attempting to "force" the Kingdom into history here and now.[9] A popular contemporary Roman Catholic hymn bids us to "build the City of God." Sorry, but I must decline. Christians who think themselves obliged to build the City of God suffer from a theological misapprehension whose political consequences, history has taught us, can run from the picaresque through the foolish to the grotesque.

No, that fevered urgency for a political construction of the Kingdom is not the way Christians ought to think of their worldly obligations. Knowing that the Son, the "first-born among many brethren" (Rom. 8:29), has been raised to glory, and knowing that he, not we, will build the City of God, we can relax a bit about the world and its politics: not to the point of indifference or insouciance or irresponsibility, but in the firm conviction that, in the extremity of the world's agony and at the summit of its glories, Jesus remains Lord. Our primary responsibility as Christian disciples is to remain faithful to the bold proclamation of *that* great truth, which is the truth that the world most urgently needs to hear.

Moreover, it is in pondering that salvific truth that we discover the courage to live out the "hope that is within" us (I Pet. 3:15). The world, to put it bluntly, can be a pain in the neck, and the politics of the world, even more so: which means that the frenzied "politics of the Kingdom" is not the only temptation set before Christians-in-the-world. The temptation to an eschatological indifference is at least as old as the Second Letter to the Thessalonians; the temptation to cynicism also has a venerable pedigree. From where, then, do we draw the courage to engage the world and its politics, in a manner befitting those "born of water and the Spirit" (John 3:5)? Hans Urs von Balthasar finds the source of what he calls "the courage to pursue the path of history"[10] in the conviction that "the Word became flesh and dwelt among us, full of grace and truth" (John 1:14):

> Only Christianity has the courage to affirm the present, because God has affirmed it. He became a man like ourselves. He lived in our alienation and died in our God-forsakenness. He imparted the "fullness of grace and truth" (John 1:17) to our here and now. He filled our present with his presence. But since the divine presence embraces all "past" and all "future" in itself, he has opened up to us all the dimensions of time. The Word that became flesh is the "Word in the beginning"; in him we have been "chosen before the foundation of the world." It is also the "final word," in which everything in heaven and on earth shall be caught up together: Alpha and Omega. . . . [Thus] it is not possession, but a being-possessed, that lends wings to Christian hope. It vibrates with the thought that the earth should reply to heaven in the way that heaven has addressed earth. It is not in his own strength that the Christian wants to change the earth, but with the power of grace of him who —transforming all things—committed his whole self for him.[11]

Because the world was formed by the Word, the world, even in the grasp of sin, has an innate intelligibility; it is not the arena of absurdity or madness. Because the world has been *transformed* by the incarnate Word who *dwelt among us,* the Christian disciple cannot despise or despair of it. For the world has been impressed with "a new spiritual form, chiselled on the very stone of existence": the form of the Incarnate and Crucified One, who is also and forever the Risen One.[12] The worldly vocation of a Christian can take the form of a contemplative withdrawal from the world, in which the contemplative dies to worldly things as a sacrificial offering for the salvation of the world.

But for most Christians, the obligation to engage the world in which the Word dwelt, "full of grace and truth," will be fulfilled in the form of action informed by contemplative prayer and reflection.[13] And so we come to the question of the Church's hope for the world.

THE PUBLIC DIFFERENCE THE CHURCH MAKES

"The Church's hope for the world": to put it another way, what does that Church ask of the world? And does that asking suggest certain hopes—or, perhaps better, prudential judgments—about the right ordering of that part of the world that is the *polis,* the political community, society organized politically for common, purposeful action?

Here, it might seem, is where we discover the "Church's agenda for the world." But there is no such agenda. Or at least there is no agenda such as that suggested by Christian Coalition congressional scorecards, U.S. Catholic Conference "political responsibility" statements, "JustLife" candidate-evaluation criteria, or the sundry public-policy pronouncements of the mainline/oldline justice-and-peace curias. These artifacts may be interesting or boring, enlightening or obfuscating, wise or stupid. But they are not, in the strict sense of the term, *ecclesial* statements. They may be statements *from* the Church, or from some faction *within* the Church; but they are not statements *of* the Church. The Church is not one political possibility, one political ideology, among many thousands of such possible contestants in the public arena.[14] If the Church is to become, in its presentation of itself to the world, what (as Balthasar puts it) it "already is and is to be, namely, the leaven that facilitates the ultimate unification of the world in its totality, the enzyme and organism of the eschatological salvation that has appeared in Christ";[15] if, in other words, the Church is to be faithful to its origin in Christ, in the blood and water that flowed from the side of the Crucified One (John 19:34)—then the Church cannot have an agenda commensurate with other "political" agendas.

But that does not mean that the Church has nothing to ask of the world. And what it asks of the world implies certain things about the right ordering of the political community.

A Space for Mission

The first thing the Church asks of the world is the space—social, legal, political, even psychological—in which to carry out its distinctive ministry of word and sacrament.

The Church asks the world to let the Church be the Church. Put more sharply, the Church expects and, if circumstances warrant, the Church *demands* that it be allowed to be what it is: a reality "in the nature of a sacrament—a sign and instrument . . . of communion with God and unity among all men."[16] The first thing the Church asks the world is that the Church be allowed to be itself.

This is, to be sure, no small thing. Nor is it a private matter. For the first thing the Church asks of the world has real-world implications, especially for that part of the world we call the state, the juridical embodiment of the political community. The state that can grant the Church the space it requires is a state that neither claims nor seeks any final authority over the Church's ministry of word and sacrament. This requires a *limited* state, one whose powers are circumscribed by custom (i.e., by moral-cultural *habit*) and by law. Thus the first thing the Church asks of "the world" is that that part of the world called "the state" adopt for itself a self-limiting ordinance.

This first request implies a deep critique of the totalitarian temptation, in both its hard (Fascist or Communist) and its softer (modern bureaucratic) embodiments. The latter is worth dwelling on for just a moment.

We all understand that something was fundamentally wrong when Nazi Germany attempted to co-opt the Church for political ends, or when the Soviet Union under Lenin, Stalin, and their heirs tried to obliterate the Church, and to co-opt, suborn, and manipulate what was not obliterated. We understand also that the persecution of the Church in China, Sudan, and Saudi Arabia today is an evil that bespeaks a fundamentally disordered political community. But we should also realize that the modern bureaucratic state's temptation to expand the reach of its regulatory power can, even in established democracies, constitute a denial of the first thing the Church asks of the world. When the U.S. Department of Housing and Urban Development "asks" the Roman Catholic Archdiocese of Los Angeles to change the name of a large shelter for the homeless that is the recipient of modest federal funds from the "St. Vincent de Paul Shelter" to the "Mr. Vincent de Paul Shelter," something is seriously awry—not, to be sure, so desperately awry as when Christian children are kidnapped in the south Sudan and sold into slavery, but awry nonetheless. The state's disinclination to grant the first request the Church makes of the world implies a disinclination to recognize the limits of its own competence and power. And that is bad news for democracy, as well as for the mission of the Church.

By being itself, the Church also serves a critical demythologizing function in a democracy. That the Church's hope is focused on Christ and his Kingdom relativizes all worldly expectations and sovereignties, thus erecting a barrier against the coercive politics of worldly utopianism. Rousseau had it backwards when he argued that Christian convictions "made any reasonable civil order impossible."[17] The true relationship is this: by locating the finality of our hope (and thus the object of our highest sovereign allegiance) in the time beyond time, the Church helps create the space for a free, vigorous, and civil interplay of a variety of proposals for ordering public life, none of which is invested with ultimate authority. Democracy is impossible when politics is absolutized. Thus Christian eschatology helps to make democracy and the politics of persuasion possible.

If a *limited state* is one implication of the first thing the Church asks of the world, then the second implication is *pluralism*. The two are closely related. For the limited state is one that recognizes that the political community is not the only community to which human beings owe allegiance.

The Church's claim for an "open" space for its mission and ministry implies the possibility of a plurality of communities within society to which men are bound with strong ties of commitment and affection. Moreover, the Christian believes that in a rightly ordered polity there is no essential contradiction (although there will always be tensions) between the obligations of discipleship and the obligations of citizenship. Thus the community of the Church helps demonstrate that genuine pluralism, far from leading to social chaos, contributes to the public order that every state is obliged to promote. The Christian claim for "free space" is not simply anti-totalitarian in its public implications; to put the matter more positively, the Church is bullish on pluralism. Pluralism is essential for the Church's public functioning; pluralism is also essential for any political community that aspires to freedom. For there can be no freedom without the free mediating institutions of civil society. These are, as Tocqueville recognized, the first "political institutions" of a democracy, precisely because they establish the crucial distinction between society and the state, and also society's moral "priority" over the state.[18]

Pondering the Possibility of Redemption

The second thing the Church asks of the world is that the world consider the possibility of its redemption.

As we know from the martyrologies, the world does not always take kindly to the Church's proposal that it might need redemption, and that the redemption it needs has been effected in Christ. Indeed, this has been an exceptionally costly proposal to make in the twentieth century, which is the greatest century of martyrdom in the history of the Church—a fact that barely registers on the consciousness of most North American Christians. Pope John Paul II sees in the twentieth-century rebirth of a "church of martyrs" both a preparation for the springtime of evangelization that should characterize the twenty-first century, and the fulfillment of the Church's longing for unity. The "most convincing form of ecumenism," the Pope wrote in 1994, "is the ecumenism of the saints and of the martyrs. The *communio sanctorum* speaks louder than the things that divide us."[19] In their common shedding of blood for the cause of Christ, Protestants, Orthodox, Anglicans, and Catholics have achieved a Christian unity that still eludes the Church in the world.[20]

As we have seen, all Christians are called to be martyrs, not necessarily to the shedding of blood, but in the original Greek sense of the martyr as "witness."[21] That to which the Christian bears witness is the truth about God and man revealed in the life, death, and resurrection of Jesus Christ. And that is the truth the Church asks the world to consider: Jesus Christ, who "fully reveals man to himself and brings to light his most high calling";[22] Jesus Christ, the "answer to the question that is every human life."[23]

In late-twentieth-century America, the Church's proclamation of this truth and the Church's invitation to the world to consider the possibility of its redemption meet less with a direct refusal than with a kind of societal indifference. God, Christ, redemption, sanctification: surely all these are beyond the pale for serious, mature, modern adults, concerned as they are with authenticity and autonomy. The Christian claim may be a useful myth, capable of producing citizens (especially lower-class citizens) with desirable behavioral characteristics. But that the Christian claim poses *the* issue involved in understanding the truth of the world: well, excuse us, we have other things to do.

Even worse than indifference is the calculated insouciance toward the Christian proposal common among a certain sort of intellectual in affluent societies today. This insouciance is rooted in a cavalier attitude toward the very possibility that human beings can know the truth of things.[24] Despite its self-conscious worldliness, this epistemological flippancy constitutes a real and present danger to "the world." For its public expression is the decadence of debonair nihilism, and debonair nihilism has awful public consequences: it creates a toxic social and cultural environment whose primary victims are not the well-off but those on the margins of society, who have far less room for error in the conduct of their lives. As we have seen in our inner urban communities, one result of principled skepticism and debonair nihilism among the intellectualoids and the wealthy is a vast breakdown of social order among the poor. If this chaos were to spread beyond the communities to which it is now largely confined, the further result would almost certainly be a breakdown of democratic order, as the state reached for an authoritarian solution to an intolerable problem.

Thus in challenging the world to remain open to the possibility of its redemption, the Church is helping to nurture—indeed to revivify —certain moral understandings about the cultural foundations of democracy and the civil liberties we associate with democracy. You cannot have a democracy without a critical mass of democrats, i.e., people who have committed themselves to the ethos of democratic civility. And there is a huge chasm between this ethos and the insouciance of debonair nihilism and principled hedonism.

To put it another way, a world that has peremptorily dismissed the question of its possible redemption is unlikely to be able to secure the cultural foundations on which a civil, democratic society can be built and sustained. Perhaps in other times and places, this was not so.[25]

But today, the world's premature dismissal of the question of its redemption often results from a deep-rooted skepticism about any matters of truth and falsehood, and this creates a situation in which citizens cannot give a persuasive account of why the democratic regime is morally superior to other arrangements.[26] The principal challenge to this skepticism and its attendant moral confusions (and social pathologies) is the Christian Church, or, more precisely, Christian orthodoxy. The Nicene Creed contains no blueprint for conducting politics. But the Church that can faithfully recite the Nicene Creed and defend its plausibility as The Way Things Are can give a much thicker account of its commitment to the dignity of the human person and to the politics of human freedom than what is on offer in most academic philosophical circles today.

Eucharistic Church, Public Church

This kind of witness in and for the world requires a particular kind of ecclesial community. The Church capable of proposing that the world consider the possibility of its redemption in Christ is emphatically not a Church conceived in mundane terms as another "voluntary organization" with a political task. Rather, the Church that can ask the world to consider itself redeemable (and redeemed) is one that conceives itself eucharistically, as the Body of Christ. And as Christ's Body it shares Christ's destiny, which is not a destiny to power but one in which "being given" means being broken and shared out.[27]

This is, to be sure, a post-Christendom Church; but that seems appropriate, in itself as well as in a post-Christendom world. Such a Church is also a Church at risk; but that, as Balthasar reminds us, has always been the Church's situation. For in being broken and shared out for "the world," he says,

> . . . [the] Church will suffer the loss of its shape as it undergoes a death, and all the more so, the more purely it lives from its source and is consequently less concerned with preserving its shape. In fact, it will not concern itself with affirming its shape but with promoting the world's salvation; as for the shape in which God will raise it from its death to serve the world afresh, it will entrust [that] to the Holy Spirit.[28]

The book of Acts, the inspired portion of the history of the Church, ends with the account of a shipwreck, the result of which is the furtherance of the Church's evangelical mission to the nations.[29] Reflection on that imagery should be reassuring as the Church considers how it might, today, propose to the world the possibility of its redemption.

A public Church eucharistically conceived also enables us to grasp that the *Letter to Diognetus* was expressing a central Christian truth, not merely a pious sentiment, when its author affirmed that, for Christians, "every foreign country is their fatherland." That is obviously not the case in worldly terms, even for the most assiduous of what we would now call "inculturators." But it is certainly true when Christians gather with their fellow believers in a foreign country around the eucharistic table of the Lord. In the 1990s, I have been privileged to be a faculty member at a seminar on modern Catholic social thought and the democratic prospect, held annually in Poland for students from throughout central and eastern Europe. Each year I am more and more impressed by the distinctive perspectives these students bring to social and political questions from their different national histories and cultural backgrounds. And yet I am even more struck by our unity around the eucharistic table. On the basis of its eucharistic *communio,* the Church cannot "give" the unity of an ordered and free political community to "the world"; if such a *polis* is possible, it will have to be organized in specifically political terms. But the eucharistic community of Christians for whom every foreign country is a homeland is a powerful countercase to the claims of the radical dividers and multiculturalists, for whom *Vive la différence!* has become the first principle of anthropology.

The kind of eucharistically centered Church that can propose to the world the question of its redemption also challenges implicitly (and, at a secondary level of witness, explicitly) a claim variously advanced by Marxists, deconstructionists, authoritarian Confucians, and activist Muslims: namely, that the notion of "universal human rights" is a species of Western cultural imperialism, and that there are no "universal human rights" because there is no universal human nature. This is an important public witness to make today, for if there is no universal human nature and no universal moral law, then there can be no universal conversation about the human future; there can only be a Hobbesian world in which all are at war with all.[30]

From a Christian point of view, the unity of the human race will be fully realized only in the Kingdom of God. And the human unity that believers experience in the Body of Christ cannot be "transferred" in one-to-one correspondence to "the world." But the *fact* of our unity in Christ across the barriers of sex, race, ethnicity, and culture is a powerful reminder to a sullen and cynical world that the claims of the dividers—who are all monists, either monists of a single ideology or monists of indifference—are not the only word on the human condition and the human prospect. Much less are they the final word.

The Causes for Which We Must Contend

There is, then, no Christian *agenda* for the politics of the world. But the Church's *hope* for the world includes a number of causes for which we are bound to contend in the world of politics, because of what we believe we know about man through the revelation of God in Christ.

The most important of these is *religious freedom*.

Here we return to the first thing the Church asks of the world. The Church cannot be the Church if it attempts to put the coercive power of the state behind its truth claims, or if it acquiesces in the state's assumption of that role. Coerced faith is no faith. As the *Letter to Diognetus* puts it, the God of Christians "saves by persuasion, not compulsion, for compulsion is no attribute of God."[31] The Church's defense of religious freedom is thus not a matter of institutional self-interest. Religious freedom is an acknowledgment in the juridical order of a basic truth about the human person that is essential for the right ordering of society. A state that claims competence in that interior sanctuary of personhood and conscience where the human person meets God is a state that has refused to adopt the self-limiting ordinance essential to right governance (not to mention democracy). Religious freedom is the first of human rights because it is the juridical acknowledgment (in constitutional and/or statutory law) that within every human person is an inviolable haven, a free space, where state power may not tread; and that acknowledgment is the beginning of limited government. In defending religious freedom, therefore, the

Church defends both the truth about man and the conditions for the possibility of civil society.32

The second cause for which the Church must contend is *pluralism*. What we call "pluralism" today is really "plurality": the sociological fact of difference. Plurality is a given in the world, and within most modern societies. Plural*ism* is a signal cultural accomplishment, the transformation of difference and division into an ordered conversation about the greatest of all political questions, first identified as such by Aristotle: "How, then, ought we to live together?"33 The question has an inescapable moral core, disclosed in the verb "ought." And so in the Aristotelian tradition (later adopted in various forms by various Christian political thinkers), politics is always an extension of ethics. To contend for the creation of a genuine pluralism of participation and engagement is one public face, so to speak, of the Church's challenge to the world in the matter of the world's possible redemption. For to build a genuine pluralism means to reject any monism of indifference or insouciance about the moral-cultural health of the public square.34

Finally, the Church must contend for the possibility of *participation* in public life. Here we return to Christian anthropology. As the Catechism of the Catholic Church puts it, "Participation is the voluntary and generous engagement of a person in social interchange. It is necessary that all participate, each according to his own position and role, in promoting the common good. This obligation is inherent in the dignity of the human person."35

The Church's defense of participatory democratic freedoms can be justified as a prudential judgment about the relative merits of various political systems. But the most secure ground for the Church's defense of democracy is its understanding of the revealed truth about man as the *imago Dei:* a *person,* not an autonomous Self, with intelligence and free will and thus capable of reflection and decision. The Church certainly does not hold that everyone is obliged to engage in the daily business of politics. But because the Church proposes to the world a vision of the human person in which the defense of individual liberties is intimately related to the responsibility of promoting the common good, the Church must contend for the possibility of active political participation by those who discern a vocational obligation to those tasks. In this respect, the Church is not simply anti-totalitarian and pro-pluralist; the Church is "populist."36

The Heart of the Matter

This construal of the "public Church" will undoubtedly strike some as terribly minimalist, perhaps even irresponsible. What about the environment, or the status of women, or welfare reform, or parental choice in education, or humanitarian intervention in Bosnia, or a flat tax, or the National Endowment for the Arts, or abortion, or euthanasia? These are indeed important issues; the life issues among them bear directly on whether the American republic will continue to exist in moral-cultural continuity with its Founding. But we damage the integrity of the Church and its public witness when we suggest, explicitly or implicitly, that politics, understood as the quest for power in the world, engages Christian *hope,* understood as one of the three theological virtues. I think I can make a fairly persuasive case for my position on any of the issues listed just above, from environment to euthanasia, and those positions will be informed by what I understand to be the relevant "middle axioms" of Christian social ethics. But the outcome of these questions—which is to say, the politics of these questions—does not touch, directly, "the hope that is within" me (to return to First Peter). If it did, there would be something defective about my hope.

The Church that conceives its public witness in these terms is the most "relevant" Church imaginable. Political analysts working strictly within the boundaries of the social sciences are now coming to understand the truth of Pope John Paul II's assertion that, in the free society today, the really interesting and urgent questions have to do with culture, not with the structures of politics and economics.[37] The political scientist Francis Fukuyama, who notoriously proposed in 1989 that, in democratic capitalism, we had reached "the end of history," now argues that neither democratic politics nor the market can function properly absent the tempering and guidance provided by moral habits, or what an older generation would have called "virtues." Democracy and the market, in other words, are not machines that will run of themselves; nor can democracy and the free economy be sustained on the basis of liberal-individualist principles alone. Thus Fukuyama discerns a paradox at the heart of the modern free society:

If the institutions of democracy and capitalism are to work properly, they must co-exist with certain *premodern cultural habits* that ensure their proper functioning. Law, contract, and economic rationality provide a necessary but not sufficient basis for both the stability and prosperity of postindustrial societies; they must as well be leavened with reciprocity, moral obligation, duty toward community, and trust, which are based in habit rather than rational calculation. The latter are not anachronisms in a modern society but rather the sine qua non of the latter's success.[38]

A Church that recognizes the "priority of culture" in the postmodern circumstances of the free society, and whose social witness addresses that society at the deepest level of its self-understanding, is thus positioned squarely on the cutting edge of the debate over the future of freedom. Far from being hopelessly out of it, such a Church, one whose social witness is drawn from the most profound source of the "hope that is within" us, may sometimes find itself uncomfortably "relevant."

But that, too, can be one of the costs of discipleship.

3

The Paradoxes of Disentanglement:
Christianity and Democracy
in America

According to an ancient tradition that has taken numerous modern forms, I am a dangerous man, a subversive, a threat to the public order: not because my political inclinations run to anarchism or to fantasies of dictatorship, but because I am an orthodox Christian.

This is not, of course, how *I* usually experience the relationship between my Christianity and my life as a citizen of the United States of America and the state of Maryland. For me, that relationship is better described by words like "energized," "frustrated," "appalled," "comforted," and "bemused." Moreover, the recording angel, observing the routines of my life, would not be likely to describe me as a threat to American democracy: I pay my taxes; I vote; I obey the laws (though I confess to a propensity for jaywalking, a disinclination to let the county Department of Ecology and Recycling tell me when I may cut my lawn, and a barely concealed contempt for the 55 m.p.h. speed limit); I make arguments about public policy in a civil manner; I work through the normal political processes to help elect candidates I favor, and I accept the results of elections in which my candidates lose; I present myself for jury duty when called. As a speculative matter, I could, I suppose, become a threat to the American regime, in the sense that I would work to overthrow it—but that would be the result of a fundamental change in the character of the regime, not in my religious convictions.

Nevertheless, as a student of the history of Christianity, of church/state relations in America, and of the theory of democracy, I have to be impressed by the number of intelligent thinkers who were or are firmly convinced that people like me are perils to public order—that Christians, when they act like Christians, are threats to democracy.

In his splendid book *The Christians as the Romans Saw Them*,[1] Professor Robert Wilken, now of the University of Virginia, explores the nature of the threat that early Christianity and its truth claims seemed to pose to the guardians of the established order of Rome. These charges are worth revisiting here, if only as a reminder of the abiding truth in the familiar aphorism *plus ça change, plus c'est la même chose.*

Pliny the Younger, for example, in a letter to Trajan described Christianity as a "degenerate sort of cult carried to extravagant lengths." Celsus, the late-second-century philosopher whose critique of Christianity occasioned one of the great works of patristic apologetics, the *Contra Celsum* of Origen, thought that Christians were socially *outré,* persons of limited intelligence whose faith was the religion of the stupid and indeed of stupidity. Moreover, Christians were sectarians who privatized religion and damaged public life by transferring religious values from the public realm to the sphere of private association. According to Celsus, the Christian doctrine of the Incarnation and the Christian claim that men were saved only by the name of Christ was a denial of the unity of the one God and undermined the authority of the one emperor. Porphyry, the biographer of Plotinus and the editor of his *Enneads,* asked, "How can men not be impious . . . who have apostasized from the customs of our fathers, through which every nation and city is sustained?"

Closer to our own times, Jean Jacques Rousseau had this to say about Christianity: "Far from winning the hearts of the citizens for the state, it removes them from it, as from all earthly things. I know of nothing that is more actively opposed to the social spirit." Christianity, Rousseau continues in the concluding chapter of his *Contrat Social,* is a purely spiritual religion, "which is occupied only with heavenly things; the native land of the Christian is not of this world." Moreover, he argues, the political defect of Christianity goes straight back to the founder of the firm (so to speak); as Rousseau put it, "Jesus came in order to set up a spiritual kingdom on earth; thereby the theological system was separated from the political system, and this in turn meant that the state ceased to be *one* state, and that inherent tensions emerged, which have never ceased to agitate the Christian peoples." The result is "a continuous struggle between the jurisdictions . . . which has made any reasonable civil order impossible in the Christian states." Christianity has created circumstances in which men have "two legislations, two sovereigns, two native lands," and thus are subjected to "antithetical obligations." So the Christian can never be both a pious believer and a good citizen. Christianity is, in the final analysis, *"insociable":* the true Christian cannot be integrated into society.[2]

The *dicta* on religion in the past twenty-five years of Supreme Court First Amendment decisions show a striking similarity to Rousseau's frettings. For the Court has not been content to render legal decisions about controverted matters; it has, in the course of that judging, painted a portrait of religious conviction that is quite remarkable (some might say, appalling). Indeed, if one knew nothing about American religion except what one had read in the decisions of the Supreme Court since *Everson* in 1947, one would have to conclude that religious conviction is indeed a danger to the democratic order, for religion, according to the Court, is inherently divisive. (Justice Blackmun went so far as to suggest, in the 1992 case *Lee v. Weisman,* that religion is potentially homicidal.) Why? Because it is inherently coercive. And why is it inherently coercive? Because it is inherently irrational. (Blackmun, again in *Lee v. Weisman,* sharply contrasted "rational debate" and "theological decree.") On the Court's understanding of it, religion is something the democratic state can tolerate if consenting adults engage in it behind closed doors. But as Justice Stevens suggested in *Grumet v. Board of Education of Kiryas Joel* in 1994, it's probably bad for the kids.[3]

Vanilla Is Not the Answer

These ancient and modern objections to religion—examples of which could, of course, be multiplied exponentially—are not met by softening the claims of Christian orthodoxy, thereby turning Christianity into a vaguely agreeable and unexceptionable set of behavioral injunctions largely having to do with tolerance, of an "anything goes, so long as no one else gets hurt" sort. H. Richard Niebuhr's lampoon of the attempt to retool the Gospel to "fit" the regnant cultural assumptions of his day is justly famous for its demolition of the vacuity of a certain modernist Christianity: "A God without wrath brought men without sin into a kingdom without judgment through the ministrations of a Christ without a Cross."[4]

Well, brethren, no thank you. The only Christianity worth considering, in itself and in relation to public life, is the kind that, in Henrik Ibsen's phrase, is far more deep-down-diving and mud-upbringing. A Christianity that takes itself seriously as the bearer of great truths about the human person, human community, and human destiny is something to contend with; a Christianity indistinguishable from the editorial page of the *New York Times* is hardly worth anyone's bother.

How, then, are we to conceive the intersection of a robust Christian orthodoxy with public life today, which in the American case means the intersection of Christianity and democracy? The previous chapter asked, "What does the Church ask *of* the world?" Here we want to explore what the Church does *for* the world, and specifically for the democratic project.

The question of the relationship between Christianity and democracy has engaged several of the finest theological and philosophical minds of our times. I am thinking of Jacques Maritain, whose *Christianity and Democracy,* written in exile during some of the hardest days of World War II, pointed western Europe toward a post-totalitarian future;[5] of Reinhold Niebuhr and his incisively ironic maxim, "Man's capacity for justice makes democracy possible; but man's inclination to injustice makes democracy necessary";[6] of John Courtney Murray, whose reflections on the American Catholic experience of the issue paved the way for the Second Vatican Council's landmark Declaration on Religious Freedom, so aptly styled in Latin *Dignitatis Humanae;*[7] and of Karol Wojtyła, a former docent of philosophical ethics at the Catholic University of Lublin, now Bishop of Rome under the title John Paul II, whose work at Vatican II on *Dignitatis Humanae* and on the Pastoral Constitution on the Church and the Modern World *(Gaudium et Spes)* has borne fruit both theologically and politically.

With the work of these giants as grist for my theological mill, what I propose to do here is to describe (and defend) what it is that putatively dangerous people like me bring to the ongoing experiment in self-governance that is American democracy. This is not, I hasten to add, an essentially utilitarian defense of "useful" religion. Rather, I want to draw out some of the implications of Christian truth claims about the human person, human community, and human destiny for the conduct of our democracy. These claims are, I believe, true: they describe The Way Things Are. That they have important *public* implications is also, I think, true. But their public *utility* is not the final warrant of their validity.

The list could be added to, subtracted from, multiplied, and/or divided. For the sake of concision, and in good trinitarian fashion, I would like to suggest that Christian orthodoxy—the things it teaches and the behaviors it warrants—has three crucial impacts on the American democratic experiment.

Desacralizing Politics

The first thing that orthodox Christianity does for America involves what we might call "making space for democracy."

This question was first broached above, in relation to what it is the Church asks of the world. Now is the time to explore the question in greater depth, and with reference to its New Testament *locus classicus*. The words have become so familiar to us that we may have lost an appreciation of their revolutionary import. So let us revisit the twenty-second chapter of Matthew's Gospel:

> Then the Pharisees went and took counsel how to entangle him in his talk. And they sent their disciples to him, along with the Herodians, saying, "Teacher, we know that you are true, and teach the way of God truthfully, and care for no man; for you do not regard the position of men. Tell us, then, what you think. Is it lawful to pay taxes to Caesar, or not?" But Jesus, aware of their malice, said, "Why do you put me to the test, you hypocrites? Show me the money for the tax." And they brought him a coin. And Jesus said to them, "Whose likeness and inscription is this?" They said, "Caesar's." Then he said to them, "Render therefore to Caesar the things that are Caesar's, and to God the things that are God's." When they heard it, they marveled; and they left him and went away. [Matt. 22:15-22]

It is, as I said, a revolutionary text, the public implications of which have been working themselves out for almost two millennia. During those centuries, Christians have not reached agreement on either the theological nuances of the text or its practical implications. Some see it as a call to a radical withdrawal from contact with the "principalities and powers"; others find in it a biblical warrant for a "two kingdoms" social ethic; no doubt someone, somewhere, is using Matthew 22 to support a flat-rate income tax. But virtually everyone would agree, I think, that the story of Caesar's coin teaches two things that have decisively influenced both the Church and the world.

The first thing to be noted about the text ("chronologically," so to speak) is that Jesus gives Caesar his due. Caesar's authority is not denied. Nor did the primitive Church deny that authority even after Caesar, in the person of his procurator, Pontius Pilate, had executed the Church's Lord. The First Letter of Peter, widely regarded by biblical scholars as being based on an ancient Christian baptismal sermon, enjoined the newly christened to "be subject for the Lord's sake to every human institution, whether it be to the emperor as supreme, or to the governors as sent by him to punish those who do wrong and to praise those who do right" (I Pet. 2:13-14). Similarly, St. Paul enjoined the Romans to "be subject to the governing authorities. For there is no authority except from God, and those that exist have been instituted by God" (Rom. 13:1). Caesar, in brief, is not to be denied what is rightly his.

But the second crucial aspect of this text (and its parallels in the Gospels of Mark and Luke) is that Jesus, by juxtaposing Caesar and God and thus dedivinizing the emperor, declares the priority of fidelity to God. As Paul later reminded the Romans in the earliest days of Christian "social ethics," there are no legitimate things of Caesar's that are not his by reason, ultimately, of God's authority. But Jesus also insists, plainly, that there are things that are God's and not Caesar's. As we noted before, because God is God, Caesar is not God. If he attempts to occupy the ground that properly belongs to God alone, Caesar must be resisted.

This gospel incident has had a pronounced impact on the history of nations. The Church's defense of its liberties in resistance to imperial and then royal absolutism in the early Middle Ages was one working-out of the meaning of Jesus' injunction not to render unto

Caesar those things that were not legitimately his. And that resistance, by helping to create conditions for the possibility of social pluralism in medieval Europe, decisively shaped the cultural context from which grew the modern quest for democracy in its Anglo-American form.[8]

Matthew 22:15-22 also influenced the collapse of Communism in Europe, especially in Poland. For five years after the accession of the Communist government of Poland in 1948, the Polish Church, under the leadership of Cardinal Stefan Wyszyński, tried with great deftness to reach a *modus vivendi* with the regime that did not involve a fundamental compromise of the freedom of the Church. But in May 1953 the regime ordered the implementation of a decree giving the state the authority to appoint and remove priests and bishops; all clergy were also required to take an oath of loyalty to the Polish People's Republic. Which meant, in practice, that the Church was to become a wholly owned subsidiary of the Polish state.

Cardinal Wyszyński now chose the path of confrontation, and in a historic sermon at Warsaw's St. John's Cathedral he threw down the gauntlet: "We teach that it is proper to render unto Caesar the things that are Caesar's and to God that which is God's. But when Caesar seats himself on the altar, we respond curtly: he may not." Later, the entire Polish episcopate issued a memorial that concluded with the boldly defiant words, "We are not allowed to place the things of God on the altar of Caesar. *Non possumus!*"

That act cost Cardinal Wyszyński his freedom during three years of imprisonment and internal exile under house arrest, but he eventually won his point. Moreover, I believe that the *Non possumus!* of the Polish episcopate in 1953 was a crucial marker along the road that led, by a long and complex path, from the abrogation of freedom in east central Europe after World War II to the restoration of democracy in those lands in 1989. Wyszyński's successful defense of the independence of the Church made completion of the totalitarian project in Poland impossible. And out of that resistance church came, in time, the overwhelming majority of the men and women who made the Solidarity revolution of 1980, and later the Revolution of 1989.[9]

Much more is involved here than rallying the troops, of course. Because Caesar is not God, the political is not a realm of ultimacy or of totality. By dedivinizing Caesar, the Christian claim desacralizes politics, which is an achievement of great *public* importance. Sacral politics, often a form of utopian politics, seems inevitably to become a violent politics of coercion. But by desacralizing the public realm, the Christian claim helps clear the social space on which a politics of persuasion can form, and a juridical state whose primary function is securing the basic rights of its citizens can be built. Because Caesar is not God, civil society is possible. Because Caesar is not God, the state is at the service of society, rather than the other way around. Because Caesar is not God, we can be democratic citizens of a limited, constitutional state.

Christianity thus brings what Archbishop Christoph Schönborn, the Dominican theologian who served as general editor of the new Catechism of the Catholic Church, has described as a "leavening of division" to public life.[10] The desacralization of politics that is implied in the dedivinization of Caesar is, in contemporary terms, a crucial barrier against the totalitarian temptation, and against the tendency of all modern bureaucratic states to extend indefinitely the reach of their coercive power. When a pious grandmother in Queens insists that the state cannot mandate teaching the techniques of anal and oral sex to primary school children, as when Cardinal Wyszyński and the Polish episcopate issued their historic *Non possumus!,* as when Gregory VII faced down the Holy Roman Emperor Henry IV in the eleventh-century investiture controversy, we are hearing echoes of that confrontation between Jesus and his critics two thousand years ago on the matter of Caesar and God.

By establishing what we might term the "penultimacy of the political," orthodox Christianity makes a considerable contribution to the never-ending project of "making space for democracy." Indeed, if by "politics" we mean the ongoing and public deliberation of that great question, "How ought we to live together?" then Christianity's insistence on the penultimacy of the political helps make genuine *politics* possible.

Making Democrats

The second impact that Christian orthodoxy and the behaviors it warrants have on the American democratic experiment has to do with the kind of a people we are and aspire to be as democrats.

Americans have been powerfully reminded in recent years that you cannot have a democracy without a sufficient number of democrats: without a sufficient critical mass of men and women who have internalized the habits of the heart and the habits of the mind—the *virtues,* if you will—that are essential to democratic self-governance. Contrary to some of the expectations of the past, American democracy is not "a machine that will run of itself." The machine can, for a time, compensate for the inadequacies of the citizenry. But over the long haul, the machine needs mechanics—and mechanics of a certain cast of mind and soul—to make it work such that the machinery serves the ends of human flourishing. The machine needs mechanics who will continue to affirm the superiority of this kind of machine over others, because of how they conceive their own moral worth and that of their neighbors.

Certainly Christian orthodoxy does not constitute the *only* set of religious and moral warrants capable of turning tyrants, which is what we all are at birth, into democrats. But I think it undeniable that democrats, like Christians, are made, not born. The *ethos* of democracy has to be learned. Christian personalism, and a Christian analysis of the human condition, can powerfully promote attitudes toward "the other" that are essential to the democratic *ethos,* and thus to the proper functioning of the democratic experiment.

Clive Staples Lewis was a fine novelist and a brilliant literary critic who also happened to have been the most successful Christian apologist of the twentieth century—a man whose books continue to sell millions of copies every year. On June 8, 1941, this layman with no formal theological training preached in Oxford's University Church of St. Mary the Virgin, the former pulpit of John Henry Newman and Edmund Pusey. Lewis's sermon, entitled "The Weight of Glory," ended like this:

> There are no *ordinary* people. You have never talked to a mere mortal. Nations, cultures, arts, civilizations—these are mortal, and their life is to ours as the life of a gnat. But it is immortals whom we joke with, work with, marry, snub, and exploit—immortal horrors or everlasting splendors. This does not mean that we are to be perpetually solemn. We must play. But our merriment must be of that kind (and it is, in fact, the merriest kind) which exists between people who have, from the outset, taken each other seriously—no flippancy, no superiority, no presumption. And our charity must be a real and costly love, with deep feeling for the sins in spite of which we love the sinner—no mere tolerance, or indulgence which parodies love as flippancy parodies merriment. Next

to the Blessed Sacrament itself, your neighbor is the holiest object presented to your senses.[11]

C. S. Lewis was a man who probably would have been far more comfortable living in the thirteenth century than in the twentieth; deeply skeptical about modernity, he never read newspapers, resented the intrusions into his privacy caused by modern communications technology, and took no part in politics. But in "The Weight of Glory," he described rather precisely some of the core qualities we should want to see embodied in democratic citizens today: a commitment to democratic equality that is sustainable in and out of season, because it is grounded in something far deeper than a consequentialist or utilitarian calculus and is thus able to discriminate between serious and spurious claims of inequality; a willingness to engage the "other" seriously, across the many barriers of difference that separate us in a society characterized by dramatic plurality; a commitment to truth-seeking and truth-telling, regardless of the consequences ("living in the truth," as the human-rights resistance in Czechoslovakia put it in the 1980s[12]); a certain seriousness—a certain *gravitas*—about life, but without the kind of bogus solemnity that characterized the public ceremonial of totalitarian states; a respect for the legitimately private space of others; a charity that displaces naked ambition as the motive for public service.

Lewis challenged the congregants at St. Mary the Virgin to live their Christianity seriously for its own sake. But that basic Christian stance of reverence toward others, who are never, ever "mere mortals," can also help form the kind of political community in which people "have, from the outset, taken each other seriously"—seriously enough to engage in the public discourse that is the lifeblood of democracy; seriously enough to engage a real argument around the question, "How *ought* we to live together?"

To adopt a formulation from Paul Tillich, democratic politics requires a democratic political culture, and culture is formed by cult, by religion, by that which, in the root sense of the Latin *religio,* binds us together. The question is not, then, whether piety has much to do with politics, but *what kind* of piety, informing what kind of politics. Christian orthodoxy is in this sense a "piety" that, by engendering reverence toward the neighbor, the "other," as a unique subject who is also the object of the salvific will of God, helps form the kind of citizens who can make a democracy work—particularly amidst racial, ethnic, and religious differences and the inevitable tensions they create.

This latter point is worth pausing on for a moment. One of the not-so-subtle attitudes at work in contemporary debates about public piety in America is the fear that vibrant religious conviction, publicly expressed in debates over public policy, inevitably leads to religious intolerance and thence to civic strife. Certainly that has happened, and it continues to happen in other venues with which we are all familiar from the newspapers. But surely the more interesting datum about the American experience is that in the United States today—in this vibrantly, maddeningly, diversely, and, it appears, incorrigibly religious society—religious tolerance is *religiously* warranted.

The roots of religious tolerance in contemporary America are not to be found in a pragmatic bargain ("This is the best way to do things . . .") reflecting a utilitarian calculus of interest (". . . because all the other ways are messier"). Rather, religious tolerance in today's America is *religiously* grounded. Tens of millions of Americans believe it is the will of God that we not kill one another over our differences as to what constitutes the will of God.[13] And that conviction is strongest, I believe, among those whose Christian conviction is most robust. Viewed solely through the lens of empirical political science, "religious tolerance" in America today is another way of describing the social management of plurality. But that same social science would also vindicate the claim that the warrants legitimating that "tolerance" are, in the main, religious. Religious tolerance in contemporary America is, in the main, a *religious* accomplishment. And while it has had important interreligious dimensions that we should remember and respect, the basic demographics tell us that the religious accomplishment of religious tolerance in America is, in the main, a Christian accomplishment.

That accomplishment is, to be sure, never secure, and thus never to be taken for granted. The convictions that undergird it must continually be renewed and refreshed. Moreover, the religious accomplishment of religious tolerance is set firmly on the path to a secure future only when it has begun to build a genuine pluralism out of what today passes for pluralism, which is all too often a monism of indifference.

We are used to thinking of "pluralism" as a demographic fact. But, as we noted before, the demographic fact is *plurality*. As the late John Courtney Murray taught us, *pluralism,* genuine pluralism, is never a mere sociological fact: it is, rather, a great moral-cultural accomplishment. For true pluralism means, not the avoidance of differences, or an indifference to differences, but the thoughtful engagement of differences within a community of civic friendship. Pluralism is the achievement of an orderly conversation, which is another way of saying a "civil society."

And what impels us to "lay down our arms . . . and . . . take up argument," as Murray nicely put it?[14] Again, there are many possible ways to build the kind of character that allows one to "take up argument" and thereby become a democratic citizen. But surely one way is via the Christian claim that we are called *to* argument and *out of* barbarism by the grace of Christ, the Logos of God, who is himself the guarantor of the intelligibility and ultimate benignity of the created order. "Next to the Blessed Sacrament itself, your neighbor is the holiest object presented to your senses." Not a bad aphorism, that, for a democrat amidst plurality, seeking to help turn that plurality into pluralism.[15]

Giving an Account

In the third place, Christian conviction makes an important contribution to the *legitimation* of our democratic regime in that Christian religious convictions and moral norms enable Christians to give an account of their democratic commitments.

Serious political action is political action undertaken after serious moral reflection and with serious moral justification. In the Declaration of Independence, as we all remember, Thomas Jefferson prefaced the moral case for American independence (and the bill of particulars against George III) by bowing toward a "decent respect to the opinions of mankind." Jefferson's willingness to give an account—or, as he put it, to "declare the causes" of the colonists' actions—ought to characterize the democrat making the case for democracy in any age.

That certainly ought to be the case in the American democracy, because, as Lincoln insisted, America is, was, and (certain contemporary critics notwithstanding) always will be a "proposition country":

a political community formed and sustained by certain intellectual and moral convictions. Who is the American, this new man, asked Crève-coeur. He is, replied Lincoln at Gettysburg, the bearer of a proposition that was the product of moral convictions. To be able to give an account of those convictions is no small part of the responsibility of citizenship, at least in these United States.

What is a good citizen? Richard John Neuhaus has put the matter succinctly:

> A good citizen does more than abide by the laws. A good citizen is able to give an account, a morally compelling account, of the regime of which he is part. He is able to justify its defense against its enemies, and to convincingly recommend its virtues to the next generation so that they, in turn, can transmit the regime to citizens yet unborn. This regime of liberal democracy, of republican self-governance, is not self-evidently good and just. An account must be given. Reasons must be given. They must be reasons that draw authority from that which is higher than the self, from that which is external to the self, from that to which the self is ultimately obliged.[16]

Father Neuhaus went on to ask, provocatively, whether an atheist could meet this test of good citizenship. Now there are many ways of being an atheist, and it is not without piquancy to recall that atheism—being *a-theos,* without God, or more precisely, the gods—was the charge leveled against the early Christians, who were thereby regarded as subversives in times of Roman persecution. Neuhaus, however, was particularly concerned about the distinctive contemporary form of being *a-theos,* without God, which he styled the "atheism of unreason": a way of being *a-theos* that "denies not only the possibility of truth claims about God but the possibility of claims to truth at all."[17]

Here we return to the debonair nihilism and principled skepticism noted in the previous chapter. In this conceptual world, if such it may be called, denying God is as nonsensical as affirming God. There is no "truth" per se; there is only the truth that the relevant "community of discourse" agrees to take as true. One has to wonder, Neuhaus concluded, whether it is at all possible for someone who is *a-theos* in this fashion to be a good citizen, in the full-orbed sense of the term. For the atheist of unreason cannot, by his or her own self-understanding, give a morally persuasive or compelling account of the democratic regime, an account that has a genuinely public grip beyond the community of selves that just happens to find it true.[18]

This judgment provoked an interesting response from a more old-fashioned-style atheist, Paul Kurtz, a former philosophy professor at SUNY-Buffalo and the author of *Humanist Manifesto II*. Kurtz rumbled, in response to Neuhaus's argument, "Is this the opening salvo of a campaign to deny atheists their rights?" To which Father Neuhaus responded, "Relax, Mr. Kurtz. Your rights are secured by my understanding of the truth, even if mine are not by yours."[19]

In an intellectual and cultural climate in which, as Alasdair MacIntyre argued a decade and a half ago, it is extraordinarily difficult to say "You *ought* to do this," rather than "I'd *prefer* that you do this,"[20] we seem to be stymied by Pontius Pilate's famous question to Jesus in John 18:38, "What is truth?" Pilate believed, perhaps cynically, perhaps sincerely, that his question was a real conversation-stopper. So do many of our contemporaries, not least those in the academy. In fact, though, for a democracy that must give an account—to itself, to its competitors and enemies, and to succeeding generations—of the truths about the human person and human community on which it was founded, Pilate's question ought to get the needed conversation started, not bring it to a premature halt.[21]

In his 1993 encyclical letter *Veritatis Splendor,* "The Splendor of the Truth," Pope John Paul II has some interesting things to say about the relationship between truth and freedom, things to be explored in more detail in a later chapter. Suffice it to say here that, contrary to the regnant media caricature of John Paul, the Polish pope in fact celebrates the modern world's emphasis on political freedom. (As a man who spent the first forty years of his adulthood living under, and struggling against, Nazis and Communists, how could he not?) But what happens, the Pope asks, when freedom gets untethered from truth? Can freedom stand by itself, without decomposing into license? This is a question of great importance, for if freedom becomes license, then freedom becomes its own undoing, as every aspect of personal and social life becomes simply the assertion of power. And that means, among many other things, the death of democracy. For when truth is democratized—which is to say, when the truth is thought to be no more than the will of each of us or a majority of us—then democracy, unable to give a finally compelling account of its own truth, is left defenseless before its enemies.[22] Democracy is not, to repeat, a machine that will run of itself.

Americans, whose political history as an independent nation began with the assertion of certain "self-evident truths," ought not to find the Pope's reassertion of a relationship between freedom and truth all that foreign. And in considering whether moral truth that is religiously informed and derived constitutes some sort of threat to democracy, we might well revisit James Madison's famous *Memorial and Remonstrance,* one of the key texts in forming the American constitutional tradition of religious freedom. We have become so accustomed to the notion of "rights" as trumps, sundered from any sense of duties, that we may miss Madison's understanding of religious freedom as an inalienable right that is ordered to a prior and supervening duty. But here is the *Memorial and Remonstrance:*

> It is the duty of every man to render to the Creator such homage and such only as he believes to be acceptable to him. This duty is precedent, both in order of time and in degree of obligation, to the claims of Civil Society. Before any man can be considered as a member of Civil Society, he must be considered as a subject of the Governor of the Universe: And if a member of Civil Society, who enters into any subordinate Association, must always do it with a reservation of his duty to the General Authority; much more must every man who becomes a member of any particular Civil Society, do it with a saving of his allegiance to the Universal Sovereign.[23]

Christians are not the only people capable of "giving an account" of their democratic commitments. Other accounts are given, and some of them have considerable public purchase. Still other accounts are thin indeed, and one would fear for the future of the United States if these thin accounts were to become dominant in the populace (as they already are among too many intellectuals). But the Christian claim that we can give such an account, a defense, of the American proposition and experiment, a defense based on biblically warranted moral understandings, puts Christians in a position to offer a more robust legitimation of the American democratic regime than some, and perhaps many, others. And that is a matter of no small public consequence in a proposition country such as this.

The Paradox

During the past two hundred years or so of Western history, a form of "Christendom" has come to an end. History has determined that the Church, for the foreseeable future, will not be able to claim a privileged (still less, determinative) role in the formulation of public policy; nor, in most cases, will the Church have state power buttressing its truth claims. The union of altar and throne is over. The last king has not been strangled with the guts of the last priest, as Voltaire wished. But "the priests" no longer constitute an "estate," and the Church is no longer a partisan political actor.

For some Christians, this has seemed a loss; some even consider it a catastrophe. I do not presume to know the future that has been created by the end of this type of Christendom. But I do think I can see a profound paradox emerging in these early days of "post-Christendom." And that paradox is a challenge to rethink the question of winners and losers at the end of modernity.

I believe it is very good for the Church that a form of Christendom implying a deep entanglement of the *auctoritas* of the Church with the *potestas* of the state is over and done with. The end of this style of Christendom frees the Church for its essential tasks of evangelization, worship, and service. And the end of Christendom gets the Church out of the coercion business, a great stain on its record that Pope John Paul II has called Christians to repent of publicly in preparation for the turn of the millennium.[24] When the same pope, in rejecting coercive evangelization, writes that "the Church proposes; she imposes nothing," he knows, and all the rest of us know, that this has not always been the case. But that it now is the case for one billion Roman Catholics is very good news for the Church and the world, in the twenty-first century and into the third millennium of the Common Era. The Church has no business putting the coercive power of the state behind its truth claims; nor does the Church have any business resacralizing politics, of any ideological hue. The end of that entanglement is, to repeat, a very, very good thing for the Church.

On the other hand, and here is our paradox, I am not at all convinced that this disentanglement that we call "the end of Christendom" has been quite the undifferentiated blessing it was expected to be for those persons and institutions charged with the tasks of governance. The machine, to repeat it one last time, will not and cannot run of itself. Democracy must be attentive to the maintenance and moral health of that social space we call "civil society," lest a flat majoritarianism decay into a subtle totalitarianism, and lest the encroachments of the bureaucratic state get out of control: who will be the caretakers of civil society? Democracy needs a critical mass of democrats, and democrats are made, not born: how shall we "grow" the democrats we need to sustain our democracy? The American democracy in particular must be able to render an account of itself: who will offer a compelling moral justification for this strange, sloppy, confused, maddening, exhilarating, tawdry, and glorious way of doing the public business? It is good, indeed it is essential, that the democratic state not be a sacred state. But the democratic state needs the disentangled Church—the "post-Christendom" Church—in order to remain a law-governed democracy in which freedom serves the ends of genuine human flourishing.

Perhaps, as a matter of abstract speculation, it could be different. But we live in the real world, in which the atheism of unreason and the moral relativism that is its bastard have profoundly affected our culture and our civil society. When three justices of the Supreme Court of the United States can reduce the "heart of liberty" to "the right to define one's own concept of existence, of meaning, of the universe, and of the mystery of human life,"[25] we are in deep trouble. Here there is no civil society, no community of democratic discourse. Here, rather, is a congeries of monads, who can hardly be considered citizens since they are related and mutually engaged only by their capacity to contest one another's "concept of existence" by lawsuit. Here there is only the state, and the individual. And we ought to know, from the history of this most sanguinary of centuries, where that eventually leads.[26]

See, then, how far the United States has come from the *Memorial and Remonstrance*. The Court seems to believe that all moral judgments are, somehow, sectarian religious judgments; and since judgments of this sort are, on the Court's understanding, inherently private, they cannot be in play in the public square. So the result is not only a religiously naked public square but a morally denuded American *agora* in which, by definition, there can be no account given in defense of the regime.

This is not a situation the United States can endure indefinitely.

A Church committed to maintaining its critical distance from state power, a Church that has internalized Dostoevsky's critique in "The Grand Inquisitor," claims no monopoly on virtue in public life. On the contrary, such a "post-Christendom" Church is committed to fostering the emergence of other strong centers of civic piety and public morality. But the "disentanglement" of "post-Christendom" forces the democratic polity to take far more seriously the question of the sources of civic piety and the means for its nurturance. This suggests that the democratic state must also deliberately foster the maintenance of institutions beyond itself, institutions that relativize the state's claims and on whose transmission of the *ethos* of democracy the democratic state depends.

Such a self-denying discipline is much easier for the eucharistic Church, which understands that its nature is to be broken and shared, than for any state; states are not accustomed to say to any other power, *Domine, non sum dignus.* And so, it may well be that the far greater burden of the end of Christendom is borne by the democratic state than by the Church. The Church, now, can give a carefully and deeply argued account of why it supports and defends the democratic project in history. But can American democracy? The Church, now, understands why it must discipline itself. But does American democracy?

4

Christian Conviction and Democratic Etiquette

A disentangled public Church is not a disengaged Church. Thus the next question to be addressed, once we have agreed to a certain "post-Christendom" mode of Christian being-in-the-world, is: how? How do we engage in a public discourse that keeps sharp the two-edged sword of gospel truth while strengthening the bonds of democratic civility? How do we distinguish between being evangelists of the Gospel and being citizens with prudential judgments informed by strong religious and moral convictions?

According to a bit of street wisdom that has worked its way into the national vocabulary, "You got to walk the walk, not just talk the talk." We might, on the matter of explicitly Christian rhetoric and the American public square, consider reversing the injunction and asking: How *do* we talk the talk so that we, and others, can walk the walk of a freedom ordered to truth and fulfilled in goodness? How do we talk so that moral judgments born of Christian religious conviction can be heard and considered by all Americans—or at least by all those willing to acknowledge that moral judgment plays a crucial role in the public-policy process?

How Christians are to "talk the talk" in American public life is a question that will not go away, because it cannot. This is a fact of demographics, as well as a reflection of the nation's historic cultural core. For the foreseeable future, the United States will remain at once a democracy, a deeply religious society, and a vibrantly, maddeningly,

65

and in some respects depressingly diverse culture. And just as in decades if not centuries past, the American public square will continue to exhibit a striking diversity of "vocabularies," many of them religious, others determinedly secular.

Raising the Decibel Level

How can Christians of various theological persuasions talk with one another as they deliberate their public responsibilities? And then, how can these diverse Christian communities contribute to a public moral discourse that sounds more like counterpoint than a cacophony? Is there a "grammar" that can bring some discipline to the polyglot public debate over how we ought to live together? Can such a "grammar" avoid producing a muddled theological Esperanto?

Questions like this have been hardy perennials in the garden of American public controversy for many decades. But they have been rendered more urgent over the past twenty years by two phenomena, distinct in their provenance but related in their public consequences.

The first is the return of conservative, evangelical, and fundamentalist Protestants to the public square from the cultural hinterlands to which they were consigned (and to which they often consigned themselves) in the aftermath of the Scopes trial of 1925. For almost fifty years after that great trek to the margins of the public discourse, "the evangelicals" were content to remain in their enclaves, worshipping their God and educating their children as they saw fit, asking only to be left alone by the larger society. By the late 1970s, however, the Carter administration's Justice Department and Internal Revenue Service, through their assault on Christian day schools, had demonstrated the impossibility of sustaining that strategy. The result was the defensive/offensive movement we have come to know as the "religious new right."[1] That this movement has dramatically sharpened the debate over the place of Christian conviction in public discourse needs no elaboration.

And second, the return of the evangelicals and fundamentalists from cultural exile was paralleled in the 1980s by a new assertiveness on the part of American Roman Catholics (and especially several prominent bishops). On issues such as abortion, pornography, school choice, and the claims of the gay/lesbian/bisexual movement, Catholic bishops, activists, and intellectuals who insisted on acting like Catholics in public soon found themselves engaged, not simply in political or electoral battles, but in heated confrontations with several of the key idea-shaping and values-transmitting institutions in our society: the prestige press, the academy, and the popular entertainment industry. One memorable moment in this struggle came on November 26, 1989, when a *New York Times* editorial solemnly warned Catholic bishops that their resistance to abortion-on-demand threatened the "truce of tolerance" by which Catholics were permitted to play a part in American public life. Even by *Times* standards, this was a high point in chutzpah.[2]

Thus through the evangelical insurgency and the revitalization of Catholics in the public square—through the activism and interaction of two groups who had long eyed each other with suspicion (if not downright hostility) but who now found themselves in common cause on a host of fevered public issues—American democracy was faced, yet again, with the problem of how it could be *e pluribus unum* in fact as well as assertion. And for their part, American Christians had to consider how their most deeply held convictions could be brought to bear on public life in ways that were faithful both to those convictions and to the canons of democratic civility. Given that the United States remains, in Chesterton's famous phrase, a nation with the soul of a church, the two questions were not unrelated.

Mars Hill Revisited

So far as we know, the Apostle Paul was not overly vexed about the public policy of Athens in the first century of the Common Era. His invocation of the "unknown god" to the men gathered on the Areopagus (Acts 17:16-34) was an evangelical tactic aimed at religious conversion, not an attempt to persuade his hearers on matters of deficit financing, health care, or defense appropriations in Greater Athens. But the evangelical instinct that led the apostle to seek a language—a "grammar"—through which the Athenians could grasp (and be grasped by) the claims of the Gospel is something on which we might well reflect, as we ponder such decidedly secondary questions as deficit financing, health care, and defense appropriations in the American republic.

Paul was a man at home with at least two moral-intellectual "grammars": the Judaic, in which he had been rabbinically trained, and the Hellenistic, which dominated elite culture in the Mediterranean world at the time. No doubt Paul regarded the Judaic grammar as superior to the Hellenistic. But he did not hesitate to employ the latter when he deemed it necessary for the sake of the Gospel.

This grammatical ecumenicity, as we might call it, was memorably captured in Paul's familiar boast, "I have become all things to all men, that I might by all means save some" (I Cor. 9:22b). Again, the questions with which we are wrestling here are of considerably less consequence than the salvation of souls. But if, in *that* supremely important cause, the Apostle to the Gentiles could appeal to his audiences through language and images with which they were familiar—if Paul could expropriate an Athenian idol as an instrument for breaking open the Gospel of Christ, the Son of the living God—then perhaps it is incumbent upon us, working in the far less dramatic precincts of public policy, to devise means of translating our religious convictions into language and images that can illuminate for all our fellow citizens the truths of how we ought to live together, as we have come to understand those truths through faith and reason.

There is a danger in this, of course: Christians eager to be heard in the public square may, through an excess of "grammatical" ecumenicity, so attenuate their message that the sharp edge of truth gets blunted and thus debased. Flaccidity in the cause of a misconceived public ecumenism has contributed to the decline of the academic study of religion in America, as well as to the collapse of mainline/oldline Protestantism.[3] Some would suggest that a similar disposition to excessive public correctness, as defined by the tastemakers of our society, has misshaped certain interpretations of the Roman Catholic "consistent ethic of life."

Moreover, it can often seem as if our cultural moment demands uncompromising confrontation rather than polite dialogue. When unborn human beings have less legal standing than an endangered species of bird in a national forest; when any configuration of "committed" adults is considered in enlightened circles to constitute a "marriage"; when senior senators bloviate about "sexual harassment" in kindergarten while national illegitimacy rates approach 30 per cent of all births: well, one is reminded of Orwell's observation, two generations ago, that "we have now sunk to a depth at which the restatement of the obvious is the first duty of intelligent men." There are some hard home truths to be told on the various Mars Hills of the American republic, and the teller of such truths is certain to bring down upon his head the odium of those committed to the establishment of the republic of the imperial autonomous Self. Under such circumstances, the old country wheeze that tells us we may as well get hung for a sheep as for a goat retains its pertinence.

The Good News

But the good news is that the bad news is not all the news there is. For we may also see, in certain signs of these times, a new public recognition of the enduring reality of religious conviction and a new willingness to concede a place for religiously based moral argument in the American public square. The warm reception given Yale law professor Stephen L. Carter's critique of the secularism of our elite culture, our law, and our politics suggests that seeds first planted by Richard John Neuhaus in *The Naked Public Square* are beginning to flower, however variously or confusedly.[4] The broad bipartisan, ecumenical, and interreligious support that made possible the passage of the Religious Freedom Restoration Act in 1993 was also an important signal (though it remains to be seen just how the creative minds on the federal bench will bend RFRA to various agendas of their own devising).

Then there is the fact that, in the mid-1990s, Americans have a president who, unlike his predecessor, is unabashedly public about his Christian faith, and who seems to understand that the engagement of differing religious convictions within the bond of democratic civility is good for America. It is far from self-evident that President Clinton's policies (and appointments) are entirely congruent with his religious and moral rhetoric; nor can one dismiss as mere partisanship the suggestion that this rhetoric was designed in part to divide the white evangelical vote and thus help secure the president's reelection. But politicians will always be politicians, and those of us who take the bully pulpit seriously can still applaud the fact that the president of the United States has publicly acknowledged that "we are a people of faith" and that "religion helps to give our people the character without which a democracy cannot survive."[5] However wide the gap between the chief executive's talk and his administration's walk, it surely means something that President Clinton experiences no embarrassment about using religious language in public.[6]

At the very least, the president's public appeal to biblical religion ought to remind us just how far from our roots we have strayed when the "naked public square" could even be considered a plausible embodiment of the American democratic experiment. In a nation whose coins and currency proclaim that "In God We Trust"; whose Supreme Court sessions open with the plea (ever more poignant in recent years) that "God save this honorable court"; whose House of Representatives and Senate begin their daily work with prayer; whose presidents have, without exception, invoked the blessing of God in their inaugural addresses — in such a country, it is the proponents of established secularism who should be on the historical, cultural, constitutional, and moral defensive. If President Clinton's use of explicitly religious language does no more than make clear who ought to be prosecuting and who defending in this matter of religion and public life, he will have done the country a service.

Lincoln's Biblical Witness

Still, the sheer fact that religiously based public moral argument is deemed O.K. in certain influential quarters does not suggest the end of our problem, any more than the national celebration of the work ethic of Cal Ripken, Jr., the Baltimore Orioles' nonstop shortstop, suggested a massive embrace of old-fashioned values. What we may have today, through a confluence of forces — not least the crisis of the urban underclass, which has finally focused the elite culture on problems of moral formation — is an opening through which to begin the slow and laborious process of reclothing the naked public square. Save in some tenured bunkers where cultural vandals make merry while the cities burn and children shoot children over basketball shoes, it is now widely acknowledged that the denuding of that square has been bad for the country. The question is how, and in what garments, it will be reclothed.

Abraham Lincoln, and specifically his Second Inaugural Address, provides an important historical model. In this speech Lincoln interpreted the national agony of a sanguinary civil war in explicitly biblical terms, citing Matthew ("Woe unto the world because of offenses; for it must needs be that offenses come: but woe to that man by whom the offense cometh") and the Psalmist ("The judgments of the Lord are true and righteous altogether") to buttress his general hermeneutic claim that the workings-out of the American democratic experiment were caught up in a divinely ordered plan for human history.

Now, can anyone reasonably argue that, in his deliberate choice of biblical language and in his appeal to the notion of a providential purpose in history, Lincoln was excluding anyone from the public debate over the meaning and purpose of the War Between the States? Can anyone reasonably contend that Lincoln's attempt to prepare the United States for reconciliation by offering a biblically based moral interpretation of the recent national experience constituted an unconstitutional "imposition" of belief and values on others?

We recognize Lincoln's Second Inaugural as perhaps the greatest speech in America's history precisely because, with singular eloquence and at a moment of unparalleled national trauma, it spoke to the entire country in an idiom that the entire country could understand. No one was excluded by Lincoln's use of biblical language and imagery; all, irrespective of confessional conviction (or the lack thereof), were included in the great moral drama whose meaning the president was trying to fix in the national consciousness.

It is arguably true that, even in the midst of civil war, the United States (North and South) was a more culturally coherent nation than our America today; and it is certainly true that no statesman of Lincoln's eloquence and moral imagination is on the horizon of our public life. Yet there is still an important lesson here: that biblical language and imagery in public discourse ought to be used not to divide but to unite; not to finish off an opponent with a rhetorical *coup de grâce,* but to call him (and all of us) to an examination of conscience on the promise and perils of the American democratic experiment.

As the Second Inaugural amply attests, this principle does not preclude hard truth-telling. But Lincoln spoke as one who understood the frailty of all things human, and especially of all things political; he did not suggest, even amidst a civil war, that all righteousness lay on one side and all evil on another; he acknowledged that the nation was under judgment; and he spoke, not as a Republican, and not even as a Northerner, but as an American seeking to reach out to other Americans across chasms of division at least as broad and deep as any we face today.

Such an approach—in which Christian conviction speaks through and to the plurality of our national life, enabling plurality to become a genuine pluralism—ought to commend itself to us, first and foremost, on Christian theological, indeed doctrinal, grounds.

The treasure of the Gospel has been entrusted to the earthen vessels of our humanity for the salvation of the world, not for the securing of partisan advantage. We debase the Gospel and the Body of Christ when we use the Gospel as a partisan trump card. Our first loyalty—our overriding loyalty—is to God in Christ, in the power of the Holy Spirit. Because of that loyalty, Christians are "resident aliens" in any *polis* in which they find themselves, as we have seen in reflecting on the *Letter to Diognetus*. But it is precisely because our ultimate allegiance is to a Kingdom not of this world that we can contribute to the working-out of an American democratic experiment that has understood itself, from the outset, to be an experiment in limited government, judged by transcendent moral norms, and open to the participation of all men and women who affirm belief in certain "self-evident" truths about human persons and human community.

The experiment could fail; it requires a virtuous people in order to succeed. All this was implied in the Second Inaugural, and that helps explain the enduring power of Lincoln's address. Like Lincoln, we should make it clear in whatever we say and do in public that our purpose is to reunite America through a new birth of freedom, not simply to throw their rascals out and get our rascals in.

There are also practical considerations to be weighed here. Playing the Gospel as a trump card is not offensive only to Jews, Muslims, Buddhists, and secularists; it is also offensive to other Christians—even (perhaps especially) those who may be otherwise inclined to make common cause with us on public-policy issues. In brief, playing the Gospel as a trump card makes Christians less effective witnesses to the truths they hold about the way in which we ought to live together. Moreover, and to go back to our primary concern, the suggestion that Christian orthodoxy yields a single answer to virtually every contested issue of public policy is an offense, not simply against political common sense, but against Christian orthodoxy.

A Grammar for Ecumenicity

Lincoln's Second Inaugural, and its unchallenged position in the pantheon of American public rhetoric, ought to have secured a place for biblical language and imagery in our public life, despite the frettings of radical secularists. But, having seen in Lincoln a model for the use of explicitly biblical language in public discourse, perhaps we should think also about natural law.

This is not the place to explore the differences among the various natural-law theories, or the points of tangency (and distinction) between Roman Catholic natural-law theory and Calvinist concepts of common grace. Rather, the question before us is how Christians contribute to the evolution of a genuine pluralism out of the plurality of vocabularies in American public moral discourse today; the question is how today's cannonading is transformed, in John Courtney Murray's pungent phrase, into a situation of "creeds at war, intelligibly."[7] And the issue is a serious one, for society will descend into a different kind of war, Hobbes's dread war of "all against all," unless we can talk together in such a way that we make sense to one another —or at least enough sense to conduct the public argument that is the lifeblood of a democracy.

"Natural law" here means the claim that, even under the conditions of the Fall, there is a moral logic built into the world and into us: a logic that reasonable men and women can grasp by disciplined reflection on the dynamics of human action.[8] The grasping of that logic is, Christians would say, aided by the effects of grace at work in human hearts; and the Gospel may draw out of the natural law certain behavioral implications that are not readily discernible to the secular eye.[9] But the point is that such a moral logic exists, that it is available to all men through rational reflection, and that it can be intelligibly argued in public.

We saw that logic at work in the American public debate over possible U.S. military action in the Persian Gulf during the months between Iraq's invasion of Kuwait in August 1990 and the beginning of Operation Desert Storm in January 1991. From one end of the country to the other, and in venues ranging from radio talk shows to taxicabs to barber shops to bars to the halls of Congress, men and women instinctively argued in the natural-law categories of the just war tradition. Was ours a just cause? Who could properly authorize the use of force? Did we have a reasonable chance of success? Was military action a last resort? How could innocent civilian lives be protected? The country did not reach instinctively for these questions because the just war tradition had been effectively catechized in our schools over the past generation (alas); rather, it did so because they are the "natural" questions that any morally reflective person will ask when contemplating the use of lethal force for the common good. Moreover, the rather high level of public moral argument over the Gulf crisis—perhaps the highest since a similar natural-law argument had been publicly engaged during the debate over the 1964 Civil Rights Act—suggests that this instinctive moral logic may have a unique capacity to bring grammatical order to the deliberations of a diverse society.

To commend the development of the skills necessary for conducting public debate according to the grammar of the natural law is not to deny explicitly Christian or Jewish or Muslim moral discourse a place in the American public square. All Americans have the right to bring their most deeply held convictions into play in our common life; that is, or ought to be, the commonly accepted meaning of the First Amendment's guarantee of the "free exercise" of religion. But to be effective in the public square those convictions should be translated into idioms that all the hearers can grasp, whether they are of the same, another, or no religion. And one "grammar" that can serve this purpose is the natural-law tradition. Two examples may help illustrate the point.

The abortion license created by the Supreme Court in 1973 remains the single most bitterly contested issue in American public life. Christian orthodoxy regards elective abortion as a grave moral evil, an offense against the entire structure of Christian morals.[10] And there is no doubt that the steady proclamation of that truth, in love, has been a crucial factor in the perdurance of the pro-life movement over the past generation. The overwhelming majority of those active on behalf of the right-to-life of the unborn are committed to that cause, despite fierce opposition from the elite culture, because they understand that the Lord requires this of them.

But how are we to make our case to those who do not share that prior religious commitment, or to those Christians whose churches do not provide clear moral counsel on this issue? And how do we do this in a political-cultural-legal climate in which individual autonomy has been virtually absolutized?

We best make our case by insisting that our defense of the right-to-life of the unborn is a defense of civil rights and of a generous, hospitable American democracy; that abortion-on-demand gravely damages the American democratic experiment by drastically constricting the community of the commonly protected; that the private use of lethal violence against an innocent is an assault on the moral foundations of any just society. In short, we best make our case for legal protection of the unborn by deploying natural-law arguments that translate our Christian moral convictions into a public idiom more powerful than the idiom of autonomy.

A similar strategy commends itself in the face of the gay and lesbian insurgency. Again, the position of orthodox Christian morality is clear: homosexual acts violate the structure of the divinely created form of love by which men and women are to exercise their sexuality in unitive and procreative responsibility. Thus "homosexual marriage" is an oxymoron, and other proposals to grant homosexuality "equal protection" with heterosexuality are an offense against biblical morality: what many would call an abomination before the Lord.[11]

But given the vast disarray wrought by the sexual revolution, by the plurality of moral vocabularies in America, and by the current confusions attending Fourteenth Amendment jurisprudence, we make a more powerful case against the public-policy claims of the gay and lesbian insurgency by arguing on natural-law grounds: that it is in the very nature of governments to make discriminations; that the relevant question is whether any proposed discrimination is invidiously unjust; and that the legal preference given to heterosexual marriage is good for society because it strengthens the basic unit of society, the family, and because it is good for children.[12] Given the immense damage done to the urban underclass by the breakdown of family life, this is, alas, an easier argument to make today than it was twenty years ago. But as that asphalt *Via Dolorosa* comes to impress itself more indelibly on the national conscience, we may well find that natural-law-based appeals to public responsibility for the welfare of children and families give us a vocabulary superior in political potency to the rhetoric of autonomy. We may also find a new possibility for building a conservative-liberal coalition on these grounds, facing these intensely controverted issues.

Similar models of argumentation can be developed for other "social issues," including censorship, school curricula, school choice, sex education, and public health. In all these cases, it should be emphasized again, the goal is not to weaken our faith-based moral claims or judgments but to articulate them in ways that can be heard, engaged, and ultimately accepted by those who do not share our Christian commitment.

In Praise of Good Manners

Finally, a word about democratic etiquette. If patriotism is often the last refuge of scoundrels, then what currently passes for civility can be the last refuge of moral weakness, confusion, or cowardice. Moreover, as Mr. Dooley pointed out a while ago, "pollytics ain't beanbag." That enduring reality, and the gravity of the questions engaged in the American *Kulturkampf*, remind us that genuine civility is not the same as docility or "niceness."

But there is a truth embedded in the habit of democratic etiquette, and we should frankly acknowledge it. The truth is that persuasion is better than coercion. And that is true because public moral argument is superior—morally and politically—to violence.

All law is, of course, in some measure coercive. But one of the moral superiorities of democracy is that our inevitably coercive laws are defined by a process of persuasion, rather than by princely ukase or politburo decree. This morally superior mode of lawmaking embodies four truths: that men and women are created with intelligence and free will, and thus as subjects, not merely objects, of power; that genuine authority is the right to command, not merely the power to coerce; that those who are called to obey and to bear burdens have first the right to be heard and to deliberate on whether a proposed burden is necessary for the common good; and that there is an inherent sense of justice in the people, by which they are empowered to pass judgment on how we ought to live together.[13]

Thus in observing, even as we refine, the rules of democratic etiquette, Christians are helping to give contemporary expression to certain moral understandings that have lain at the heart of the central political tradition of the West since that tradition first formed in Jerusalem, Athens, and Rome (to take symbolic reference points). And, not so inconsequentially, we are thereby taking a stand against the totalitarian temptation that lurks at the heart of every modern state, including modern democratic states. To be sure, that is not the most important "public" thing we Christians do. But it is an important thing, nonetheless.

Beyond "Accommodation"

Two obstacles make the difficult transition from plurality to genuine pluralism in contemporary America even more difficult.

The first obstacle is the legal and cultural sediment of the Supreme Court's jurisprudence about the First Amendment religion clause over the past fifty years. There is not space here to review this sorry history. Suffice it to say that the Court's strange decision to divide what is clearly one religion clause into two religion clauses, and its subsequent tortuous efforts to "balance" the claims of free-exercise and no-establishment through Rube Goldberg contraptions like the three-part "Lemon test,"[14] have led the justices into a jurisprudential labyrinth of exceptional darkness and complexity. Worse, they have created a legal and cultural climate in which the public exercise of religious conviction is too often understood as a quirk to be tolerated, rather than a fundamental human right that any just state is obliged to acknowledge.[15] The justices' increasingly bizarre balancing act has elevated no-establishment and subordinated free-exercise to the point where a new establishment, the establishment of secularism, threatens the constitutional order. And until the First Amendment's religion clause is stitched together once again, in law and in the popular understanding of the law—until, that is, no-establishment is understood as the means to the goal of free-exercise—our law will remain profoundly confused and our political culture too often inhospitable to people of faith.[16]

Thus, for example, one cannot applaud Professor Stephen L. Carter's suggestion that the answer to the trivialization of religious belief and practice in contemporary American law and politics is something like maximum feasible toleration for religion in public life. No: the free and public exercise of religious conviction is not to be "tolerated"

—it is to be welcomed as the first of freedoms and the foundation of any meaningful scheme of human rights. "Toleration," as we have seen, has to do with how we think and act in a public square where religiously informed moral judgments are in vigorous conversation. That conversation itself, however, is not something we simply "tolerate." It is something we ought to celebrate.

In brief: until we reverse, both in law and in our popular legal-political culture, the inversion of the religion clause that the Court has effected since the *Everson* decision in 1947, the already difficult problem of bringing a measure of democratic order and civility into our public moral discourse will be endlessly exacerbated.

Christian Self-Discipline

The second obstacle along the path to genuine pluralism is a certain lack of theological and political discipline on the part of the religious right.

Now this may seem a classic case of "blaming the victim." After all, the fall of 1993 witnessed a campaign for lieutenant governor of Virginia in which the Democratic Party and many reporters portrayed the Republican candidate, an avowed Christian, as a high-tech Savonarola panting to impose a theocracy on the great Commonwealth, the Mother of Presidents, through such lurid policies as . . . well, school choice, informed consent prior to an elective abortion, parental notification of a minor's intention to seek an abortion, equalization of the state's personal income-tax exemption with that allowed by the federal government, tort reform, and a lid on state borrowing. All of which took place just eight months after a *Washington Post* reporter blithely described evangelicals as "largely poor, uneducated, and easy to command." Which in turn took place a mere seven months after the prestige press batted nary an eye when Jesse Jackson, at the 1992 Democratic National Convention, told the Christmas story in such a way as to criticize those who would have objected to Mary's aborting Jesus.

In these circumstances, in which fevered warnings are issued about the machinations of the religious right while not a word is said about the agenda of the religious left (and its influence on no less a personage than Hillary Rodham Clinton), it may seem passing strange to suggest that the challenge to the establishment of secularism in America must be complemented by a demand for increased self-discipline on the part of the religious right. Yet that is what is needed. And here is why.

It is needed, first and foremost, for theological reasons. A partisan Gospel is an ideological Gospel, and, as many of us insisted against the claims of liberation theology in the 1970s and 1980s, an ideologically driven Gospel is a debasement of the truth of God in Christ. "Christian voter scorecards" suggesting that the Gospel provides a "Christian answer" on the balanced-budget amendment, congressional term limits, voting rules in the House of Representatives, and the federal debt ceiling demean the Gospel by identifying it with an ideological agenda.

Another set of concerns arises from democratic theory. I have no quarrel with describing our current circumstances as an American "culture war." But the suggestion, offered by Patrick J. Buchanan at the 1992 Republican Convention, that a culture war is to be equated, willy-nilly, with a "religious war" must be stoutly resisted. The two are not the same. A culture war can be adjudicated, and the warring parties can reach a reasonable accommodation through the processes (electoral, legislative, and juridical) of democratic persuasion. This is not the case with a religious war.

Moreover, the very phrase "religious war" suggests that the answer to the issue at the heart of the culture war—namely, the establishment of officially sanctioned secularism as the American democratic creed —is an alternative sanctified creed. But under the conditions of plurality that seem to be written into the script of history (by God, some of us would say), such a substitution cannot be the answer. The alternative to the naked public square is the reconstitution of civil society in America. And civil society requires the achievement of a genuine pluralism in which creeds are "intelligibly in conflict."

Any number of forces have declared war on the religious right. For its part, however, the religious right should decline that definition of the conflict, and get on with the task of rebuilding civil society in America. This strategy would be both theologically appropriate and, one suspects, very good politics.

Finally, a greater measure of theological and political self-discipline is to be urged on the religious right because it is just possible that the right might win. And thus it had better start thinking now about how it wants to win: as a force of reaction, or as a movement to revitalize the American experiment. The choice here will have a lot to do with how conservatives, evangelical Christian or otherwise, govern in the future.

To say that the religious right just might win is not necessarily to predict the outcome of, say, the 1998 congressional elections, or the millennial presidentiad two years later. And it is possible that our current moral-cultural ills might lead to a kind of national implosion, perhaps in the next decade. To say that the religious right might win is, rather, to express an intuition about the current correlation of cultural forces in the American democracy. Irving Kristol seems to have been on to something when he argued (a mere twelve days after President Clinton's inauguration) that cultural conservatism was the wave of the future in the United States.[17] The secularization project, though it dominates the network airwaves and the academy, has largely failed. Americans are arguably more religious today than they were fifty years ago. And this growth is not to be found in those precincts where mainline/oldline churches have been acquiescing to secularization. On the contrary, the churches making the most serious doctrinal and moral demands on their congregants are the ones that are flourishing. All of this on the positive side, coupled with, on the negative side, the undeniably disastrous effects of the sexual revolution, the welfare state, and the absolutization of individual autonomy, suggests that the revival of "traditional moral values" as the common ethical horizon of our public life in the late twentieth and early twenty-first century is not impossible.

In these circumstances, the evangelical and fundamentalist components of the religious right and their Catholic allies must practice the public arts of grammatical ecumenicity. Religious conservatives must learn how to translate religiously grounded moral claims into a public language and imagery capable of challenging the hegemony of what Mary Ann Glendon has styled "rights-talk."[18]

For the cultural-conservative coalition that can revitalize American civil society and American politics will include Christians of Protestant, Roman Catholic, and Orthodox commitment; Jews who have broken ranks with the reflexive secularism and cultural liberalism that have come to inform so much of American Jewry's approach to the public square; a few secular people; and, just perhaps, a considerable number of Muslims. Grammatical ecumenicity within this coalition is essential to maintaining its strength in the cultural and political battles in which it will be engaged. And such ecumenicity will be even more essential for exercising the powers of governance so that the reconstitution of America as a nation *e pluribus unum* involves a widening, rather than a theologically and democratically inappropriate narrowing, of the *unum*.

In talking the talk, in truth and in charity, with force and with wit, so that others can enter the great conversation over the "oughts" of our common life, religious conservatives can make a signal contribution to the reclothing of America's naked public square. And in doing that, they will be serving the Lord who stands in judgment on all the works of our hands, most especially our politics. For orthodox Christians, politics is, or ought to be, penultimate. Talking the talk in the terms suggested here helps keep politics in its place. And that, too, is no mean contribution to the reconstruction of civil society in America at the end of the twentieth century.

5

John Paul II: The Lion Beyond Winter

On October 5, 1995, a 75-year-old Pole dressed in the manner of a sixteenth-century Dominican friar walked with some difficulty to the great marble rostrum of the United Nations General Assembly, there to address the world, or at least a goodly part of it. Behind this elderly cleric were arrayed several senior U.N. officials, including the secretary-general, Boutros Boutros-Ghali. In the world according to CNN, the Pole in the white soutane, the second son of a retired Hapsburg army officer, may have seemed something of an anachronism, while Dr. Boutros-Ghali and his colleagues, nattily attired and beaming, looked to be the very flower of late twentieth-century modernity.

The truth of things was rather different.

For in one of the great ironies of our time, the septuagenarian Pole, Karol Józef Wojtyła, more familiarly known as Pope John Paul II, walked onto that stage representing one of the world's most powerful, dynamic, and effective institutions, while the secretary-general and his confreres on the dais represented something that seemed, on its fiftieth anniversary, old, hackneyed, ineffective, bureaucratically stifling, and intellectually moribund—the adjectives that the founding fathers of modernity had once applied to the Roman Catholic Church.

But when the Pope addressed the United Nations in 1995, much more was going on than a grand symbolic refutation of the claim that modernization inevitably means radical secularization. For on the threshold of the third millennium the Catholic Church, under the leadership of John Paul II, has become far, far more than a symbol of stubborn religiosity.

In sharp contrast to the sorry record of the U.N., for example, the Church has become the world's foremost institutional defender of basic human rights. U.N. peacekeeping flounders around the world; Vatican peacemaking has been effective in venues ranging from Latin America to southern Africa. John Paul II is now widely recognized as the single most influential figure in the non-violent collapse of European Communism; as we shall see in the next chapter, the Pope has also been an important influence on the "third wave" of democratization that has changed the political landscape of central and eastern Europe, Latin America, and parts of east Asia.

Moreover, this recent past is prologue to a future of considerable possibility. The twenty-first century, André Malraux famously said, will be religious, or it will not *be*. Over one billion human beings, of virtually every race and ethnicity under the sun, are Roman Catholics. The social doctrine of their Church is, arguably, the most sophisticated body of moral reasoning about the free society on offer in a world poised on the edge of a new millennium. How that teaching shapes those billion lives, and how those billion people live out their Catholicism, will have an enormous impact on the social and political contours of the twenty-first century, and beyond.

Voltaire must be turning over in his grave. But then, Voltaire never imagined a pope quite like John Paul II.

Always Looking Forward

In August 1994, Roman journalists, the local rumor-mongers, and various other ecclesiastical hangers-on were mounting a death-watch along the Via della Conciliazione, the broad avenue running from Hadrian's tomb, the Castel Sant'Angelo, into St. Peter's Square. According to the chatter in the bars and trattorias, John Paul II was finished, and the only arguments were about the probable cause of his demise (cancer? Parkinson's disease? the aftereffects of Mehmet Ali Agca's bullets?), the identity of his successor, and the lasting impact, if any, of his pontificate.

Yet over the next nine months, between September 1994 and May

1995, John Paul II published an international bestseller *(Crossing the Threshold of Hope),* dramatically altered the course of the U.N.-sponsored World Conference on Population and Development in Cairo, gathered and addressed the largest crowd in human history (at Manila, in January 1995), saw his encyclical on abortion and euthanasia featured on the cover of *Newsweek* (and, even more astonishingly, respectfully treated in the *New York Times*), called the Church to prepare for the "Great Jubilee" of the year 2000 by publicly repenting of its sins and errors, boldly proposed that Orthodox and Protestant Christians help him think through the kind of papacy that makes sense in the third millennium of Christian history, and completed a grueling ten-day pilgrimage to Africa after briefer trips to the Czech Republic, Poland, and Belgium and a two-week holiday hiking in the mountains of the Val d'Aosta.

Not a bad run, that: especially for a 75-year-old who has survived an assassination attempt, cancer, and Italian medicine while working extraordinarily long hours, day in and day out, for the past seventeen years. But then John Paul didn't think he was dying in the late summer of 1994; and neither did those who were privileged in those days to share in his sharp, witty, and wholly future-oriented conversation. John Paul's expectation that there was still important work for him to do has surely been borne out by subsequent events.

But the extraordinary pace of the Pope's pastoral and intellectual activity in the mid-1990s does not explain why the London *Independent,* no papal apologist, described him in January 1995 as "the only truly global leader left." Why, then, when the Pope mounted the General Assembly rostrum in October 1995, did he seem, not a romantic anachronism, but a man perched adventuresomely on the cutting edge of history?

Revitalizing Peter's Commission

At one level, the answer has to do with the dramatic changes that John Paul II has wrought in the modern exercise of an ancient office. The centralization of authority in the Catholic Church in the mid- and late-nineteenth century created a largely executive papacy, with the pope functioning as something like the CEO of RC, Inc. In varying degrees, mid-twentieth-century popes chafed under this model of papal leadership. Pius XII (1939-58) retained the baroque style of his immediate predecessors, but invited a lot of the world into the Vatican to hear him discourse on a mind-boggling array of subjects, from midwifery to atomic warfare. John XXIII (1958-63) began to break out of the gilded cage, traveling on a few occasions to major Italian shrines. Paul VI (1963-78) took his message to the U.N., the World Council of Churches, Uganda, Manila, and the Holy Land. But with John Paul II, a decisive transformation of the world's oldest institution has taken place.

Except for a few recalcitrant Italians, no one still thinks that the pope's primary responsibility is to micro-manage the central administrative machinery of the Catholic Church. Using emblematic modern instruments like radio, television, DC-10s, helicopters, Mercedes-Benz "popemobiles," compact discs, and the Internet, John Paul has revived and revitalized the historic ministry of Peter, recorded in Acts, as the first among the Church's public teachers, or evangelists. The extraordinary volume of his official writings has guaranteed that John Paul's papacy will be remembered as one of the great teaching pontificates in history. But it is the intensely personal dimension he has brought to this catechesis, through his pilgrimages to every continent, that has caught the imagination of tens of millions of people around the world.

Because John Paul II has left such an imprint on contemporary history, it is important to emphasize that evangelism, not tourism and not politics-as-usual, has been the hallmark of his relentless travels. The Polish pope takes quite seriously the injunction of Jesus to Peter, that his task as leader of the apostolic college was to "strengthen your brethren" (Luke 22:32); the travels of Peter's 263rd successor have given the fulfillment of that commission a uniquely global reach. From the favelas of São Paulo to the Eskimo hinterlands of northwest Canada, from small African villages to the concrete canyons of Manhattan, John Paul has been, first and foremost, a pastor, calling the People of God who are the Body of Christ to a more compelling expression of the fullness of Christian faith.

The Pope is no quietist, however, and his evangelism is shaped by the conviction that Christian truth has an inescapably *public* character. In the following chapters, for example, we shall see how John Paul has made the Second Vatican Council's Declaration on Religious

Freedom the intellectual and moral cornerstone of a full-bodied Catholic theory (and critique) of democracy. Thus the Pope's public ministry has embodied, on a global political chessboard, the two things the Church asks of the world: space for its mission, and a hearing for its message.

I Ias this involved an inconsistency, perhaps even a contradiction? John Paul has, after all, persistently urged Catholic priests to avoid partisan politics. The charge of inconsistency is frequently mounted from the Catholic left (and from the leaders of repressive regimes). But it misses the fundamental theological point. For the Pope, commitment to the Gospel *demands* a defense of the dignity and worth of human life. In this sense, John Paul has been the least "political" of modern popes, if by "political" we mean acting internationally according to the established canons of diplomacy. When religious freedom and other basic human rights are threatened, John Paul has challenged dictators to their faces, privately or publicly—as a rogues' gallery that includes Ferdinand Marcos, Augusto Pinochet, Alfredo Strocssner, Wojciech Jaruzelski, and the brothers Ortega could attest.

But if by "political" we mean to recall once again that ancient Aristotelian question, "How *ought* we to live together?" then John Paul's global evangelism has been intensely "political"—though in a distinctively evangelical key. When Karol Wojtyła was a young man of twenty during the Nazi occupation of Poland, he was a leading figure in Kraków's underground Rhapsodic Theater. Performing clandestinely without props or costumes, in shuttered apartments above the streets where Nazi sound trucks blared the news of the latest eastern-front triumphs, the future pope learned the power of what the Rhapsodic players called the "living word" to cut sharply and cleanly through the static of lies and propaganda.[1] It is a lesson John Paul has applied in Managua and Manila, Warsaw and Santiago, and in the run-up to the September 1994 Cairo population conference, to considerable effect.[2]

The Pope's "public" project has remained remarkably consistent for seventeen years, even as changed historical circumstances have shifted the focus and, to some extent, the impact of the message. During the endgame of the Cold War, the issues and the imagery were clear-cut: there was the Pope in June 1979, preaching before a million Poles in Warsaw's Victory Square, calling upon the Holy Spirit to "renew the face of the earth—of this land!" And the people responded with the spontaneous, rhythmic chant, "We want God! We want God!"

In the post–Cold War period, and with his eye fixed on the developed societies of the West, John Paul has been pressing what might be termed a "postmodern" agenda of cultural reform and renewal. As the son of a nation that preserved itself for well over a century (between 1793 and 1919) through its language, literature, music, and religion when its independent political and economic life was snuffed out, John Paul II is convinced that "culture [is] . . . a greater power than all other forces" (as he told UNESCO in 1980). The Pope has now applied that conviction to the question of how our hard-won political and economic freedom can be lived responsibly. As we shall see in chapters seven and eight, John Paul believes that only a vibrant, publicly assertive moral culture can discipline and temper democratic polities and market economies so that democracy and the market serve the ends of genuine human flourishing.

The initial American reception of this "new" papal challenge was, perhaps, somewhat chilly; no doubt the message was distorted by a media lens through which every critique of the sexual revolution becomes a repressive assault from the fever swamps. But as concern for the character deficit in American society has mounted, what once seemed off-putting to some now looks increasingly prophetic. Americans are rediscovering the old truths that democrats are made, not born, and that a certain critical mass of virtue is indispensable to the functioning of democracy. Which happens to be exactly what John Paul has been urging.

On the Far Side of Modernity

Not only has John Paul II reshaped the functions of the papacy; he has also fundamentally reoriented the Catholic intellectual encounter with modernity. Eschewing both the bunker strategy of the pre-modern Know Nothings and the eager acquiescence of the hyper-modernizers, Karol Wojtyła has long been a leader in that small band of world-class Catholic intellectuals who, for some four decades, have used modern critical methods of scholarship and philosophical analysis to scout the intellectual terrain on the far side of modernity. During his pre-papal years as a member of the faculty of

Christian philosophy and an instructor in ethics at the Catholic University of Lublin (the only such institution in the Communist world), Professor Dr. Wojtyła was regarded as a dangerous radical by some of his colleagues. But then, as now, and in his dual role as intellectual and pastor, he was simply (simply!) seeking to articulate the classic affirmations of the Creed and of Christian morality in a language and conceptuality that challenges those he terms the "masters of suspicion": the epigones of the Enlightenment who deny the very possibility that human beings can grasp and articulate the truth of things.

Those who miss the Pope's root philosophical-theological conviction—that the reality created by the Word of God is an intelligible reality—also tend to miss his most pressing ecclesial concern, which has to do, not with some putative "crisis of authority," but with a crisis of *faith:* faith in God, to be sure, but also a crisis of faith in man and in the future of the human drama.

Like Aleksandr Solzhenitsyn, another prophetic figure who brings a distinctive Christian-Slavic angle of vision to the analysis of contemporary history, Karol Wojtyła has thought deeply about the meaning of modernity's forgetting God—which for the Pope, as for the great Russian chronicler, is a phenomenon with incalculable *public* consequences. Thus when John Paul II reads the bloody history of the twentieth century through this distinctive lens, he sees in the carnage unmistakable evidence of what happens when a genuine humanism that affirms the dignity and value of every human person is displaced by hubris masquerading as humanism. And what happens, of course, is that men and women are reduced to being the objects of others' manipulative and often lethal power, in the service of racial, ethnic, ideological, or class ends.

The Pope's first encyclical, *Redemptor Hominis,* powerfully proclaimed an alternative vision of human possibility: a Christologically informed humanism in which "Christ, the new Adam, in the very realization of the mystery of the Father and his love, fully reveals man to himself and brings to light his most high calling."[3] Here is the Christian claim confidently posed, again, as the antithesis of the alienation that faith is alleged to visit upon us. And here we may also see presaged the Christological-humanistic thrust of John Paul's entire pontificate.

Morality and Authority

The most controversial aspect of John Paul II's papacy, at least for the American media, has been his teaching on sexual morality and on the life issues of abortion and euthanasia. Here, alas, vast confusions about the content of Catholic doctrine and the nature of religious authority have combined to make an already contentious dialogue between the Church and the modern world even more difficult.

Tad Szulc's unfortunate book, *John Paul II: The Biography,*[4] was an example of these confusions at work. Szulc, like many of his brethren in the American press (and, it must be said, like many liberal Protestant and Catholic leaders), could not seem to grasp the fact that John Paul, as pope, is the custodian of a body of religious and moral convictions. He is not an autocrat laying down the law on the basis of his own private conclusions about theology and morality. Rather, for Catholics, he is Peter among us, interpreting the authentic tradition of the Church. That tradition can develop over time (as we shall have ample occasion to reflect upon in the following chapter). But as John Henry Newman taught the Church, authentic development is always in essential theological continuity with what has gone before.

Thus, on the matter of abortion and euthanasia, John Paul's position is not a question of the personal convictions of Karol Wojtyła, moral philosopher and docent of Lublin. Rather, the pro-life position that the Pope has passionately articulated is a matter of a fundamental and unchangeable—hence non-negotiable—moral truth and has been so understood for centuries (as we saw in our reflections on *Diognetus*). Moreover, this truth has enormous civilizational consequences, which is all the more reason to regret the fact that John Paul's critics (like Tad Szulc) often seem wholly innocent of the public dimensions of the abortion controversy, and ignore the implications for a law-governed society of a constitutionally warranted right to lethal violence for private ends. In pressing these issues so hard, the Pope believes he is defending both the innocent and the possibility of democratic self-governance. It is a conviction that his critics would do well to engage, rather than to ignore or ridicule or dismiss as clerical misogyny.

Conquering Fear

John Paul II is an immensely attractive personality who is without question the most familiar figure in the world. Yet the man *Time* magazine dubbed "John Paul Superstar" after his first visit to the U.N. and the United States in the fall of 1979 has transcended celebrity. Rather, the Pope seems poised on the cutting edge of history because he is defining a bold, new, morally challenging humanism in a period often dominated by the pleasure principle and the rough calculus of utility. John Paul's undergraduate university in Kraków, the Jagiellonian, was founded in 1364; there, Copernicus first detected the flaw in Ptolemy's geocentric view of the universe. Unlike some of his papal predecessors', Karol Wojtyła's theological convictions are certainly not threatened by the Copernican revolution in cosmology. But he is profoundly concerned about late modernity's tendency to instrumentalize, and thus degrade, the human person, a trend he sees at the root of a host of contemporary evils. Thus it is possible to think of Wojtyła as the man who left Kraków for Rome to restore, not geocentricity, but the dignity of the human person as the focal point of modern thought.[5]

As we have seen, Wojtyła the priest and bishop is also a professional philosopher deeply versed in his discipline's classic, medieval, modern, and contemporary expressions. What I called above his effort to scout the intellectual terrain on the "far side of modernity" is, viewed from another angle, a bold attempt to revivify the humanistic tradition, which he believes to have been profoundly wounded by several hundred years of principled intellectual skepticism (what they call in the academy the "hermeneutics of suspicion") and by a twentieth century of incomparably dehumanizing brutality. Again echoing the analysis of Solzhenitsyn, John Paul believes that the political crisis of the twentieth century began when European civilization "fell into a rage of self-mutilation"[6] in 1914 and set loose a train of evil events whose effects have only now begun to recede. But that political crisis of crises had deeper philosophical, indeed spiritual, roots. The wanton slaughter of 1914-18; the rise of Communism, Fascism, and Nazism; World War II, the Holocaust, and the Gulag; forty-five years of Cold War lived under the threat of nuclear annihilation—all this grimly vindicated, in blood and tears,

Chesterton's adage that when a man ceases to believe in God, he doesn't believe in nothing, but in anything. Ideas do have consequences, and the consequences of the hermeneutics of suspicion have been extraordinarily lethal. Launched in the Renaissance on the basis of a new confidence in the human prospect, secularist modernity has ironically given birth to a great fear: a fear of man and his proclivities, a fear for the future of civilization.

The spiritual core of John Paul II's project, in both its ecclesiastical and its public dimensions, is to conquer that great fear through a new and more securely grounded affirmation of human possibility.

For Karol Wojtyła, Christian believer, the conquest of fear comes through conversion to Christ, "the one Mediator between God and men":

> As the image of the invisible God, Christ is the perfect man who has restored to the children of Adam the divine likeness which had been deformed by sin. In his human nature, free from all sin and assumed into the divine Person of the Word, the nature shared by all human beings is raised to a sublime dignity: "By this incarnation the Son of God united himself in some sense with every man. He labored with human hands, thought with a human mind, acted with a human will, and loved with a human heart."[7]

This Christological humanism is a theme to which the Pope has returned tirelessly over seventeen years; thus in his 1995 remarks to a papal commission preparing for the Great Jubilee of 2000, he mused, "To what a lofty vocation, dear friends, humanity is called." From another source, this might seem a pleasant piety; from someone whose humanism is built on a religious faith tested and found true in the dark night of resistance to Nazism and Communism, it is a compelling affirmation.

And, for John Paul, just as a belief in human dignity is not something for Catholics or Christians only, so the task of reconstructing a new humanism for the twenty-first century is broad-gauged, ecumenical, and interreligious. Wojtyła's deep commitment to this enterprise is one of the hallmarks of his pontificate; its conceptual roots take us back, once again, to his pre-papal work as philosopher and ethicist at Lublin.

The objective of Wojtyła's principal philosophical work as a leading figure in the modern school of phenomenology was to display the human person in all his dimensions—physical, intellectual, psychological, spiritual—as a free and responsible moral agent. Viewed from one angle, this emphasis on freedom *and* responsibility is Wojtyła's answer to the biological, cultural, and political-economic determinisms of our time. But it is also his method for opening up the transcendent horizon of the human experience.

For it is in the dynamics of free and responsible moral agency, Wojtyła argues, that the transcendent—"the extraordinary side of the ordinary," as he once put it—breaks open for human beings. To borrow the Pope's book title: the "threshold of hope" is not only ahead of us but also above us. And we discover that threshold when we reflect on the inner dynamics of moral action, which has as its goal the highest possible realization of the good. Contrary to the solipsistic absolutizing of the self that has characterized contemporary notions of human subjectivity (and is summed up, in a word, in the American addiction to "autonomy"), Wojtyła-the-philosopher argues that a true humanism, commensurate with what is most noble in the human person, is born in that greatest of human dramas: the struggle to surrender the self that we are to the pursuit of the self we ought to become.[8]

Putting it in these terms does scant justice to the richness and complexity of Wojtyła's philosophical product, but it perhaps illustrates the fatuity of the charge that the Pope's mind is pre-modern and narrowly sectarian. On the contrary, it is Wojtyła's passion for the depth of the human experience (and his contempt for the hollowing out of the human person that flies under the flag of "autonomy") that has led him into active conversation with the philosophers and social scientists whom he invites to seminars at his summer residence at Castel Gandolfo, in the Alban Hills outside Rome. (1994's decidedly ecumenical gathering included Leszek Kołakowski, Edward Shils, Bernard Lewis, Paul Ricoeur, Charles Taylor, and Bronisław Geremek.) As both philosopher and pope, Karol Wojtyła has no trouble with the notion that the Church ought to open its windows to the modern world. But, as Richard John Neuhaus has put it, John Paul also challenges the modern world to open its windows to the worlds of which it is part, which include the worlds of transcendent truth and love.[9]

Toward the Great Jubilee

The Pope once said that the three greatest surprises of his life were his election to the papacy, his surviving Mehmet Ali Agca's attempt to kill him in 1981, and the collapse of Communism without massive bloodshed in 1989. Had the Italian candidates not deadlocked in October 1978, Wojtyła might have retired in mid-1995 as archbishop of Kraków or primate of Poland; had Agca's point-blank shots followed a path only millimeters different, the bullets would have severed John Paul's abdominal aorta, killing him almost instantly. In either case, the history of the 1980s and 1990s would have been rather different. Some will see in all of this an incredible string of luck; Karol Wojtyła and many others see the hand of Providence at work.

And in that calm confidence we may find yet another reason for the Pope's magnetism: he is a man who knows precisely who he is, what he believes, and what he is about. *Vocation*—the notion that God has a distinctive purpose and responsibility in mind for every human life—is something that Karol Wojtyła has always taken with great seriousness. In a lesser soul, this could breed a stunning arrogance; in Wojtyła, it has bred a man who embodies in a singular way the great truth that Augustine captured in the *Confessions:* "Thou has made us for Thee, and our heart is restless until it rests in Thee."

No one has a sure knowledge of the rest of the script that has been written for Karol Wojtyła, but it would indeed seem to point toward the Great Jubilee of 2000. Between now and then, what might the millennial Pope have on his agenda?

John Paul laid out ambitious plans for the Catholic Church's celebration of the Great Jubilee in a 1994 apostolic letter, *Tertio Millennio Adveniente.* Perhaps most provocatively, he called the people of the Church to an "examination of conscience" for "not having shown the true face of God," and for thereby contributing to "religious indifference," the "widespread loss of the transcendent sense of the human person," and "grave forms of injustice and exclusion."[10] Conversely, the Pope urged the Church to reflect on the fact, ignored by most North American Catholics, that we live in the greatest period of persecution and martyrdom in Christian history.[11] More programmatically, the Pope reiterated his "fervent wish" to go to Sarajevo, Lebanon, and Jerusalem, and expressed a desire to mark the year 2000 by visiting "the places on the road taken by the people of God of the Old Covenant, starting with Abraham and Moses, through Egypt and Mount Sinai, as far as Damascus, the city which witnessed the conversion of St. Paul."[12] The year 2000 should also be marked, the Pope suggested, by "a meeting of all Christians," to be prepared "in an attitude of fraternal cooperation with Christians of other denominations and traditions."[13]

In the last half of the last decade of the second millennium, one hallmark of John Paul's public project will continue to be a robust defense of the universality of human rights, a moral claim now under attack from gerontocratic Chinese Communists, Singaporean authoritarians, Islamic activists, and Western deconstructionists. John Paul II is committed to the principle of universality on theological, philosophical, and political grounds. As both Christian believer and philosophical analyst of the dynamics of the "acting person," John Paul is fully persuaded that certain basic rights—foremost among them, the right of religious freedom—constitute the inalienable moral heritage of all human beings. Moreover, he understands that the denial of universality is rooted in the denial of a universal moral law. But that radical relativism is, in turn, a prescription for a Hobbesian world in which all are at war with all. The public stakes involved in the defense of universality (which must also involve a critique of the wild proliferation of "rights-talk" in the U.N. and other international venues) are very high indeed, and John Paul II may be expected to take a large role in that debate.[14]

The Pope has also been laying great stress on Christian unity as the millennium approaches. Richard John Neuhaus has argued that the Pope's bold ecumenism, a fruit of the Second Vatican Council that John Paul celebrated in the 1995 encyclical *Ut Unum Sint* ("That They May Be One"), has in fact reconfigured the ecumenical enterprise at the end of the twentieth century:

> After the [Second Vatican] Council, there was much talk about the Catholic Church "joining" the ecumenical movement that dates from the 1910 Edinburgh Missionary Conference and is today represented by the World Council of Churches (WCC). Because of the asymmetry of size and ecclesiological self-understandings, there was never a possibility of the Catholic Church simply joining the WCC as another church among the churches. *Ut Unum Sint* formally clarifies what most observers—Protestant, Orthodox, and

Catholic—have recognized to be the case in the last several decades, namely, that since the Council the Catholic Church has reconstituted the ecumenical movement. In some respects, the Catholic Church today *is* the ecumenical movement; at the very least it is the spiritual and institutional center of the movement toward Christian unity in our time.[15]

In concrete terms, John Paul seems to believe that it just may be possible to heal the breach of the eleventh century between Rome and Eastern Orthodoxy sooner rather than later. Whether Orthodoxy, variegated and fractious, is in a position to respond to the Pope's initiatives is another question. But John Paul has made it abundantly clear on several occasions that he believes there are neither theological nor jurisdictional roadblocks to full communion between the Roman Catholic and Orthodox churches. Were that reunification to be accomplished, it would have the most profound public implications for post-Communist eastern Europe.

In inter-religious terms, John Paul is committed to a deepening of the Catholic-Jewish dialogue, to which he has devoted considerable attention during his pontificate. His successful negotiation of full diplomatic relations between the Holy See and Israel, while not in itself a theological breakthrough, broke a crucial psychological barrier, beyond which the Pope envisions a richer, more profound theological encounter between Jews and Catholics. Perhaps even more challenging will be the attempt to find a *modus vivendi* with activist Islam. Commenting on the 1995 dedication of a new grand mosque in Rome, the Pope celebrated the fact that "in Rome, the center of Christianity and the See of Peter's successor, Muslims should have their own place of worship with full respect for their freedom of conscience," while noting that "it is unfortunately necessary to point out that in some Islamic countries similar signs of the recognition of religious freedom are lacking." On the edge of the third millennium, John Paul concluded, "the world . . . is waiting for these signs."[16]

The Nature of Greatness

History has honored only two of the 264 popes—Leo I (440-461) and Gregory I (590-604)—with the title "the Great." Like John Paul II, Leo and Gregory led a Church confronted by the claims of barbarians: in Leo's case, the Huns; in Gregory's, the Lombards. Leo the Great successfully turned Attila back from Rome; Gregory the Great effected a truce with the invading Lombards and set about the work of converting them to orthodox Christianity.

Will history come to think of Karol Wojtyła as "John Paul the Great"? If it does, the reasons will have much to do with a third successful papal intervention in the face of the barbarians: in this case, the "masters of suspicion" whose radical deconstruction of reason has had such grave public consequences. When "humanism" had become an intellectual husk to some and a term of opprobrium to others, the world was given a pope whose profound faith and penetrating intellect illuminated new possibilities of a mature hope in the human prospect. Hope, *pace* Václav Havel, is not the same as optimism. But to have restored hope in the century of Auschwitz and the Gulag is an accomplishment as momentous as any in the history of the papacy during the second millennium.

To the specifics of that achievement, and its imprint on history and public life, we now turn.

6

Catholicism and Democracy: Parsing the Other Twentieth-Century Revolution

In a conversation in the mid-1980s, Sir Michael Howard, then the Regius Professor of Modern History at Oxford, suggested that there had been two great revolutions in the twentieth century. The first had taken place when Lenin's Bolsheviks expropriated the Russian people's revolution in November 1917. The other was going on even as we spoke: the transformation of the Roman Catholic Church from a bastion of the *ancien régime* into perhaps the world's foremost institutional defender of human rights. It was a fascinating reading of the history of our century. I also sensed, in Sir Michael's telling of the story, just a *soupçon* of surprise: fancy that—the Vatican as defender of the rights of man!

There are, to be sure, reasons to be surprised by the contemporary Vatican's aggressive defense of human rights, and by Pope John Paul II's endorsement of democracy as the form of government that best coheres with the Church's vision of "integral human development." In the worlds of political power, those surprised would have to include the Brezhnevite and post-Brezhnevite generations of Communist leaders in central and eastern Europe, as well as Ferdinand Marcos, General Augusto Pinochet, and General Alfredo Stroessner. Yet in another way there should be no surprise. Key themes in classic Catholic social ethics—personalism, the common good, and the principle of subsidiarity—are not simply congruent with liberal democratic forms of governance: they would seem to require democratic polities for their effective embodiment, at least under today's circumstances.

That would come as news indeed to Pope Gregory XVI or Pope Pius IX, whose attitudes toward liberal democracy in the nineteenth century were decidedly chilly. What has happened between then and now, between the mid-nineteenth and late twentieth centuries, between an official Catholic skepticism bordering on hostility about democracy and a Catholic endorsement of democracy that not only threatens tyrants but actually helps to topple them? And where might the encounter between Catholicism and democracy be headed in the twenty-first century?

CATHOLICISM AGAINST SECULAR LIBERALISM

The hostility of the mid-nineteenth-century papal magisterium to certain liberal concepts of the rights of man (as defined, for example, in the creed of the French Revolution) and the Church's deep skepticism about the liberal democratic state in its teething phase are well known to students of the period. The general position was neatly summed up in Pius IX's 1864 Syllabus of Errors, whose last condemned proposition was that "the Roman Pontiff can and should reconcile himself to and agree with progress, liberalism, and modern civilization." Eighteen years earlier, however, Giovanni Maria Mastai-Ferretti had been elected as Pius IX in part because he was thought to have a more tolerant attitude toward modern thought and institutions than his predecessor, Gregory XVI (1831-46), who in the 1832 and 1834 encyclicals *Mirari Vos* and *Singulari Nos* had flatly condemned liberalism (including "this false and absurd maxim, or better this madness, that everyone should have and practice freedom of conscience") as essentially irreligious.[1]

But events—particularly the Italian *Risorgimento,* whose liberal anti-clerical leadership made no pretense about its intention to dislodge traditional ecclesiastical authority throughout Italy—hardened Pius IX in his views. By the time of the First Vatican Council (1869-70), the pope who had been elected twenty-three years earlier as something of a reformer had become, throughout the world, the very symbol of intransigent resistance to the ideas and institutions of modernity.[2]

Reasons for the Resistance

Personal factors and the churnings of Italian politics undoubtedly bore on the retrenchment strategy of Pius IX. But it seems more fruitful to focus on the substantive reasons why official Catholicism in the nineteenth century found itself in resistance to the Continental liberal project.

First, there were the enduring effects of the shock that the French Revolution sent through European Catholicism—a shock of greater intensity than any other the Church had absorbed since the Reformation. There was, to be sure, the crazed bloodiness of the Terror itself. Beyond that, however, and even beyond Napoleon's persecution of Pope Pius VII, the leadership of Roman Catholicism saw the lingering specter of Jacobinism as an ideological force that threatened the very foundations of European civilization.[3] That civilization in its public aspects had been rooted in the notion that states, as well as individual men, were accountable to transcendent moral norms, generally held to be revealed by a God who was sovereign over states as well as over individuals. By its defiant insistence on the autonomous reason of man as the first, and indeed only, principle of political organization, Jacobinism threatened more than the position of the Church as mediator between the sovereign God and his creatures. In the Church's view, the Jacobin spirit would inevitably lead to the implosion of civilization and its subsequent collapse into mobocracy, or what J. R. Talmon has called totalitarian democracy,[4] and events in France and elsewhere made it clear that this hard judgment was not unfounded. Thus in the minds of a church leadership that had long identified, not merely its institutional prerogatives, but civilization itself with the moral understandings that (in however attenuated a form) underlay the structures of the *ancien régime*, a damning equation formed: liberalism = Jacobinism = (anticlericalism + The Terror + anarchy). Discriminating or not, fair or not, the brush of Robespierre tarred the revolutionaries of 1848, the leaders of the Italian *Risorgimento* (Cavour, Mazzini, Garibaldi, and the like), and in fact the entire Continental liberal project.[5]

The second factor that colored the mid-nineteenth-century Church's appraisal of liberalism and democracy was the Church's own internal situation. The answer that Roman Catholicism devised to the political threat posed by the rise of post-monarchical states in Europe and to the advance of liberal ideas was centralization: the concentration of effective authority over virtually all matters, great and small, in the person (and, of course, staff) of the Roman pontiff. The pope would be the judge of orthodoxy and orthopraxis; the pope would manage the Church's affairs with sovereign states through an expanding network of papal diplomats, concordat arrangements, and so forth. *Ubi Petrus, ibi ecclesia* ("Where Peter is, there is the Church") is an ancient theological maxim. But it was given new breadth in the nineteenth century in response to the ideological (and indeed physical) threats posed by the forces of what the Syllabus called "progress, liberalism, and modern civilization."

There is, of course, an irony, here: the Church's answer to the threat of "progress, liberalism, and modern civilization" was to adopt a quintessentially modern (i.e., highly centralized and bureaucratically controlled) structure. Nonetheless, the new emphasis on centralized authority, coupled with the traditional understanding of the divinely given prerogatives of the Roman pontiff, and further complicated by the dependence of the Papal States (pre-1870) on European monarchs for physical security, created a situation in which the Church's leadership was rather unlikely to feel much affinity with liberal democracy.

A third obstacle that kept the Church from looking kindly on liberal democracy was that liberalism in the latter part of the nineteenth century was widely perceived in Vatican circles as a package deal that included Darwinism, which seemed to threaten the distinctiveness of human beings in creation; "higher criticism" or the "historical-critical method," which seemed to challenge the integrity of the Bible and its status as the revealed word of God; and socialism, which seemed to threaten the Church's traditional teaching on the right of private property. To these perceived threats in the order of ideas must be added the physical threat of revolutionary Marxism as it showed itself in, say, the 1870 Paris Commune.

The most fundamental reason for the Church's resistance to the liberal democratic project in the nineteenth century should not, though, be located on this institutional/ideological axis. The threats noted above were real, in both institutional and personal terms (ask Pius VII or Pius IX), and those threats did act as a lens through which ideas and events were, in some cases, misperceived. All that can be conceded. But beneath it all lay, I believe, an evangelical concern.

Rightly or wrongly, the central leadership of nineteenth-century Roman Catholicism truly believed that religious freedom—a key plank in the platform of liberal democracy—would inevitably lead to religious indifference and, given the right circumstances, to government hostility toward religion. The secularization of western Europe in the nineteenth century was a complicated business,[6] and it would be a serious mistake to attribute it solely (or even primarily) to the collapse of the old altar-and-throne arrangements that had obtained since the Peace of Westphalia ended the European wars of religion in 1648. On the other hand, and from the Vatican's point of view at that time, secularization had proceeded apace with the collapse of those arrangements. Those of us with the luxury of hindsight should perhaps be less quick to dismiss as mindless the inferences that were drawn. There was, after all, at the beginning of the nineteenth century, the Napoleonic persecution of the Church; and after 1870 there was the pressing problem of the violently anti-clerical Third French Republic. This government hostility toward religion made it all too easy to read the historical record backwards, from the depredations of the Commune and the later anti-clericalism of the Third Republic, to the *Declaration des Droits de L'Homme et du Citoyen.*

We should not, in short, dismiss Roman resistance to the liberal democratic project as merely institutional self-interest. Some liberal democratic states did put grave difficulties in the path of the Church's evangelical and sacramental mission, and larger conclusions were shortly drawn.

On the other hand, the Roman authorities were slow to seize the opportunities presented by what might be called the Catholic Whig tradition, which looks to Thomas Aquinas for its inspiration and which had, in Lord Acton, a powerful spokesman in the mid- and late-nineteenth century. But given Acton's negative views on the utility of the definition of papal infallibility at the First Vatican Council (itself, *inter alia,* an act of defiance against the epistemological spirit of the age), the British historian was an unlikely broker between this tradition, which taught the possibility of genuine progress in history when that progress is mediated through rightly ordered public institutions holding themselves accountable to transcendent moral norms, and the Roman Curia.

In any case, the Catholic Whig tradition, a revolutionary liberal tradition in its own right, if in sharp contrast to the Jacobinism with which the Vatican typically associated liberalism, would not have all that long to wait, as history goes, for its moment to arrive.

THE TURN TOWARD DEMOCRACY BEGINS

What accounts for the shift in official Catholic teaching between 1864 and 1965, between the rejection of the modern constitutional state in the Syllabus of Errors and the Second Vatican Council's acceptance of the juridical state in *Dignitatis Humanae* (the Declaration on Religious Freedom) and *Gaudium et Spes* (the Pastoral Constitution on the Church in the Modern World)?[7] Many factors were in play, of course, but one has received relatively little attention in most church histories: the fact of America.

In the United States the Church was confronted with a genuine *novum:* a liberal, pluralistic society and a liberal democratic state that were good for Roman Catholics. Religious liberty and the constitutional separation of the institutions of church and state in America had led, not to religious indifference, but to a vibrant Catholicism that unlike its western European counterparts still held the allegiance of the working class. Moreover, while anti-Catholicism was a fact of life in the United States and Catholic immigrants not infrequently received a rough welcome, the U.S. government had never conducted an overt program of persecution on the basis of religious conviction.[8]

This was, as can be imagined, somewhat difficult to handle for those in Rome who were still committed to a restoration of the *ancien régime,* or were simply skeptical about the American experiment. A bold, public attempt to press the argument for religious freedom and the democratic state took place in Rome on March 25, 1887, when the newly created Cardinal James Gibbons of Baltimore took possession of his titular Church of Santa Maria in Trastevere, and preached to his Roman congregation in these terms:

Scarcely were the United States formed when Pius VI, of happy memory, established there the Catholic hierarchy and appointed the illustrious John Carroll first Bishop of Baltimore. This event, so important to us, occurred less than a hundred years ago. . . . Our

Catholic community in those days numbered only a few thousand souls . . . and were served by the merest handful of priests. Thanks to the fructifying grace of God, the grain of mustard seed then planted has grown to be a large tree, spreading its branches over the length and width of our fair land. . . . For their great progress under God and the fostering care of the Holy See *we are indebted in no small degree to the civil liberty we enjoy in our enlightened republic.*

Our Holy Father, Leo XIII, in his luminous encyclical on the constitution of Christian States, declares that the Church is not committed to any particular form of civil government. She adapts to all; she leavens all with the sacred leaven of the Gospel. She has lived under absolute empires; she thrives under constitutional monarchies; she grows and expands under the free republic. She has often, indeed, been hampered in her divine mission and has had to struggle for a footing wherever despotism has cast its dark shadow . . . but in the genial air of liberty she blossoms like the rose!

For myself, as a citizen of the United States, and without closing my eyes to our defects as a nation, I proclaim, with a deep sense of pride and gratitude, and in this great capital of Christendom, that I belong to a country where the civil government holds over us the aegis of its protection without interfering in the legitimate exercise of our sublime mission as ministers of the Gospel of Jesus Christ.

Our country has liberty without license, authority without despotism. . . . But, while we are acknowledged to have a free government, we do not, perhaps, receive due credit for possessing also a strong government. Yes, our nation is strong, and her strength lies, under Providence, in the majesty and supremacy of the law, in the loyalty of her citizens to that law, and in the affection of our people for their free institutions.[9]

Gibbons's proud assertions sound mild to our ears, but in their own day they were intended as a challenge and were understood as such, by celebrants and detractors alike. As Gerald Fogarty, S.J., puts it, "Here was the gauntlet of the benefit of American religious liberty thrown down by the new world to the old. . . ."[10]

Pope Leo XIII (1878-1903) was happy to acknowledge the practical benefits of the American arrangement in the American circumstance. But he was not yet prepared to concede the moral superiority of the liberal (i.e., confessionally neutral) state over the classic European arrangements. In his 1895 encyclical letter to the American hierarchy, *Longinqua Oceani,* Leo cautioned against any temptation to universalize the American experience and experiment:

> . . . the Church amongst you, unopposed by the Constitution and government of your nation, fettered by no hostile legislation, protected against violence by the common laws and the impartiality of the tribunals, is free to live and act without hindrance. Yet, though all this is true, it would be very erroneous to draw the conclusion that in America is to be sought the type of the most desirable status of the Church, or that it would be universally lawful or expedient for State and Church to be, as in America, dissevered and divorced. The fact that Catholicity with you is in good condition, nay, is even enjoying a prosperous growth, is by all means to be attributed to the fecundity with which God has endowed his Church, in virtue of which unless men or circumstances interfere, she spontaneously expands and propagates herself; but she would bring forth more abundant fruits if, in addition to liberty, she enjoyed the favor of the laws and the patronage of the public authority.[11]

Thus the situation in the late nineteenth century: the American arrangement and the liberal democratic, confessionally neutral state it represented *tolerari potest* (could be tolerated). Indeed, the accomplishments of the Church under such a new arrangement could be gratefully acknowledged. This was a large step ahead of the rejectionist posture of Pius IX and the Syllabus. But it still stopped considerably short of the stage at which the confessionally neutral state—i.e., the state that acknowledges religious freedom as an inalienable right grounded in the nature of the human person and reflecting the inherent limits of the state's competence—is preferred to a benign altar-and-throne (or altar-and-desk) arrangement.

The path to that more developed position, which is the basis of the contemporary Catholic rapprochement with democracy, would be traversed over the next sixty years. The vigor of American Catholicism continued to play an exemplary role in ensuring that the issue remained alive. And the providential loss of the Papal States also meant that popes from Leo XIII on were able to consider, from a far less encumbered political and theological position, the relative merits of various forms of modern governance.

The Pressures of History

As the nineteenth century gave way to the twentieth, other realities of modern life began to influence the Church's perspective. One was the rise of totalitarianism in both its Leninist and Fascist forms, and the threat posed to Roman Catholicism by both of these modern political movements. Confronted by raw political power in the service of demonic ideology, the Church was led, not only to look toward the democracies for protection, but to look toward democracy itself as an antidote to the totalitarian temptation. This was particularly true in the immediate post–World War II period, when Vatican diplomacy, often in cooperation with U.S. diplomats and occupation forces, worked to strengthen Christian Democratic parties in Germany and Italy. In the Italian case, this represented a shift indeed, for Pope Pius XI (1922-39) had summarily ended the proto–Christian Democratic experiment led by Don Luigi Sturzo in the early twentieth century—with unfortunate results.[12] Now, in a world where even constitutional monarchy was clearly on the wane, Christian Democracy both in theory and in practice seemed to many Vatican minds (including that of Giovanni Battista Montini, later Pope Paul VI) the best available alternative to either Leninist or Fascist totalitarianism. Montini was influenced in this judgment by his regard for the philosophical work of the French neo-Thomist Jacques Maritain, whose *Christianity and Democracy,* written during the summer of 1942, became a kind of theoretical manifesto for the Christian Democratic movement.[13]

The Church's turn toward Christian Democracy was also facilitated by the decline of anti-clericalist bias among European liberals, and by the difference between liberals and radicals that was horribly clarified by totalitarian persecution. The Vatican may still have had its differences with liberals, but after the ruthless persecution of Christianity under Lenin and Stalin, the Ukrainian terror famine, and the Holocaust, it was no longer possible even to suggest that modern radical dictators such as Stalin and Hitler were but exceptionally virulent forms of a general liberal virus. In the French situation, cooperative efforts during World War II between Catholic intellectuals and a few religious leaders, and the wider Resistance movement (with its secularist and Marxist leaderships), helped break down some of the stereotypes that had plagued life under the Third Republic.[14] In Italy, the tradition of Don Sturzo, embodied in such major post-war figures as Alcide de Gasperi and Aldo Moro, could be reclaimed, just as in Germany Konrad Adenauer was able to tap the Christian Democratic tradition of the old Catholic Center party.[15] In the post–World War II period, then, there were new facts of national and international life that validated Gibbons's thesis beyond the borders of the United States. These new facts created the sociological conditions for retrieving Pius VII's views on the potential compatibility of Catholicism and democratic political institutions.

Finally, and perhaps most significantly for the history of ideas, the evolution of Catholic social teaching itself pushed the Church toward a more positive appraisal of liberal democracy. The key development here was Pius XI's emphasis on *subsidiarity,* a principle that was central in the encyclical he issued in 1931 for the fortieth anniversary of Leo XIII's groundbreaking social encyclical *Rerum Novarum.* The key passage in Pius XI's letter, *Quadragesimo Anno,* was the following:

> It is true, as history clearly shows, that because of changed circumstances much that formerly was performed by small associations can now be accomplished only by larger ones. Nevertheless, it is a fixed and unchangeable principle, most basic in social philosophy, immoveable and unalterable, that, just as it is wrong to take away from individuals what they can accomplish by their own ability and effort and entrust it to a community, so it is an injury and at the same time both a serious evil and a disturbance of right order to assign to a larger and higher society what can be performed successfully by smaller and lower communities. The reason is that all social activity, of its very power and nature, should supply help [*subsidium*] to the members of the social body, but may never destroy or absorb them.
>
> The state, then, should leave to these smaller groups the settlement of business and problems of minor importance, which would otherwise greatly distract it. Thus it will carry out with greater freedom, power, and success the tasks belonging to it alone, because it alone is qualified to perform them: directing, watching, stimulating, and restraining, as circumstances suggest or necessity demands. Let those in power, therefore, be convinced that the more faithfully this principle of subsidiary function is followed and a

graded hierarchical order exists among the various associations, the greater also will be both social authority and social efficiency, and the happier and more prosperous too will be the condition of the commonwealth.[16]

The Elements of Subsidiarity

As it has worked itself out in subsequent Catholic social teaching, the principle of subsidiarity has consisted of the following substantive elements:

1. The individual human person is both the source and the end of society: *civitas propter cives, non cives propter civitatem* ("The city exists for the benefit of its citizens, not the citizens for the city").

2. Yet the human person is "naturally" social, and can achieve the fullness of human development only in human communities. (This is sometimes referred to, particularly in the writings of John Paul II, as the principle of *solidarity*.)

3. The purpose of social relationships and human communities is to give help *(subsidium)* to individuals as they pursue, freely, their obligation to work for their own human development. The state or society should not, save in exceptional circumstances, replace or displace this individual self-responsibility; society and the state provide conditions for the possibility of exercising self-responsibility.

4. There is a hierarchy of communities in human society; larger, "higher" communities are to provide help *(subsidium)*, in the manner noted above, to smaller or "lower" communities.

5. *Positively*, the principle of subsidiarity means that all communities should encourage and enable (not merely permit) individuals to exercise their self-responsibility, and larger communities should do this for smaller communities. Put another way, decision-making responsibility in society should rest at the "lowest" level commensurate with the effective pursuit of the common good.[17]

6. *Negatively*, the principle means that communities must not deprive individuals, nor larger communities deprive smaller communities, of the opportunity to do what they can for themselves.

Subsidiarity, in other words, is a formal principle "by which to regulate competencies between individual and communities and between smaller and larger communities." Because it is a formal principle, its precise meaning in practice will differ according to circumstances; because it is rooted in "the metaphysics of the person, it applies to the life of every society."[18]

There is both a historical and a substantive connection between the identification of the principle of subsidiarity and the Roman Catholic Church's increasingly positive appraisal of democracy in the mid-twentieth century. Historically, the very concept of subsidiarity was developed in the German *Königswinterer Kreis,* a group of Catholic intellectuals interested in questions of political economy. This group had a deep influence both upon the author of *Quadragesimo Anno,* the Jesuit Oswald von Nell-Breuning, and upon the evolution of Christian Democracy in pre- and post-war Germany.[19]

The substantive connection was closely related to the historical connection. *Quadragesimo Anno* was written under the lengthening shadow of totalitarianism. If its predecessor encyclical, *Rerum Novarum,* had been issued at least in part to warn against the dangers inherent in Manchesterian liberalism, *Quadragesimo Anno* was written in response to the threat posed by the overweening pretensions of the modern state:[20] thus the importance of the principle of subsidiarity, which tried to set clear boundaries to state power. The question then arises: Under modern circumstances, what form of governance is most likely to acknowledge, in practice as well as in rhetoric, the limited role of the state, the moral and social importance of what Edmund Burke called the "small platoons," and the principle of *civitas propter cives?*

In contemporary practice, liberal democracies have best met the test of these moral criteria. That was not quite what Pius XI, with his corporatist vision, had in mind in 1931, but it was certainly what Pope Pius XII (1939-58) had in mind by the mid-1940s. Pius XII was not a "global democrat," in any romantic sense of the term. He did seem to think, however, that democracy provided the best available modern form of government in the developed world, not least because it would provide a powerful barrier against the totalitarian temptation.

VATICAN II ON CHURCH AND STATE

The proximate origins of what I have elsewhere called the "Catholic human rights revolution,"[21] which led to the Church's overt support of the democratic revolution in world politics, should be located in the Second Vatican Council's Declaration on Religious Freedom *(Dignitatis Humanae)*. The Declaration, issued in 1965, reflected aspects of the American experience and experiment, and a brief sketch of that background is in order.

One of the chief intellectual architects of *Dignitatis Humanae* was the U.S. Jesuit theologian John Courtney Murray. Beginning in the late 1940s, Murray conceived and orchestrated a creative extension of Catholic church/state theory. The official Roman position, when Murray first took up the topic, was precisely where Leo XIII had left it in *Longinqua Oceani:* the "thesis," or preferred arrangement, was the legal establishment of Catholicism on either the classic altar-and-throne or the modern Francoist model; the American arrangement, i.e., religious freedom for all in a confessionally neutral state, was a tolerable hypothesis. Moreover, in a confessionally neutral state, the Church ought (according to the official position) to work for the day when it would enjoy the benefits of state support. The "thesis," with its rejection of religious freedom as a fundamental human right, was grounded on the moral-theological maxim that "error has no rights." This meant, in public terms, that "erroneous" religious communities, such as the sundry forms of Protestantism in America, should not, under "ideal" circumstances, receive the tolerant (if tacit) blessing of the state, a view defended by prominent American Catholic theologians like Joseph Clifford Fenton and Francis Connell, C.SS.R., of the Catholic University of America and the *American Ecclesiastical Review*.[22]

Murray's challenge to this position, and his creative extension of Catholic church/state theory, involved the retrieval and development of a largely forgotten current in Catholic thought that antedated the altar-and-throne model. Murray found the *locus classicus* of this forgotten current in a letter sent by Pope Gelasius I to the Byzantine emperor Anastasius in 494, in which the pope had written, "Two there are, august emperor, by which this world is ruled on title of original and sovereign right—the consecrated authority of the priesthood and the royal power." This "dualism," Murray argued, was not a radical "two kingdoms" construct so much as a declaration of independence for both Church and state. The Church's freedom to exercise its ministry of truth and charity was a limit on the powers of government; the state's lack of authority in matters spiritual "desacralized" politics. And this, as we have seen above, helped open up the possibility of a politics of consent, in place of the politics of divine right or the politics of coercion. The Gelasian tradition, Murray concluded, frowned on a unitary church/state system for the sake of the integrity of both religion and politics.

After considerable theological and ecclesiastical-political maneuvering, and in no small part because of the witness of the persecuted Church in central and eastern Europe, Murray's Gelasian retrieval prevailed at Vatican II. Enriched by a personalist philosophical approach that taught that persons had rights, whether their opinions were erroneous or not, Murray's view was incorporated into *Dignitatis Humanae,* with a palpable effect on the Church's subsequent stance toward democracy.

The Nature of Religious Freedom

Just how is the definition of religious freedom as a fundamental human right connected to the affirmation of democratic forms of governance? The connection has to do with the very nature of religious freedom, which has both an "interior" meaning and a "public" meaning. Its interior meaning can be stated in these terms: Because human beings, as persons, have an innate capacity for thinking and choosing and an innate drive for truth and goodness, freedom to pursue that quest for the true and the good, without coercion, is a basic human good. This innate quest for truth and goodness, which is the basic dynamic of what John Paul II has called the "interior freedom" of the human person, is the object or end to be protected by that human right we call the right of religious freedom. The right of religious freedom, in other words, is, in the juridical order, an acknowledgment of a basic moral claim about the constitutive dynamics of human being-in-the-world. As the Council put it, religious freedom means that "all men are to be immune from coercion on the part of individuals or of social groups and of any human power, in such wise that in matters religious no one is to be forced to act in a manner contrary to his beliefs."[23] Therefore religious freedom can be considered the most fundamental of human rights, because it is the one that corresponds to the most fundamentally human dimension of human being-in-the-world.

This, then, is the interior or personalist meaning of religious freedom. There is also a public meaning. According to the analysis above, religious freedom can be considered a crucial aspect of civil society: religious freedom is a basic condition for the possibility of a *polis* structured in accordance with the inherent human dignity of the persons who are its citizens. The right of religious freedom, as we have had occasion to note before, establishes a fundamental barrier between the person and the state that is essential to a just *polis*. The state is not omnicompetent, and one of the reasons we know that is that, in acknowledging the right of religious freedom, the state gives juridical expression to the fact that there is a *sanctum sanctorum*, a privileged sanctuary, within every human person, where coercive power may not tread.

In *Gaudium et Spes,* for example, the bishops of the Second Vatican Council describe conscience as "the sanctuary of man, where he is alone with God whose voice echoes in him."[24] This affirmation of the sanctuary of conscience is not to be understood in relativist terms as endorsing a putative "right to be wrong"; nor did the council fathers have in mind some "right to *do* wrong," based on the individualist notion that a human being has the right to think whatever he likes, and to behave accordingly, simply because he thinks it. The free man of conscience is also and always obliged to listen to the "voice of God" —the voice of truth—echoing within him. Thus John Paul II notes that the dialogue of conscience is always a dialogue "with God, the author of the [natural moral] law, the primordial image and final end of man."[25] Religious freedom, in other words, is not dependent on epistemological skepticism or indifferentism.[26] And the state, by acknowledging the "prior" right of religious freedom, also acknowledges its own inability to write or edit the script of the dramatic dialogue that takes place within the sanctuary of human conscience.

The right of religious freedom includes, as the Council taught, the claim that "within due limits, nobody [should be] forced to act against his convictions in religious matters in private or in public, alone or in association with others."[27] This claim is also helpful in establishing that distinction between society and the state which is fundamental to the liberal democratic project. As we have seen, in both theory and practice democracy rests upon the understandings that society is prior to the state, and that the state exists to serve society, not the other way around. Social institutions have a logical, historical, and one might even say ontological priority over institutions of government.[28] Among the many social institutions that have persistently claimed this priority are religious institutions and, in the Gelasian tradition, the Christian Church.

Thus the public dimension of the right of religious freedom is a crucial barrier against the totalitarian temptation, in either its Leninist or its mobocracy forms. Some things in a democracy—indeed, the basic human rights that are the very building blocks of democracy—are not up for a vote, in the sense that their truth is not to be measured by majority acquiescence.[29] Democratic politics is not merely procedural politics; democracies are substantive experiments whose successful working-out requires certain habits (virtues) and attitudes, in addition to the usual democratic procedures. The public meaning of the right of religious freedom reminds us of this, in and out of season. And thus the importance of the right of religious freedom for unbelievers as well as believers, for the secularized U.S. new-class elite as well as for the 90 per cent of the American people who remain stubbornly unsecularized.[30]

In short, and as Murray himself put it, at Vatican II and in *Dignitatis Humanae* Roman Catholicism embraced "the political doctrine of . . . the juridical state . . . [i.e.] government as constitutional and limited in function—its primary function being juridical, namely, the protection and promotion of the rights of man and the facilitation of the performance of man's native duties."[31] The juridical or constitutional state is ruled by consent, not by coercion or by claims of divine right. The state itself stands under the judgment of moral norms that transcend it, moral norms whose constitutional and/or legal expression can be found in bills of rights. Moreover, religious freedom, constitutionally and legally protected, desacralizes politics and thereby opens up the possibility of a politics of consent. Where, in the modern world, could such constitutionally regulated, limited, consensual states be found? The question, posed, seemed to answer itself: in democratic states.

Thus the path to an official Roman Catholic affirmation of democracy had been cleared, and the obligatory ends of a morally worthy democratic *polis* specified, in this American-shaped development of doctrine on the matter of the fundamental human right of religious freedom.

THE CONTEMPORARY DISCUSSION

Pope John Paul II has deepened and intellectually extended the Catholic human-rights revolution during his pontificate: first, by explicitly connecting it to the democratic revolution in world politics, and then by undertaking a searching evaluation and critique of democratic theory on the edge of the third millennium.

It is interesting to remember that the pope who has effected this decisive extension of Catholic social doctrine has never lived under a fully democratic regime (inter-war Poland having been something of a truncated democracy, especially after 1926). Yet in a sense his intense interest in questions of democracy reflects his experience in Poland, where the "parchment barriers" (as James Madison would have called them) of Communist constitutions illustrated how important it is that rights be secured by the structure of governmental institutions, as well as by the habits and attitudes of a people. Here, again, we see how the totalitarian assault on human rights in the twentieth century has been, paradoxically, a prod to the extension of Catholic human-rights teaching.

In the first ten years of his pontificate, though, John Paul II also had to contend with various theologies of liberation, and it was in his dialogue with liberation theology that the new Catholic "theology of democracy" began to take distinctive shape.

Whether liberation theology represents a genuinely distinctive phenomenon in Catholic history, or merely the old Iberian fondness for altar-and-throne arrangements in a unitary state moved from right to left on the political spectrum, is an intriguing question. In any event, and while liberation theology was and is more complex than what has typically been presented in the secular media, the sundry theologies of liberation have tended to share a pronounced skepticism, at times verging on hostility, toward what they consider the bourgeois formalism of liberal democracy. Thus by the early 1980s these theologies had taken a sharply different path, in defining the nature and purposes of public Catholicism, than that taken by the Roman magisterium.

In an attempt to close this widening breach between official Catholic social teaching and the theologies of liberation, the Congregation for the Doctrine of the Faith issued two documents on liberation theology, one in 1984 and the other in 1986. The 1984 Instruction on

Certain Aspects of the "Theology of Liberation," issued by the Congregation with the Pope's personal authority, acknowledged that liberation was an important theme in Christian theology. It frankly faced the overwhelming facts of poverty and degradation in much of Latin America and argued that the Church has a special love for, and responsibility to, the poor. But the Instruction rejected a number of key themes of the various theologies of liberation: the locating of sin primarily in social, economic, and political structures; the class-struggle model of society and history and related analyses of structural violence; subordination of the individual to the collectivity; the transformation of good and evil into strictly political categories, and the subsequent loss of a sense of transcendent dimension to the moral life; the concept of a partisan Church; and an "exclusively political interpretation" of the death of Christ.[32]

For our purposes here, though, the most crucial passage in the 1984 Instruction was this:

> One needs to be on guard against the politicization of existence, which, misunderstanding the entire meaning of the Kingdom of God and the transcendence of the person, begins to sacralize politics and betray the religion of the people in favor of the projects of the revolution.[33]

Against the core dynamic of the Catholic human-rights revolution, the theologies of liberation seemed to be proposing a return to the altar-and-throne arrangements of the past—this time buttressed by the allegedly "scientific" accomplishments of Marxist social analysis. With this new monism came, inevitably, the use of coercive state power against individuals and against the Church. The politics of consent was again being threatened by the politics of coercion. In short, the theologies of liberation had broken with the modern retrieval of the Gelasian tradition as it had evolved in the teaching of the Second Vatican Council and the social teaching of John Paul II.

The 1986 Instruction on Christian Freedom and Liberation pushed the official Roman discussion even further toward an open endorsement of the moral superiority of democratic politics:

> . . . [T]here can only be authentic development in a social and political system which respects freedoms and fosters them through

the participation of everyone. This participation can take different forms; it is necessary in order to guarantee a proper pluralism in institutions and in social initiatives. It ensures, notably by a real separation between the powers of the State, the exercise of human rights, also protecting them against possible abuses on the part of the public powers. No one can be excluded from this participation. in social and political life for reasons of sex, race, color, social condition, language, or religion. . . .

When the political authorities regulate the exercise of freedoms, they cannot use the pretext of the demands of public order and security in order to curtail those freedoms systematically. Nor can the alleged principle of national security, or a narrowly economic outlook, or a totalitarian conception of social life, prevail over the value of freedom and its rights.[34]

The politicization of the Gospel—its reduction to a partisan, mundane program—and the resacralization of politics were decisively rejected by the 1984 Instruction. The 1986 Instruction taught that participatory politics was morally superior to the politics of vanguards, whether aristocratic or Marxist-Leninist. The link between these themes and the positive task of democracy-building was made in late 1987 by John Paul's encyclical *Sollicitudo Rei Socialis*.

The Case for Participation

Sollicitudo's portrait of the grim situation of Third World countries was based on a more complex historical, social, and economic analysis than could be found in the encyclical it was written to commemorate, Paul VI's *Populorum Progressio* (1968). Where Paul tended to assign primary (some would say, virtually exclusive) responsibility for underdevelopment to the developed world, John Paul II argued that responsibility for the condition of the world's underclass was not unilinear. For the development failures of the post-colonial period certainly involved "grave instances of omissions on the part of the developing countries themselves, and especially on the part of those holding economic and political power."[35] In a more positive vein, John Paul II extended the Catholic human-rights revolution in explicitly political-cultural terms, teaching that sustained economic development would be impossible without the evolution of civil society:

"the developing nations themselves should favor the self-affirmation of each citizen, through access to a wider culture and a free flow of information."[36]

Yet the enhanced moral and cultural skills of a people, important as they were, were not enough, the Pope continued. "Integral human development" could not take place if the peoples in question remained the vassals or victims of inept, hidebound, ideologically rigid, and/or kleptocratic dictatorships. Thus, true development required that Third World countries "reform certain unjust structures, and in particular their political institutions, in order to replace corrupt, dictatorial, and authoritarian forms of government by *democratic and participatory ones.*"[37] In short, in *Sollicitudo Rei Socialis,* the formal leadership of the Roman Catholic Church reconfirmed its support for the democratic revolution in world politics. As John Paul II said of this striking phenomenon of the 1980s,

> This is a process which we hope will spread and grow stronger. For the health of a political community—as expressed in the free and responsible participation of all citizens in public affairs, in the rule of law, and in respect for and promotion of human rights—is the *necessary condition and sure guarantee* of the development of the whole individual and of all people.[38]

Sollicitudo thus brought Catholic social theory into congruence with Catholic social practice during the first decade of the pontificate of John Paul II. Whether the locale was El Salvador, Chile, Nicaragua, Paraguay, Poland, the Philippines, South Korea, or sub-Saharan Africa, John Paul II was, throughout the 1980s, a consistent voice of support (and, in Poland, the Philippines, and Chile, far more than that) for replacing "corrupt, dictatorial and authoritarian forms of government" with "democratic and participatory ones." As for criticism that his preaching on behalf of human rights and democracy constituted an unbecoming interference in politics, the Pope, en route to Chile and Paraguay in 1987, had this to say to a reporter who asked him about such carping: "Yes, yes, I am not the evangelizer of democracy, I am the evangelizer of the Gospel. To the Gospel message, of course, belong all the problems of human rights, and if democracy means human rights it also belongs to the message of the Church."[39] From religious conversion, to moral norms, to institutions and patterns of governance: the Pope's sense of priorities was clear, but so too was the connection between Catholic social teaching and the democratic revolution then unfolding dramatically throughout the world.

A Critique From "Inside"

None of this should be taken to suggest that the Church had become an uncritical or naïve celebrant of the democratic possibility. As John Paul II made clear during his pastoral visit to the United States in 1987, democratic societies have to remind themselves constantly of the moral standards by which their politics are meant to be judged. The Pope put it this way, speaking, in Miami, of the United States:

> Among the many admirable values of this country there is one that stands out in particular. It is freedom. The concept of freedom is part of the very fabric of this nation as a political community of free people. Freedom is a great gift, a blessing of God.
>
> From the beginning of America, freedom was directed to forming a well-ordered society and to promoting its peaceful life. Freedom was channelled to the fullness of human life, to the preservation of human dignity, and to the safeguarding of human rights. An experience of ordered freedom is truly part of the history of this land.
>
> This is the freedom that America is called upon to live and guard and transmit. She is called to exercise it in such a way that it will also benefit the cause of freedom in other nations and among other peoples.[40]

Thus did the Bishop of Rome endorse the moral intention of the American experiment in categories reminiscent of the Catholic Whig tradition—but emphasizing Acton's postulate that freedom is not a matter of doing what you want, but rather having the right to do what you ought.[41]

This line of development in the magisterium of John Paul II displayed a particularly sharp edge, of course, in the Revolution of 1989 in central and eastern Europe: a political revolution that was, as the Holy Father has insisted, made possible by a moral revolution, a revolution of conscience and of the human spirit, in the countries of the old Warsaw Pact.[42] The experience of 1989 and the struggles of democracies both old and new in the 1990s have, in turn, driven the social doctrine of the Church under John Paul II into a new reflection on the philosophical and moral foundations of democracy. The question for the late 1990s and beyond will be, it seems: How can democratic societies foster the flourishing of human life in its many dimensions, not merely the political or economic?

The Church's encounter with democracy, from the days of Gregory XVI and Pius IX to the present, can be described as a process of transition from *hostility* (Gregory XVI and Pius IX) to *toleration* (Leo XIII and Pius XI) to *admiration* (Pius XII and John XXIII) to *endorsement* (Vatican II and John Paul II), and now, in the late 1990s, to *internal critique*. Prior to the Council, the Church was speaking to democracy from "outside"; since the Council, the Church has, in a sense, spoken to democracy from "within" the democratic experiment as a full participant in democratic life, committed, through its own social doctrine, to the success of the democratic project.

To describe the relationship in these terms is by no means to subordinate the Church to politics; it is to note, however, that as the Church's understanding of democracy has evolved, so has the Church's understanding of itself vis-à-vis democracy. Because of the teaching of the Council and of John Paul II, an "exterior" line of critique has given way to an "interior" critique. Far from being a neutral observer, and without compromising its distinctive social and political "location," the Church now believes that it speaks to democracy from "within" the ongoing democratic debate about the democratic prospect.

John Paul II has developed this "internal line" of analysis—which now constitutes the world's most sophisticated moral case for, and critique of, the democratic project—in a triptych of encyclicals: *Centesimus Annus* (1991), *Veritatis Splendor* (1993), and *Evangelium Vitae* (1995).

In *Centesimus Annus* (as we shall see in detail in the following chapter), John Paul challenged the notion, prominent in the American academy and in certain intellectual circles in post-Communist east central Europe, that democracy was necessarily hollow in its philosophical core, so that the democratic project could be reduced to a matter of "democratic" legal and political procedures:

Nowadays there is a tendency to claim that agnosticism and skeptical relativism are the philosophy and the basic attitude which correspond to democratic forms of political life. Those who are convinced that they know the truth and firmly adhere to it are considered unreliable from a democratic point of view, since they do not accept that truth is determined by the majority, or that it is subject to variation according to different political trends. It must be observed in this regard that if there is no ultimate truth to guide and direct political activity, then ideas and convictions can easily be manipulated for reasons of power. As history demonstrates, a democracy without values easily turns into open or thinly disguised totalitarianism.[43]

The question of the relation between truth and democracy, and the papal critique of the idea of the merely procedural republic, continued two years later in *Veritatis Splendor*. As we shall see in chapter eight, "The Splendor of Truth" is not a "social encyclical" but rather a lengthy reflection on the current situation of Catholic moral theology. Nonetheless, John Paul II was at pains to draw out, at some length, the public implications for democratic societies of one of the encyclical's key teachings: that there are "intrinsically evil" acts, acts that are always and everywhere wrong, irrespective of circumstances or the intentions of individuals.

This might seem, at first blush, an abstract point, or at best one that engages the private decisions of individuals. Yet John Paul argues that the reality of objective evil is a public truth with public consequences. The "truth," in this instance, is that there is a moral logic "hard-wired" into human persons, which we can discern through a careful reflection on human nature and human action. And that "truth" is, in turn, a crucial structural component of the inner architecture of civil society and democracy. Why? Because, the Pope suggests, the foundations of democratic politics can be secured only when society possesses a common moral "grammar" that disciplines and directs the public debate about public life. Truth and freedom, in short, have a lot to do with each other; and so do truth and democracy.

John Paul intensified his "internal critique" of the democratic project in *Evangelium Vitae,* his 1995 encyclical on the "life issues" of abortion and euthanasia. If *Centesimus Annus* opened the question of truth and democracy, and *Veritatis Splendor* specified the ways in which moral truth sets the cultural foundations for sustainable democratic societies, *Evangelium Vitae* discusses several of the ways in which "real existing democracies" can betray their own core values, setting in motion processes that lead to their decay and, ultimately, to their dissolution.

John Paul recognizes that "decisions that go against life"—i.e., decisions to take an innocent human life through abortion or to terminate a life through euthanasia—often reflect "tragic situations of profound suffering, loneliness, a total lack of economic prospects, depression, and anxiety about the future." These circumstances can mitigate "subjective responsibility and the consequent culpability of those who make . . . choices which in themselves are evil." But that has always been the case. What is different, indeed ominously different, today is that these choices "against life" are being described as *"legitimate expressions of individual freedom, to be acknowledged and protected as actual rights."*[44] Wrongs have become rights.

The modern quest for freedom, in the politics of nations and in the social witness of the Church, has frequently been articulated in the language of "human rights." Now, the Pope argues, a decisive turning point has been reached, and the entire edifice of freedom has been jeopardized in consequence:

> The process which once led to discovering the idea of "human rights"—rights inherent in every person and prior to any Constitution and State legislation—is today marked by a *surprising contradiction*. Precisely in an age when the inviolable rights of persons are solemnly proclaimed and the value of life is publicly affirmed, the very right to life is being denied or trampled upon, especially at the more significant moment of existence: the moment of birth and the moment of death.
>
> On the one hand, the various declarations of human rights and the many initiatives inspired by these declarations show that at the global level there is a growing moral sensitivity, more alert to acknowledging the value and dignity of every individual as a human being, without any distinction of race, nationality, religion, political opinion, or social class.
>
> On the other hand, these noble proclamations are unfortunately contradicted by a tragic repudiation of them in practice. This denial is still more distressing, indeed more scandalous, pre-

cisely because it is occurring in a society which makes the affirmation and protection of human rights its primary objective and its
boast. How can these repeated affirmations of principle be recon-
ciled with the continual increase and widespread justification of
attacks on human life? How can we reconcile these declarations
with the refusal to accept those who are weak and needy, the elderly,
or those who have just been conceived? These attacks go directly
against respect for life and they represent a *direct threat to the entire
culture of human rights.*[45]

When democracies use the language of "rights" as a tool to justify
laws permitting objectively evil acts—indeed, when those objectively
evil acts are described as "rights"—more has been lost than precision of
language: something has happened to the character of democratic practice. And that defect of character quickly shows up in public policy. As
the contemporary American experience illustrates, democracies, when
they abandon the central moral principles that give meaning to self-
governance, begin to take on some of the attributes of tyrannies. For
when those moral principles are abandoned or traduced, says the Pope,

> The State is no longer the "common home" where all can live
> together on the basis of principles of fundamental equality, but is
> transformed into a *tyrant State,* which arrogates to itself the right to
> dispose of the life of the weakest and most defenseless members,
> from the unborn child to the elderly, in the name of a public interest
> which is really nothing but the interest of one part. The appearance
> of the strictest respect for legality is maintained, at least when the
> laws permitting abortion and euthanasia are the result of a ballot
> in accordance with what are generally seen as the rule of democracy.
> Really, what we have here is only the tragic caricature of legality;
> the democratic ideal, which is only truly such when it acknowledges
> and safeguards the dignity of every human person, *is betrayed in its
> very foundations.* . . .
>   To claim the right to abortion, infanticide and euthanasia, and
> to recognize that right in law, means to attribute to human freedom
> a *perverse and evil significance:* that of an *absolute power over others and
> against others.* This is the death of true freedom.[46]

It may seem a harsh judgment. But examples of this process of
democratic decay are not hard to find in the contemporary United

States. When, for example, judicial ukase and congressional legislation combine to prevent pro-life Americans from exercising their free-speech rights, or when pro-life Americans are required by law to provide tax support for procedures that they deem to be grave moral evils, then consciences are being coerced by force in a way that threatens the integrity of the democratic experiment. Democracy is also imperiled when certain misconstrued "rights" become the pretexts for circumventing the normal legislative processes of democratic government by handing over all power on issues of life and death to "shadow governments" such as courts, regulatory agencies, and professional associations, which by their nature are less open to scrutiny, and less susceptible to change by democratic persuasion.[47]

If a single sentence could sum up the main thrust of this new "internal critique" of democracy in the social magisterium of John Paul II, it might be this: Culture is "prior" to politics and economics. In this sense, and as suggested in the previous chapter, John Paul II is a "postmodern" pope. Since *Sollicitudo Rei Socialis,* he has become markedly less interested in the old structural questions of politics and economics (democracy vs. *ancien régime* vs. totalitarianism, capitalism vs. socialism vs. the "Catholic third way"). Those questions, the Pope seems to suggest, have been largely answered. If, under the conditions of modernity, you want a free and prosperous society that protects basic human rights while advancing the common good, you choose democracy and the market (or, in the Pope's preferred phrase, the "free economy"). The really interesting and urgent questions today have to do with culture: with the habits of heart and mind that make democracy and the market work to promote genuine human goods.

In the second decade of John Paul II's pontificate, the "other twentieth-century revolution"—the emergence of the Catholic Church as the world's premier institutional defender of human rights—has been both deepened and amplified. In the name of human rights, the Church still challenges tyrants. But it now challenges democrats, too, and on the basis of the same core moral principles that form the basis of the Catholic human-rights revolution.

All of which suggests that the twentieth century's "other revolution" will continue long into the twenty-first.

7

Centesimus Annus:
The Architecture of Freedom

We live, my dear, in a time of transition." Adam's legendary comment to Eve on their way out of the Garden of Eden seems particularly apt for the years since the collapse of European Communism. Yet for some, this period has been less a time of mere transition than a time of final settling: a time when the West has achieved the "end of history" by demonstrating beyond doubt the unsurpassable superiority of liberal democratic polities and market economies. On this provocative understanding of our situation, first argued by Francis Fukuyama, all that remains to do is to fine-tune Western political and economic systems in order to solve "technical problems," assuage "environmental concerns," and satisfy "sophisticated consumer demands."[1]

In central and eastern Europe, however, the collapse of Communism has meant not the "end of history" but rather the return of history to its normal patterns and rhythms. And the victory of the West in the Fifty-Five Years' War against totalitarianism, welcome as it was, has not seen the inauguration of the kingdom of righteousness, truth, and justice here among us. Indeed, historians of the late twenty-first century may well record that the crisis of Communism was followed in short order by the crisis of liberal democracy or democratic capitalism. Moreover, and to illustrate the venerable axiom that there are many ironies in the fire, the crisis of liberal democracy, if it descends upon us with full fury, will be similar to the crisis of Com-

125

munism in one crucial respect: it will be an "anthropological" crisis, in which a false idea of the human person and human community leads to tremendous stress, and ultimately to breakdown, within our political and economic systems.

Communism failed for many reasons: it was economically inefficient, technologically backward, culturally stultifying, politically cruel. But above all, it failed because it was a heresy, a congeries of false teachings about the nature of man and human community, about human history and human destiny. Those false teachings provided the ideological rationale for the political and economic institutions that Communist societies created. And the failures of those institutions— in governance, production, distribution, and consumption—were foreshadowed by the errors of Communism as a doctrine. Marxist-Leninist theory, following a Hegelian dialectic, stressed the impact of "internal contradictions" on the rise and fall of pre-socialist societies. In yet another irony, the Marxist-Leninist project itself failed because of the "internal contradictions" of Marxism-Leninism.[2]

Similarly, the crisis of liberal democratic society that may soon be upon us (if it has not already arrived) has an "anthropological" root in a great debate over the nature of the human person. That debate is publicly focused, in the United States, on the meaning of human freedom. And on this question, a culture war of potentially explosive consequence has broken out.

THE AMERICAN CULTURE WAR

In one corner, we have those who would agree with an assertion made by Professor Rocco Buttiglione, a careful and sympathetic student of the American scene, a distinguished Italian philosopher, and an adviser to Pope John Paul II: "Nothing good can be done without freedom, but freedom is not the highest value in itself. Freedom is given to man in order to make possible the free obedience to truth and the free gift of oneself in love."[3] On this understanding of freedom and its relation to the nature of the human person, democracy is a substantive moral experiment. The procedures of democracy grow out of, and depend upon, the *ethos* of the democratic society. And if those procedures are to serve human goods, that *ethos* must reflect the truth about the human person. Thus democracy depends on an ongoing process of moral-cultural revitalization. Democratic self-governance is never finally secured; each generation must face Lincoln's question as to whether nations conceived in liberty and dedicated to equality before the law can long endure.

In the opposing corner are those who argue that freedom is constituted by the liberty to pursue one's personal gratifications, self-defined, so long as no one else (or at least no one in whom the state asserts a "compelling interest") gets hurt. This anorexic conception of freedom is not confined to the groves of academe, where tenured radicals celebrate the joys of debonair nihilism; it was succinctly formulated by the U.S. Supreme Court in a joint opinion by Justices Kennedy, O'Connor, and Souter, in June 1992: "At the heart of liberty is the right to define one's own concept of existence, of meaning, of the universe, and of the mystery of human life."[4] On this understanding of things, democracy is merely an ensemble of procedures, largely legal, by which we regulate the pursuit of our personal satisfactions. Democracy has no substantive moral core. No civil society, no community of republican virtue, no public moral conversation sustains democracy; there are only the Rules of the Game. The gratification of the unencumbered, self-constituting, imperial Self is the end toward which the American democratic experiment is ordered.

Those of us who have been writing about an American *Kulturkampf* (or "culture war") in recent years have sometimes been accused of exaggeration, even by colleagues sympathetic to our views on specific issues. But with the Kennedy/O'Connor/Souter dictum in *Casey v. Planned Parenthood,* the culture war was defined with unmistakable clarity, its gravity underscored beyond anything that any sound-bite publicist could have proposed.

For in a decision celebrated by the prestige press, the elite culture, most of the academy, and many religious leaders, the so-called moderate center of the U.S. Supreme Court declared that republican virtue, understood as a broad communal consensus on the moral coordinates of our common life, is no part of the inner constitution, the moral architecture, of "freedom" in America. Why? Because to define such a consensus and to embody it in law would, according to Kennedy, O'Connor, and Souter, be an act of "compulsion" that would deny citizens the "attributes of personhood."[5] And yet there are tens of millions of Americans who, with the Founders and Framers, believe the opposite: who believe that rights and laws ought to be grounded in prior understandings of rights and wrongs (the alternative being governance through sheer coercion); who believe that familial and public responsibility has a higher moral status in a civilized conscience than private satisfaction; who believe that the common good is a nobler horizon against which to conduct one's life than the narrow infinity described by the pursuit of the self-actualized, self-constituting self.[6]

These battle lines in the American *Kulturkampf* are, admittedly, broadly described. And if we are honest with ourselves, we might concede that the trenches in the war run through our own hearts, as well as between ourselves and others. But that there is a culture war in America today, and that the resolution of that war will determine the future of the American democratic experiment, we need not doubt. The power of ideas in history has been decisively demonstrated by the course of events in the twentieth century. How we *conceive* freedom will have much to do with how we construct and operate the political and economic *institutions* through which freedom is mediated and publicly expressed. Wise Americans since colonial days have understood that those institutions can so decay that the result is social chaos, and ultimately oppression. Whether that chaos unfolds in our time is the outcome being contested in the American *Kulturkampf,* and in the crisis of liberal democratic society that seems, ironically, to be following hard on the heels of the collapse of Communism.

John Paul II on Human Freedom

In May 1991, Pope John Paul II issued a social encyclical that quickly established itself as a landmark event in contemporary religious thought. Issued to honor the centenary of Pope Leo XIII's pioneering encyclical *Rerum Novarum, Centesimus Annus* ("The Hundredth Year") offers both a look back at the *res novae,* the "new things" that seized the attention of Leo XIII, and a look ahead at what we might call the "new new things," the new facts of public life at the end of the twentieth century and the turn of the third Christian millennium.

Like other papal documents, *Centesimus Annus* reaffirms the classic themes of Catholic social thought. But John Paul II's creative extension of the tradition makes *Centesimus Annus* a singularly bold, and singularly relevant, document—one that reconfigures the boundaries of the Catholic debate over the right ordering of culture, economics, and politics under the conditions of modernity, and one that provides a badly needed framework for the debate over the future of ordered liberty in these United States.

Centesimus Annus is not a matter for Catholics only, for the encyclical addresses itself to "all men and women of good will." Pope John Paul II understands himself to be making *public* moral arguments, in which he invites others to engage. Moreover, and as if to prove the point, non-Catholic scholars, religious leaders, and politicians have been showing an increasing interest in modern Catholic social teaching as perhaps the most well-developed and coherent set of Christian reference points for conducting the argument about how Americans should order their lives today. Indeed, John Paul II's witness to Christian orthodoxy has sometimes been more appreciated outside his church than within it. As a prominent Southern Baptist once put it to a group of Catholic colleagues, "Down where I come from, people are saying, 'You folks finally got yourself a pope who knows how to pope.'"

For these reasons, *Centesimus Annus* should be of particular interest to citizens of the United States. As a nation "conceived in liberty," as the leader of the party of freedom in world politics, and as a country involved in a grave public debate over the very meaning of freedom, the United States might well pay careful attention to what the most influential moral leader in the contemporary world has to say about the many dimensions of freedom, and about the intimate relationship between freedom and truth, particularly the "truth about man" that has been such a prominent theme in the teaching of this pope.

What John Paul II means by "freedom," of course, is not exactly what America's cultural elites have had in mind since the fevered "liberations" of the 1960s. And so an argument is upon us: What *is* this freedom that, in Miami in 1987, the Pope called a "great gift, a great blessing of God"? How is it to be lived by free men and women in free societies that must protect individual liberty while advancing the common good?

Here the Pope's concerns directly intersect the most basic issues in the American *Kulturkampf,* and so *Centesimus Annus* can shed some much needed light on our national debate over rights, responsibilities, and republican virtue.

The Problem of Freedom

Centesimus Annus is a profound meditation on man's quest for a freedom that will truly satisfy the deepest yearnings of the human heart. In this sense, *Centesimus Annus* is theology long before it is political science and economics. The encyclical is an exercise in Christian anthropology and, more specifically, a reflection on human nature as it expresses itself in history through political and economic action. John Paul II does not regard the human quest for true freedom as something peripheral to the concerns of the Church. Quite the contrary: the quest for freedom is "built in" to the very nature of man's way of being in the world, and "built in" by a God whom we are to find and worship, in freedom. Thus a Christian anthropology of freedom necessarily engages questions of the theology of freedom. For history, as Hans Urs von Balthasar reminds us, is "unfolded before us" because of the "art of the world-architect," who is God.[7]

Centesimus Annus begins with a review of the teaching of Leo XIII in *Rerum Novarum.* There, in 1891, the Church began to grapple with the new problem of freedom that had been created by the upheavals of the Industrial Revolution in economics and the French Revolution in politics: "Traditional society was passing away and another was beginning to be formed—one which brought the hope of new freedoms but also the threat of new forms of injustice and servitude."[8] That threat was particularly grave when modernity ignored "the essential bond between human freedom and truth."[9] Leo XIII understood, his successor argues, that a "freedom which refused to be bound to the truth would fall into arbitrariness and end up submitting itself to the vilest of passions, to the point of self-destruction."[10] In the last decade of this bloodiest of centuries, it is difficult to suggest that Leo XIII was unduly pessimistic about certain aspects of the modern quest for freedom.

From Leo XIII on, Catholic social teaching's answer to the "problem" of freedom has begun with a theologically and philosophically grounded moral reflection on man himself: with an insistence on the dignity and worth of each human being as a creature endowed with intelligence and will and thus made in the "image and likeness" of God (Gen. 1:26). Therefore the beginning of the answer to the rapaciousness of Manchesterian liberalism in economics was to assert, on the basis of man as the *imago Dei*, "the *dignity of the worker* . . . [and] the *dignity of work*."[11] And the beginning of the answer to the massive repression and injustice of the twentieth-century tyrannies was Leo XIII's insistence on the "necessary limits to the State's intervention" in human affairs.[12] Why are those limits "necessary"? Because "the individual, the family, and society are prior to the State, and . . . the State exists in order to protect their rights and not stifle them."[13]

The Catholic human-rights revolution of the late twentieth century thus owes a large debt of gratitude to the last pope of the nineteenth century. For it was Leo XIII who first pointed toward Christian *personalism* as the alternative to socialist collectivism (which subsumed human personality into the mass) and to radical individualism (which locked human personality into an auto-constructed prison of solipsism).

Deepening the "Rights" Debate

Since he took office in October 1978, John Paul II has been a vigorous proponent of basic human rights, particularly the fundamental right of religious freedom. This pattern continues in *Centesimus Annus*, in which the Pope decries the situation in those countries "which covertly, or even openly, deny to citizens of faiths other than that of the majority the full exercise of their civil and religious rights, preventing them from taking part in the cultural process, and restricting both the Church's right to preach the Gospel and the right of those who hear this preaching to accept it."[14]

For that reason, it is all the more striking that the human-rights language is a bit more muted in *Centesimus Annus* than in John Paul's earlier encyclicals—and far more muted than it was in Pope John XXIII's famous 1963 letter, *Pacem in Terris*. John Paul II has not suddenly become less interested in the problems of human rights. Rather, he seems determined to deepen (and, in some respects, to discipline) the debate over "rights" by linking rights to *obligations* and to *truth*.

On this latter point, John Paul argues forcefully that conscience is not
some kind of moral free agent, in which an "autonomous self" declares
something to be right because it is right "for me." No, conscience is
"bound . . . to the truth."[15] And the truth about man is not to be
confused with "an appeal to the appetites and inclinations toward
immediate gratification," an appeal that is "utilitarian" in character and
does not reflect "the hierarchy of the true values of human existence."[16]

Nor are "rights" simply a matter of our immunities from the
coercive power of others, important as such immunities are. Rights
exist so that we can fulfill our obligations. Thus, to take an example
from one sphere of life, a man should be free economically so that he
can enter into more cooperative relationships with others and meet
his obligations to work in order to "provide for the needs of his family,
his community, his nation, and ultimately all humanity."[17] Ownership, too, has its obligations: "Just as the person fully realizes himself
in the free gift of self, so too ownership morally satisfies itself in the
creation, at the proper time and in the proper way, of opportunities
for work and human growth for all."[18]

By harking back to the Christian personalism of Leo XIII, while at
the same time thickening, so to speak, the concept of rights in the
Catholic tradition, *Centesimus Annus* provides a powerful example of
Christian anthropology at work, probing the mystery of man as it
reveals itself in the many dimensions of human community. But this
is no abstract philosophical exercise. For, having set the proper framework for thinking about public life, the Pope immediately brings his
analysis of the "truth about man" to bear on one of the most stunning
events in this century of the unexpected—the Revolution of 1989 in
central and eastern Europe.

Revolution of the Spirit

"The fundamental error of socialism," says John Paul II, "is anthropological in nature":

Socialism considers the individual person simply as an element, a
molecule within the social organism, so that the good of the individual is completely subordinated to the functioning of the socioeconomic mechanism. Socialism likewise maintains that the good

of the individual can be realized without reference to his free choice, to the unique and exclusive responsibility he exercises in the face of good or evil. Man is thus reduced to a series of social relationships, and the concept of the person as the . . . subject of moral decision disappears, the very subject whose decisions build the social order.

From this mistaken conception of the person there arise both a distortion of law . . . and an opposition to private property. A person who is deprived of something he can call "his own," and of the possibility of earning a living through his own initiative, comes to depend on the social machine and on those who control it. This makes it much more difficult for him to recognize his dignity as a person, and hinders progress toward the building up of an authentic human community.[19]

Western political scientists and international-relations specialists have had a hard time agreeing on the primary cause of the dramatic events that took place in central and eastern Europe in 1989. "Delayed modernization" is one frequently encountered answer: the economic systems of the Communist world could not compete, and the only way to change them was to get rid of the political regimes that had imposed collectivism in the first place. It is, in truth, a deliciously (if depressingly) Marxist "answer" to the utter collapse of Marxism— and a worrisome indication of how deeply quasi-Marxist themes have sunk into the collective unconscious of the new knowledge class.

Pope John Paul II, however, is not persuaded by this materialistic analysis of modern history.

Centesimus Annus would be well worth careful study for its marvelous third chapter alone. For in "The Year 1989," the Pope offers a succinct, pointed, and compelling analysis of the roots of the Revolution of 1989—an analysis whose implications for Western societies we ignore at our peril. The fundamental problem with Communism (or what the Pope calls "Real Socialism") was not its economic decrepitude. Rather, Communism failed because it denied "the truth about man." Communism's failures were first and foremost failures in the order of ideas. Its faith was misplaced, and so its hope was utopian and its charity non-existent. "The God That Failed" was a false god whose acolytes murdered tens of millions of human beings and led societies and economies into terminal crisis.

Pope John Paul begins his historical analysis of 1989 in 1945, with the Yalta Agreements. "Yalta," in fact, has loomed very large indeed in the vision of the Polish pontiff. World War II, "which should have re-established freedom and restored the right of nations, ended without having attained these goals"—indeed, it ended with "the spread of Communist totalitarianism over more than half of Europe and over other parts of the world."[20] Yalta, in other words, was more than a diplomatic accommodation; it was a moral catastrophe and a betrayal of the sacrifices of the war, a betrayal rooted in incomprehension of (or indifference to) the nature of Marxist-Leninist totalitarianism. A failure of moral intuition or of will led to a failure of politics.

Thus the first truth about central and eastern Europe was that the "Yalta arrangement" could not be regarded as merely a historical datum: regrettable, perhaps, but nonetheless an unchallengeable fact of life with which one had to deal. Dealing had to be done; not for nothing did Pope John Paul spend his early priesthood in a Polish Church dominated by Cardinal Stefan Wyszyński of Warsaw, the tenacious prelate who gained Catholicism—and the remnants of Polish civil society—crucial breathing room in the 1950s. But there should be no illusions amidst such negotiations, no false expectations of a gradual "convergence" between East and West.[21] The only "dealing" that would contribute to a genuine peace would be based on the conviction that no peace worthy of the name could be built on the foundations of Yalta.

Facing Down Fear

As it began, so it would end. The origins of this bizarre and suffocating empire found their parallels, forty-four years later, in the ways in which the empire fell.

The moral catastrophe of Yalta was attacked at its roots by "the Church's commitment to defend and promote human rights," by a confrontation with Stalin's empire at the level of ethics, history, and culture. Communism, and particularly Communist atheism, the Pope said time and time again, was "an act against man."[22] And the antidote to the false humanism of Marxism-Leninism came from a truly Christian humanism in which men and women once again learned the human dignity that was theirs by birthright.

p 196

That understanding had never been completely snuffed out in central and eastern Europe. But there was fear—the pathology that bound the Yalta imperial system together. Breaking the fever of fear was thus the crucial first step in addressing the calamity of Yalta.

First in Poland, then elsewhere, millions of people in the region began to face down their fear during John Paul II's first, dramatic return to Poland in June 1979. His message during that extraordinary pilgrimage was decidedly "pre-political." It was a message about ethics, culture, and history devoted to explicating "the truth about man" that Poles knew in their bones—the truth that their regime had denied for two generations. But although it was not a message about "politics" in the narrow sense of the struggle for power, it was high-octane "politics" in the more venerable sense of the term: "Politics" as the ongoing argument about the good person, the good society, and the structure of freedom. And that upper-case Politics led, over time, to the distinctive lower-case politics of the Revolution of 1989, the revolution that reversed Yalta.

John Paul II believes that, among the "many factors involved in the fall of [these] oppressive regimes, some deserve special mention." The first point at which "the truth about man" intersected with politics was on the question of the rights of workers. The Pope does not hesitate to drive home the full irony of the situation:

> It cannot be forgotten that the fundamental crisis of systems claiming to express the rule and indeed the dictatorship of the working class began with the great upheavals which took place in Poland in the name of solidarity. It was the throngs of working people which foreswore the ideology which presumed to speak in their name. On the basis of a hard, lived experience of work and of oppression, it was they who recovered and, in a sense, rediscovered the content and principles of the Church's social doctrine.[23]

That reappropriation of "the truth about man" led to another of the distinctive elements of the Revolution of 1989—its non-violence. Tactical considerations surely played a role in the choice of non-violence by those whom we used to call "dissidents": the bad guys had all the guns, and the good guys knew it. But it is hard to explain why the mass of the people remained non-violent—particularly given the glorification of armed revolt in Polish history and culture—unless one understands that a moral revolution, a revolution of conscience, had preceded the political revolution of 1989.

The Pope was fully aware that the economic systems of central and eastern Europe were a shambles by the mid-1980s, and that this played its role in the collapse of Stalin's empire. But John Paul also argues that the economic disaster of command economies was not a "technical problem" alone; it was, rather, "a consequence of the violation of the human rights to private initiative, to ownership of property, and to freedom in the economic sector."[24] Marxist economics, just like Leninist politics, refused to acknowledge "the truth about man."

State atheism in the Eastern bloc also carried the seeds of its own destruction, according to John Paul. The "spiritual void" the state created by building a world without windows "deprived the younger generation of direction and in many cases led them, in the irrepressible search for personal identity and for the meaning of life, to rediscover the religious roots of their national cultures, and to rediscover the person of Christ himself as the existentially adequate response to the desire in every human heart for goodness, truth, and life."[25] The Communists had thought they could "uproot the need for God from the human heart." They learned that "it is not possible to succeed in this without throwing the heart into turmoil."[26]

And Communism onto the ash heap of history.

John Paul II's carefully crafted discussion of the Revolution of 1989 makes no claims for the Church's role as agent of the Revolution that would strike any fairminded reader as implausible or excessive. The Holy See was well aware of the many other factors that conspired to produce the peaceful demolition of Stalin's empire: the Helsinki process, which publicly indicted Communist regimes for their human-rights violations and created a powerful network of human-rights activists on both sides of the Iron Curtain; the fact of Mikhail Gorbachev; and the Strategic Defense Initiative (SDI), which a number of Vatican officials consider, privately, to have been decisive in forcing a change in Soviet policy.[27]

But in *Centesimus Annus,* John Paul II was determined to teach a more comprehensive truth about the Revolution of 1989—that a revolution of the spirit, built on the sure foundation of "the truth about man," preceded the transfer of power from Communist to democratic hands. The Revolution of 1989, viewed through this wide-angle lens, began in 1979. It was a revolution in which people learned

first to throw off fear, and only then to throw off their chains—
non-violently. It was a revolution of conservation, in which people
reclaimed their moral, cultural, and historical identities. It was a revolution "from the bottom up," the bottom being the historic ethical
and cultural self-understandings of individuals and nations.

Which is to say, it was a revolution that reminded the West that a
vital civil society was the essential foundation of a democracy.

The Free Economy

John Paul II's analysis of the dynamics and structure of freedom
then turns to the question of how the free society ought to organize
its economic life in light of the "truth about man":

> Not only is it wrong from the ethical point of view to disregard
> human nature, which is made for freedom, but in practice it is
> impossible to do so. Where society is so organized as to reduce
> arbitrarily or even suppress the sphere in which freedom is legiti-
> mately exercised, the result is that the life of society becomes pro-
> gressively disorganized and goes into decline.
>
> Moreover, man, who was created for freedom, bears within
> himself the wound of original sin, which constantly draws him
> toward evil and puts him in need of redemption. Not only is *this*
> *doctrine an integral part of Christian revelation;* it also has great herme-
> neutical value insofar as it helps one to understand human reality.
> Man tends towards good, but he is also capable of evil. He can
> transcend his immediate interest and still remain bound to it.
>
> The social order will be all the more stable, the more it takes
> this fact into account and does not place in opposition personal
> interest and the interests of society as a whole, but rather seeks to
> bring them into a fruitful harmony. In fact, when self-interest is
> violently suppressed, it is replaced by a burdensome system of
> bureaucratic control which dries up the wellsprings of initiative and
> creativity. When people think they possess the secret of a perfect
> social organization which makes evil impossible, they also think
> that they can use any means, including violence and deceit, in order
> to bring that organization into being. Politics then becomes a "secu-
> lar religion" which operates under the illusion of creating paradise
> in this world. But no political society . . . can ever be confused with
> the Kingdom of God.[28]

Perhaps the most striking "new thing" about *Centesimus Annus* is the way in which John Paul II draws out the implications of his Christian anthropology of human freedom, and his analysis of the dynamics of the Revolution of 1989, in the field of economics. In fact, *Centesimus Annus* contains the most striking papal endorsement of—and challenge to—the "free economy" in a century. The endorsement comes in the form of the answer to a pressing question:

> Can it be said that, after the failure of Communism, capitalism is the victorious social system, and that capitalism should be the goal of the countries now making efforts to rebuild their economy and society? Is this the model which ought to be proposed to the countries of the Third World which are searching for the path to true economic and civil progress?
>
> The answer is obviously complex. If by "capitalism" is meant an economic system which recognizes the fundamental and positive role of business, the market, private property, and the resulting responsibility for the means of production, as well as free human creativity in the economic sector, then the answer is certainly in the affirmative, even though it would perhaps be more appropriate to speak of a "business economy," "market economy," or simply "free economy." But if by "capitalism" is meant a system in which freedom in the economic sector is not circumscribed within a strong juridical framework which places it at the service of human freedom in its totality, and which sees it as a particular aspect of that freedom, the core of which is ethical and religious, then the reply is certainly negative.[29]

In other words, if by "capitalism" is meant what the West at its best means by capitalism—a tripartite system in which democratic politics and a vibrant moral culture discipline and temper the free market—then that is indeed the system that the Pope urges the new democracies and the Third World to adopt, because it is the system most congruent with a human freedom that is truly liberating.

Latin American liberation theologians, western European social democrats, east-central European traditionalists, and the defenders of the liberal status quo in American Catholicism insist that this endorsement carries many conditions with it. Of course it does and of course it should: those conditions are neither new nor surprising nor unwelcome. No thoughtful defender of the market would deny the need for its careful regulation by law, culture, and public morality.[30] What is new about *Centesimus Annus* comes in passages like these:

> The modern *business economy* has positive aspects. Its basis is human freedom exercised in the economic field, just as it is exercised in many other fields.[31]

> It is precisely the ability to foresee both the needs of others and the combinations of productive factors most adapted to satisfying those needs that constitutes another important source of wealth in modern society. Besides, many goods cannot be adequately produced through the work of an isolated individual; they require the cooperation of many people working towards a common goal. Organizing such a productive effort, planning its duration in time, making sure that it corresponds in a positive way to the demands which it must satisfy, and taking the necessary risk—all this too is a source of wealth in today's society. In this way, the *role* of disciplined and creative *human work* and, as an essential part of that work, *initiative and entrepreneurial ability* becomes increasingly evident and decisive.[32]

> Another task of the State is that of overseeing and directing the exercise of human rights in the economic sector. However, primary responsibility in this area belongs not to the State but to individuals and to the various groups and associations which make up society. The State could not directly ensure the right to work for all its citizens unless it controlled every aspect of economic life and restricted the free initiative of individuals.[33]

> Indeed, besides the earth, man's principal resource is *man himself.*[34]

Centesimus Annus thus marks a decisive break with the curious materialism that had characterized aspects of modern Catholic social teaching since Leo XIII. Wealth-creation today, John Paul II readily acknowledges, has more to do with human creativity and imagination, and with political and economic systems capable of unleashing that creativity and imagination, than with "resources" *per se*. And that, he seems to suggest, is one of the "signs of the times" to which Catholic social thought must be attentive.

In fact, one of the most distinctive characteristics of *Centesimus Annus* is its empirical sensitivity. John Paul II has clearly thought carefully about what does and what does not work in exercising what has come to be known as a "preferential option for the poor" in the new democracies, in the Third World, and in impoverished parts of the developed world. The "preferential option," the Pope seems to suggest, is a formal principle; its content should be determined, not on the basis of ideological orthodoxy (that is what was rejected in the Revolution of 1989), but by empirical facts. And for John Paul, the evidence is in. What works best for the poor is democratic polities and properly regulated market economies. Why? Because democracy and the market are the systems that best cohere with human nature, with human freedom, with "the truth about man."

It will take some time for this new direction in Catholic social thought to register on the compasses of those still committed to what the Pope calls the "impossible compromise between Marxism and Christianity,"[35] as well as by those who continue to search for a chimerical Catholic "third way" between capitalism and socialism. (At a meeting in Rome shortly after the encyclical was published, for example, the dean of the social-science faculty at the Pontifical Gregorian University told me that "Capitalism A [i.e., the capitalism the Pope endorses] exists only in textbooks." I suggested to the dean, a Latin American Jesuit, that if he really believed that, he had no business running a faculty of social science.) But the text of Centesimus Annus itself is plain; the authoritative teaching of the Catholic Church is that a properly regulated market, disciplined by politics, law, and culture, is best for poor people. It works. It allows the poor to participate in economic life, to enter what Richard John Neuhaus has called the "circle of productivity and exchange."[36] And thus it gives the poor an "option" to exercise their freedom and creativity as economic actors that is available in no other system.

The moral implications of this analysis for U.S. social welfare policy are not difficult to define. We best exercise our responsibility for and to the poor by efforts to include them in the free economy and in democratic public life. Empowerment, rather than dependency, is the goal.

Culture Wars, Revisited

If man does not live by bread alone, neither does the free society. And so Centesimus Annus next turns to the question of how the explo-

sive energies of the market are made to serve a freedom that finds its
fulfillment in goodness rather than in ephemeral goodies:

> It is not possible to understand man on the basis of economics
> alone, nor to define him simply on the basis of class membership.
> Man is understood in a more complete way when he is situated
> within the sphere of culture through his language, history, and the
> position he takes toward the fundamental events of life, such as
> birth, love, work, and death. At the heart of every culture lies the
> attitude man takes to the greatest mystery: the mystery of God.
> Different cultures are basically different ways of facing the question
> of the meaning of personal existence. When this question is elim-
> inated, the cultural and moral life of nations are corrupted.[37]

Understandably enough, much of the debate in the immediate
aftermath of *Centesimus Annus* focused on the encyclical's careful endorsement of the "free economy." But the truth of the matter is that
John Paul II is rather more concerned about the "culture" leg of the
politics-economics-culture triad than about the argument between
market economists and those still defending state-centered schemes
of development. The latter debate has been settled. The real issue
remains the ability of a culture to provide the market with the moral
framework it needs to serve the cause of integral human development.

The lessons of 1989, for both East and West, are once again on the
Pope's mind. Can the new democracies develop societies that provide
for the free exercise of human creativity in the workplace, in politics,
and in the many fields of culture without becoming libertine in their
public moral life? Will "consumerism"—that is, consumption as an
ideology, not the reality of "consumers" as a natural part of what
dissidents used to call a "normal society"—replace Marxism-
Leninism as the new form of bondage east of the Elbe River? Has it
already done so in the West? If not, how can we prevent its triumph?
If so, how can we repair the damage and put the free society on a
firmer moral foundation?

The Pope is not persuaded by libertarian arguments. "Of itself,"
he writes, "the economic system does not possess criteria for correctly
distinguishing new and higher forms of satisfying human needs from
artificial new needs which hinder the formation of a mature personality." The market cannot be left on its own. "*A great deal of educational*

and cultural work is urgently needed" so that the market's remarkable capacity to generate wealth is bent toward ends that are congruent with "the truth about man"—which is not, John Paul continually urges, an economic truth alone, or even primarily.[38]

In fact, the Pope seems convinced that consumerism-as-ideology ought to be blamed, not on the market system, but on the moral-cultural system's failures to discipline the market:

> These criticisms [of consumerism in its hedonistic form] are directed not so much against an economic system as against an ethical and cultural system. . . . If economic life is absolutized, if the production and consumption of goods become the center of social life and society's only value . . . the reason is to be found not so much in the economic system itself as in the fact that the entire socio-cultural system, by ignoring the ethical and religious dimension, has been weakened, and ends by limiting itself to the production of goods and services alone.[39]

As should be abundantly clear by now, *Centesimus Annus* is no dreary exercise in papal scolding. John Paul II knows that the things of this world are important, and that material goods can enhance man's capacity for living a freedom worthy of a creature made in the image and likeness of God. "It is not wrong to want to live better," he says. "What is wrong is a style of life which is presumed to be better when it is directed toward 'having' rather than 'being,' and which wants to have more, not in order to be more but in order to spend life in enjoyment as an end in itself." Self-command, in economic life as well as in interpersonal relationships, is the hallmark of a freedom being lived in a truly liberating way.[40]

Reconstructing Civil Society

So what is to be done to construct (or reconstruct) the moral-cultural foundations of the free society? On this front, John Paul is not inclined to look first toward the institutions of the state. Indeed, another "new thing" in *Centesimus Annus* is the Pope's severe criticism of the excesses of the welfare state, which in its extreme form he styles the "social assistance state." Here, the Pope argues, is another abuse of human freedom: "By intervening directly and depriving society of its responsibility, the Social Assistance State leads to a loss of human energies and an inordinate increase of public agencies, which are dominated more by bureaucratic ways of thinking than by concern for serving their clients, and which are accompanied by an enormous increase in spending."[41]

John Paul's preference, which is an expression of the classic Catholic principle of "subsidiarity," is for what in the American context would be called "mediating structures": "Needs are best understood and satisfied by people who are closest to [the poor, the weak, the stricken] and who act as neighbors to those in need."[42] Such mediating structures—religious institutions, voluntary organizations, unions, business associations, neighborhood groups, service organizations, and the like—are the backbone of what Václav Havel's "Charter 77" and the Solidarity movement worked to resurrect in central and eastern Europe throughout the 1980s under the rubric of "civil society." The reconstruction of this civil society is the first order of business in setting the foundations of democracy—a message that ought to be taken to heart by those in the West, too, especially those who have read their Tocqueville and have pondered the Frenchman's identification of the voluntary association as *the* distinctive and essential institutional foundation of democratic culture in America.[43]

In sum, what is needed is a public moral culture that encourages "lifestyles in which the quest for truth, beauty, goodness, and communion with others for the sake of common growth are the factors which determine consumer choice, savings, and investments."[44] We do not live in hermetically sealed containers labeled "economic life," "politics," and "lifestyle." John Paul insists that it is all of a piece. There is only one human universe, and it is an inescapably moral universe in which questions of "ought" emerge at every juncture; or as the Pope puts it, "Even the decision to invest in one place rather than another, in one productive sector rather than another, is always *a moral and cultural choice*."[45]

As with economics, so with politics. I have stressed here the importance of "1989" in the Pope's historical vision. But by 1989, the Pope means a set of events fraught with meaning for the West as well as for the East. John Paul II has vigorously positioned the Church on the side of the democratic revolution throughout the world, not because he is a geopolitician, but because he is an evangelist, a moral teacher, and a pastor. On the threshold of the third millennium, the post-Christendom

Church, he insists, "has no models to present." But, as an expression of its fundamental concern for "the truth about man," the Church "values the democratic system inasmuch as it ensures the participation of citizens in making political choices, guarantees to the governed the possibility of both electing and holding accountable those who govern them, and of replacing them through peaceful means when appropriate."[46]

Truth and Consequences

There are no guarantees about the future of the free society, particularly given the mistaken attitude toward the relationship between rights and obligations, between rights and the truth, common among Western cultural elites. It was not as Cassandra but as a friend of democracy that John Paul II laid down the challenge noted previously about the importance of a horizon of truth for the democratic experiment:

> Nowadays there is a tendency to claim that agnosticism and skeptical relativism are the philosophy and the basic attitude which correspond to democratic forms of political life. Those who are convinced that they know the truth and firmly adhere to it are considered unreliable from a democratic point of view, since they do not accept that truth is determined by the majority, or that it is subject to variation according to different political trends. It must be observed in this regard that if there is no ultimate truth to guide and direct political activity, then ideas and convictions can easily be manipulated for reasons of power. As history demonstrates, a democracy without values easily turns into open or thinly disguised totalitarianism.[47]

Still, the Pope continues, "the Church respects *the legitimate autonomy of the democratic order,*" and the Church "is not entitled to express preferences for this or that institutional or constitutional solution." Rather, the Church is the Church, and thus "her contribution to the political order is precisely her vision of the dignity of the person revealed in all its fullness in the mystery of the Incarnate Word."[48] But that vision itself, as we have seen, has public consequences, not least in terms of civic education and democratic legitimation.

Centesimus Annus is an extraordinary statement of faith and hope.

At the end of a century of tyranny, the Pope speaks a word of hope in freedom. At the end of a century of fear in which the human family has become afraid of what it might be capable of, the Pope speaks of hope in man's capacity to order his public life in ways that serve the cause of human flourishing. And those expressions of hope are not fragile optimism, because the worldly hopes expressed in *Centesimus Annus* are grounded in a transcendent hope, born of faith in the God who created man with intelligence and free will.

Given the breadth of the issues it addressed, the depth at which questions were probed, and the empirical sensitivity John Paul II shows to the "signs of the times" as they illuminate freedom's cause at the end of the twentieth century, this encyclical may well be regarded, in time, as the greatest of the twentieth-century social encyclicals. With *Centesimus Annus,* the "Pope of Freedom" did far more than mark the centenary of a great tradition: he brilliantly scouted the terrain for the next hundred years of humanity's struggle to embody in public life the truth that makes us free. His is a vision of the possibilities and the crisis of freedom that Americans, especially in this season of *Kulturkampf,* most certainly ought not to ignore.

An American Epilogue: Wojtyła Meets Murray

To my knowledge, John Courtney Murray, S.J., whose work on religious freedom we have already explored, never spoke of a public Church "after Christendom." But his call for Catholicism to contribute to the formation of a religiously informed public philosophy that would ground, discipline, and direct the American experiment in ordered liberty has many affinities with John Paul II's "public" ecclesiology. Indeed, in Murray's critical analysis of the modern American circumstance, we may find an anticipation of some of the key themes in *Centesimus Annus*'s critique of merely "proceduralist" democracy. And in Murray's prescription for a revitalization of American democracy through a retrieval of the classic moral and political understandings from which the United States was born, we may find a notable example of how the social doctrine of the Church can be "translated" into a historic American idiom without losing its moral cutting edge.

Murray believed, with Lincoln (and not unlike John Paul II), that America was a "proposition country"—a political community gathered together by certain ideas and ideals, whose very future rested on the capacity of those ideas and ideals to shape its people's lives. The "American proposition" was composed of truths that the American Founders held in common; these truths were the "inner architecture" of the American experiment in ordered liberty. Moreover, the contemporary vitality of those truths was the key to the successful working-out of our national experiment today.[49]

Five Foundational Truths

Forty years after Murray wrote *We Hold These Truths,* it is precisely these foundational truths that are being contested in the American culture war. Murray believed, and I think John Paul II would agree, that the degree to which these truths are "received" in contemporary America and inform the life of the American political community is *the* crucial index of the health of the civil society that sustains our democracy. For unless there is some consensus on the moral architecture of the American experiment, there can be no disciplined public discourse over the ways in which we order our common life. As Murray put it, if "barbarism threatens when men cease to live together according to reason . . . [barbarism] likewise threatens when men cease to talk together according to reasonable laws."[50]

What are these truths? Five of them seem to me most basic, and most urgently in need of reiteration today.

1. The first "truth" on which the American experiment is built, in terms of the ontology of the experiment as well as its functional aspects, is that *God is sovereign over nations as well as over individuals.*

This truth distinguishes the American tradition—a conservative tradition, in the sense of maintaining continuity with the central political tradition of Christian Europe—from the Jacobin/laicist tradition of late-eighteenth-century continental Europe and its nineteenth- and twentieth-century epigones. In the latter tradition (which gave rise, as we have seen, to the Reign of Terror as practiced by both Robespierre and Lenin), the "autonomous reason of man" was "the first and the sole principle of political organization."[51] In the American revolutionary tradition, by contrast, the sovereignty of God, which necessarily stands in judgment on all our works, is the first principle of political organization.

This theological affirmation has critical public consequences. First, it establishes, on as secure a foundation as possible, the penultimacy of the political. The affirmation of God's sovereignty over the nation as well as over the individuals who compose it sets limits on the boundaries of the political, even as it invests politics with its own proper dignity.

Moreover, because God is sovereign, all the works of our hands— and especially those that have to do with the exercise of power—are under judgment. When Americans pledge allegiance to the flag today and affirm "one nation, under God," we reaffirm the Founders' notion that the nation, this American experiment in ordered liberty, is under judgment. The organization of the experiment, and the laws by which it is conducted, are to be judged against a wider moral horizon than that of immediate political expediency or interest.

This is not a truth that is well understood in, say, the Supreme Court today. The recovery of it is the key to a revitalization of the American experiment that is in moral continuity with the Founding.

2. The second truth on which the American experiment is built is that *the human person has the God-given capacity to be self-governing.*

The God who gave us life and liberty also gave us the capacity to reflect on our nature and our circumstances, and to discern from that reflection our moral obligations. The social embodiment of this truth about the human person is, Murray argued, the notion of a "free people under a limited government"—the best shorthand formula, he believed, for the essence of the American experiment.

According to that familiar formula, government is not simply coercion. Government is "the right to command"; government is authority, and this authority is both derived from law and limited by law.[52] Thus the notion of the rule of law should not be understood, Murray wrote, in the positivist sense that the law is simply what the law says it is. No, the law, too, is under judgment. The law is to be judged by moral criteria that transcend it.

Here, too, is an issue on which a renewed conversation is imperative in contemporary America, most especially in terms of the controversies over abortion and euthanasia. The fact that a right-to-life movement is thriving in the United States, twenty years after the principal culture-forming institutions of our society pronounced the issue settled on behalf of a radical abortion license, is powerful testimony to the "reception" of Murray's second truth by millions of Americans. And the resistance to that movement in the academy, the media, many churches, and much of the permanent political class (a resistance increasingly mounted on the basis of "autonomy" claims) illustrates the depth and gravity of the culture war.

3. The third truth undergirding the American experiment, in Murray's analysis, is that *just governance—governance that is congruent with the dignity of human beings as persons, as moral agents—is by, through, and with the consent of the governed.*

This was, Murray argued, an ancient principle, with deep roots in the political thought of Christian medieval Europe (which, of course, was shaped by Roman law and Greek political philosophy). But in the American experiment, the ancient principle of consent was married to another principle that looms large in the social vision of John Paul II: the principle of popular participation in governance.[53]

Thus Lincoln's phrase at Gettysburg, "government *by* the people," was no mere rhetorical flourish. The people adopted their basic law, the Constitution, through elected representatives. The people made the laws of the land through other elected representatives and rotated the executive power such that the Constitution "came alive" in the rhythms of our national life. In short, as Murray put it, "the people are governed because in a true sense, they govern themselves."[54]

All of this raises serious questions today, of course, about the rise of a permanent political class, the role of the media in public life, and the conditions of civic education, and these questions bear heavily on the conduct of the American *Kulturkampf.*

4. Murray's third truth involves a real act of faith in the capacity of the people, not to settle technical minutiae, but to wrestle seriously with great issues. That faith was, in turn, built on Murray's fourth truth, the fourth building block in the intellectual/moral foundations of the American experiment: *"there is a sense of justice inherent in the people"* by which they are *"empowered to judge, direct, and correct the processes of government."*[55]

This truth, medieval in root, took concrete political form in the First Amendment's guarantees of free speech and a free press. In Murray's view, these freedoms were not rooted in the thin individualistic claim that someone has a right to say what he thinks just because he happens to think it. Rather, these freedoms had a thicker reality; they were social, *public* necessities. For, as Murray argues, people who are required to obey have the "right to be heard" about the matters on which their obedience is to be required; and people who bear burdens and make sacrifices have the right to debate and pass judgment on whether the policy requiring those sacrifices in fact serves the common good.[56]

These rights give concrete reality to the fundamental distinction between *society* and the *state,* and embody the traditional Western Christian understanding that "society" is *prior* to the state. This means, in practical, daily terms, that the state exists to serve society, not the other way around. As we have seen, that understanding of "civil society" played a crucial role in the collapse of Communism. But it is also the foundation, in our American context, of the freedom from governmental control enjoyed by the academy, the means of communication, the family, and religious institutions. It is no accident that legal encroachments on the independence of those "prior" institutions (especially church/synagogue and family) are among the most fevered issues in the American *Kulturkampf*—which, yet again, shows itself to be an argument down to first principles.

5. The fifth truth on which the American experiment was grounded was the classic claim that *"only a virtuous people can be free."*[57]

Like the Founders, and like Pope John Paul II, Father Murray understood that free government in a free society is not inevitable, only possible, and that its possibility can be realized *publicly* only when the people are governed *inwardly* by the "universal moral law." Or, as Lord Acton put it, freedom is "not the power of doing what we like, but rather the right of being able to do what we ought."[58]

On this understanding, of course, and to come straight back to the beginning, democracy is more than a political experiment, more than the "Rules of the Game." Democracy is a spiritual and moral enterprise, and its success (or failure) depends upon the virtues (or lack thereof) of the people of the enterprise. As Murray argued, men and women who would be free must learn to discipline themselves, and the governing institutions of a free society must be self-governing "from within" if they are to serve the ends of virtue—and of freedom.[59]

Thus the American ideal, as Murray understood the Founders' intention, was not simply freedom, but ordered freedom: freedom ordered from within by the virtues of the people, and ordered from without by constitutional and statutory law that holds itself accountable to the same transcendent moral law that is the ethical compass of each individual citizen. And that ideal is congenial to classic Catholic understandings of man, society, and history, especially as given contemporary expression by John Paul II.

It would be foolish optimism, bordering on culpable naïveté, to suggest that these five truths are "held" in American society today such that our public discourse and our public life are consistently disciplined by reference to them. But the very fact of the American *Kulturkampf* is itself an interesting witness to the continuing vitality of what Murray would have called this "ensemble of elementary affirmations." For the denial of these truths by those intellectual, political, and legal forces that would reduce American democracy to a framework for the pursuit of the gratification of the imperial autonomous Self has led to their rediscovery by those Roman Catholic and evangelical Protestant thinkers and activists committed to the revitalization of the United States as a substantive moral experiment in which rights and laws are tethered once again to rights and wrongs.

No one can predict the outcome of the American *Kulturkampf.* Signs of national renewal compete for our attention with new experiments in decadence. But however one calculates the odds on a revitalization of our national culture, the experience of Weimar Germany stands before us as a grim warning: the most elegantly constructed democratic institutions will crumble and fall if their moral foundations in civil society weaken. Americans may not "hold these truths" with as much certainty today as in the past. *Centesimus Annus* reminds us that we fail to grasp them at our peril, and at the peril of the American experiment itself.

8

Veritatis Splendor: *Moral Truth and the Democratic Prospect*

The Paul Revere House in Boston is a minor shrine of American democracy; the Collegium Maius of Kraków's Jagiellonian University is one of Europe's venerable intellectual centers. These two historic sites might seem to have little in common. But visitors can find in both places some useful instruction on the nature of democracy. In the Revere House, a display relating to the American patriot's civic activities includes this simple statement: "Paul Revere's public service after the war reflect[ed] his belief in the ideals of the new nation. He embraced the vision of America as a moral republic with virtuous citizens working for the common good." Over the entrance to the "Aula," the great lecture hall of the Collegium Maius, is the Latin inscription, *Plus ratio quam vis:* "Reason rather than force."

One of the superiorities of democratic governance over other forms of political organization is that it embodies the moral truth contained in the Collegium Maius motto: that the rule of law is superior to violence. All law is in some measure coercive. But in a democracy, our inevitably coercive laws are defined by a process of persuasion, argument, debate, reasoning together—democratic deliberation, in other words—rather than by princely edict or politburo decree. This is no small achievement. It means that the law, in a democracy, is authoritative, not authoritarian. And this touches directly on the question of democracy and Christian humanism.

For, as we have seen, the moral superiority of democratic lawmaking is more than a matter of aesthetics, of the fact that debate and voting are less messy than torture and terror. Rather, the arts of democratic deliberation and decision-making are morally superior to coercion because they embody the truths about the human person and about the right ordering of political community that we explored at the end of the last chapter. By giving those moral truths concrete expression in history, the art of democratic persuasion—the application of reason to the exercise of public authority—enables a society to live out what Jacques Maritain once called "heroic humanism."

Plus ratio quam vis, indeed.

But what is this "reason" that is superior to brute force? It is not simply a neutral, inert capacity, built into human beings like the hardware in a computer. No, there is a *dynamic* built into reason, just as there is with our other faculties. The faculty of sight is ordered to seeing; the faculty of hearing is ordered to listening. And the dynamic of reason is that it is ordered to the truth: to discerning both The Way Things Are and The Way Things Ought to Be. As Václav Havel has put it, we should "understand the truth of the world not as mere information about it, but as an attitude, a commitment, a moral imperative."[1] Thus the reasoning we do together in a democracy is an effort to determine, not simply for each of us as an individual but for ourselves as a political community, the truth of our situation ("How is it going with us?") and the things we need to do together to advance the common good (in familiar American terms, "How shall we secure 'liberty and justice for all'?").

Talk about "truth" and democracy did not seem to bother Paul Revere. Like many others in the founding generation of American political leaders, he believed that the American Revolution was justified because continuing the colonial arrangement between America and Great Britain would mean denying certain "truths" about the human person, and thus about the way society *ought* to be organized. And, as the example of Havel suggests, the intuition that "the truth of the world" has something to do with democratic self-governance has not completely disappeared among major public figures. Still, it has to be said that President Havel is a distinctive presence on the world political stage because he is something of an exception. For whenever the matter of "truth and democracy" or "truth and freedom" gets raised today, many people (including many intelligent and thoughtful people) get very wary indeed.

"Whose Truth?"

That was certainly the case in 1991, in the aftermath of *Centesimus Annus*. When John Paul II argued that "*obedience to the truth* about God and man is the first condition of freedom,"[2] Nobel laureate Milton Friedman, responding "as a non-Catholic classical liberal," countered that this was really a bit much. The encyclical, he agreed, was full of "good will and high motives." Yet he concluded, "I must confess that one high-minded sentiment, passed off as if it were a self-evident proposition, sent shivers down my back: 'Obedience to the truth about God and man is the first condition of freedom.' Whose 'truth'? Decided by whom? Echoes of the Spanish Inquisition?"[3] We may be sure that many others—classical liberals, not-so-classical liberals, and conservatives—shared Dr. Friedman's worries.

Thus concerns about the precise meaning of the relation between truth and freedom, between truth and democracy, should not be dismissed as merely the fretting of secularist minds, spinning their wheels in the rut of anti-clericalism. Some of that goes on, to be sure (often, alas, in American lecture halls and law courts). But there are more serious issues in play here.

One set of legitimate concerns is based on a deep sense of the human tragedy of the twentieth century, in which tens of millions of lives have been sacrificed to the idols of ideology—to some perverted and coercively imposed construction of "the truth." Others worry that the modern bureaucratic state is already too powerful, and that any talk about "truth and democracy" invests the state with yet another set of coercive powers, damaging to individual liberties and to civil society. Still others, looking at the plurality that seems built into the script of history, wonder how any agreement can be reached about "the truth" and its relation to freedom and democracy, given the diversity of views encountered even within established democratic societies.

The "Subjectivity" of Society

John Paul II had anticipated some of this criticism, and he addressed several of these concerns in *Centesimus Annus* itself. The sentence that so bothered Milton Friedman, for example, was not an abstract moral ukase. Rather, it was a considered judgment based on an empirically informed critique of two tendencies found in developed democracies: the tendency to "instrumentalize" human beings, turning them into objects to be manipulated to others' ends by others' power, and the tendency to think of human fulfillment solely in terms of the satisfaction of "my needs." As John Paul wrote,

> Exploitation, at least in the forms analyzed and described by Karl Marx, has been overcome in Western society. Alienation, however, has not been overcome as it exists in various forms of exploitation, when people use one another, and when they seek an ever more refined satisfaction of their individual and secondary needs. . . . A person who is concerned solely or primarily with possessing and enjoying, who is no longer able to control his instincts and passions, or to subordinate them by obedience to the truth, cannot be free.[4]

Those who lack self-command cannot be truly free. The insight is ancient, yet the tendency in modern democracies has been to deny it, or ignore it. And the results are all too much with us, in the form of a human degradation that spans the socioeconomic spectrum. The breakdown of the moral habits of self-command has led to new forms of dependency, even enslavement, in the American urban underclass; that same moral hollowness contributes to gross materialism, substance abuse, and drug or alcohol dependency in the yuppie suburbs.

Still, the critics would ask (and legitimately enough), just what kind of role does the Catholic Church envision for itself here, in this business of "truth and democracy"? History and the development of its own social doctrine have compelled the Church to abandon altar-and-throne alliances; has the Church now opted for a more subtle form of political power, manipulating the democratic process so that a legislature eventually imposes the Church's concept of "truth" on society as a whole?[5]

Speaking for world Catholicism, John Paul II seemed far less interested in imposing anything than in starting a conversation. As he wrote in *Centesimus Annus,* the Church "does not close her eyes to the danger of fanaticism or fundamentalism among those who, in the name of an ideology which purports to be scientific or religious, claim the right to impose on others their own concept of what is true and good." Such ideological imperialism is emphatically not the ecclesial *modus operandi* that John Paul has in mind, and the reasons why go beyond good manners:

> *Christian truth* is not of this kind. Since it is not an ideology, the Christian faith does not presume to imprison changing socio-political realities in a rigid schema, and it recognizes that human life is realized in history in conditions that are diverse and imperfect. Furthermore, in constantly reaffirming the transcendent dignity of the person, the Church's method is always that of respect for freedom.[6]

Or, to return once again to John Paul's 1990 encyclical on Christian mission, *Redemptoris Missio,*

> On her part, the Church addresses people with full respect for their freedom. Her mission does not restrict freedom but rather promotes it. *The Church proposes; she imposes nothing.* She respects individuals and cultures, and she honors the sanctuary of conscience.[7]

In short, what John Paul II proposed in *Centesimus Annus* was not the imposition on society of one denominational concept of "truth" and its relation to democracy. Rather, the Pope was urging the imperative of an ongoing public dialogue about the moral foundations of democracy and the "oughts" of our common life: a dialogue that would set the normative horizon for civil society. For a democracy that cannot give a persuasive moral account of its commitment to human freedom is a democracy in which freedom, always at risk in the world, is gravely imperiled.

Such an ongoing public moral dialogue is, the Pope argued, an expression of the "subjectivity of society," the intellectual and moral dynamism of civil society itself. For "civil society" is not simply an aggregation of individuals. A genuinely civil society is a community of public moral discourse and mutual aid, composed of persons with both rights and duties. And it is through this process of public moral argument, the Pope suggested, that plurality can be transformed into pluralism: into a respectful engagement of differences and a plumbing of the depths of those differences, so that the truth of things gets clarified for all involved. In order to be true to itself, such a public moral dialogue about how we ought to order our lives together must be conducted with a deep respect for the convictions and insights of others. And to be true to all of those others, it has to be a dialogue that does not preemptively exclude, at the outset, any conception of the truth of things: which means that religious conceptions of the truth about human beings and human society have to be welcome, on the grounds of democratic civility and equality—and that Dr. Friedman might have been just a bit overwrought in summoning up the image of the Inquisition.

Making Sense to One Another

Just as the human body dies without oxygen, the democratic body politic dies without the oxygenation of political debate, without public deliberation about how we ought to live together. Or, to vary the biological metaphor, democratic deliberation is the lifeblood of democracy. Stanch it and you kill democracy (as generations of totalitarians understood full well).

But we cannot debate the oughts of our common life unless we can make moral sense to one another. And we cannot do this without a grammar by which the conversation about those oughts is ordered.

The philosopher Alasdair MacIntyre's description of a world that has forgotten the "grammar" of science sheds some interesting light on our moral-cultural circumstances:

Imagine that the natural sciences were to suffer the effects of a catastrophe. A series of environmental disasters are blamed by the general public on the scientists. Widespread riots occur, laboratories are burnt down, physicists are lynched, books and instruments are destroyed. Finally a Know-Nothing political movement takes power and successfully abolishes science teaching in schools and universities, imprisoning and executing the remaining scientists. Later still there is a reaction against this destructive movement and enlightened people seek to revive science, although they have largely forgotten what it was. But all that they possess are fragments: a knowledge of experiments detached from any knowledge of the theoretical context which gave them significance; parts of theories unrelated . . . to the other bits; instruments whose use has been forgotten; half-chapters from books, single pages from articles. . . . None the less all these fragments are reembodied in a set of practices which go under the revived names of physics, chemistry, and biology. Adults argue with each other about the respective merits of relativity theory, evolutionary theory, and phlogiston theory, although they possess only a very partial knowledge of each. Children learn by heart the surviving portions of the periodic table and recite as incantations some of the theorems of Euclid. Nobody, or almost nobody, realizes that what they are doing is not natural science in any proper sense at all.[8]

It sounds like chaos. People would be using terms like "proton" and "neutron," the "uncertainty principle," and "general relativity" in ways that might or might not have anything to do with the original meaning. Because the words had come unglued from the truths that gave them meaning, their new use would, from our point of view, be ad hoc and arbitrary. But those using them wouldn't think they were being arbitrary, and the local postmodernists would extol the virtues of a "subjective" science, culturally conditioned all the way down.

Chaos indeed. But suppose we were to substitute the words "right" and "wrong" for "proton" and "neutron," and suppose that the subject were moral philosophy, not natural science. Wouldn't that sound uncomfortably like the situation in which many people, in both old and new democracies, find themselves today: moral language is frequently deployed in public debate, but without any agreement on the meaning of the terms or their relation to an objective order of truth? Alasdair MacIntyre believes that that is in fact our situation, and one result of it is moral emotivism: the confusions of our public moral culture have created a situation in which we cannot really say "We *ought* to do X." We can only say, "I'd *prefer* that we do X." Thus serious public moral argument has ground to a halt—which means, says MacIntyre, that "the barbarians are not waiting beyond the frontiers; they have already been governing us for quite some time."[9]

For reasons to be unfolded below, I think MacIntyre's description of our predicament is a bit too grim. But he has surely identified one of the great threats to democracies today, and one of the urgent public tasks of the Church. Without serious and sustained public conversation, deliberation, and persuasion, without public *moral* argument, democracy atrophies. And if the publicly received concept of human freedom becomes utterly detached from any normative context—if freedom and truth are thought to have little or nothing to do with each other—then democratic discourse about the commonweal becomes virtually impossible. For such debate inevitably engages issues of *ought*. And unless there is some way to talk to one another, and make sense to one another, about the *oughts* of our common life, we really do run the risk of social chaos.

After which comes, as we have seen, the reimposition of order by means of coercion.

Avoiding this chaos and its authoritarian aftermath means rebuilding the grammar of public moral argument so that we can, again, make sense to one another. And the way to do that, John Paul II argues in his 1993 encyclical *Veritatis Splendor,* is to recognize that there is a moral logic built into the world and into us. That is, there is a universal human nature, and human reason, through reflection on that nature, can discern certain fundamental truths that are the foundation of the moral life. This sounds impossibly old hat to some modern ears. Universal moral truths, applicable in Chicago, London, Prague, Kraków, Kiev, Cairo, New Delhi, and Singapore? Please. But, the Pope asks, are we really prepared to say, flatly, that there are no universally valid moral norms? Is child sacrifice or rape ever morally justifiable? What about Auschwitz and the Gulag?

No, the Pope insists, the human person, the "acting person," is truly and substantially free. God has created human beings for freedom, and the hard facts of sin notwithstanding, men and women are capable of freedom. That, John Paul believes, is the truth without which talk about morality and talk about democracy make no sense whatsoever. No doubt the modern disciplines of psychology, sociology, and cultural anthropology can shed light on the way different people in different circumstances perceive their freedom and act on it. But, as Richard John Neuhaus has put it, there is, "deep within each 'acting person' . . . an aspiration toward the good that he either follows or defies."[10] To recognize that aspiration is to begin the construction of a moral grammar that makes democratic discourse possible.

A Lesson From 1989

Those still inclined to be skeptical of these claims about how truth is related to freedom and to democracy might wish to consider the experience of the human-rights movements in east central Europe that, throughout the 1980s, prepared the ground for what became the Revolution of 1989.

Here we return to Václav Havel. In his seminal 1978 essay "The Power of the Powerless," Havel argued that the key to understanding the Communist system, and thus to devising a resistance strategy capable of challenging it effectively, was to recognize that the system was built on lies: Communism was structural mendacity, a "world of appearances trying to pass for reality."[11] And that structure of mendacity was not simply a reflection of the fact that human beings, being sinners, lie from time to time. Rather, and to borrow here from the postmodernists, Communism was a structure of lies "all the way down." The result was a systematic falsification of reality in all its aspects. As Havel put it,

> Because the regime is captive to its own lies, it must falsify everything. It falsifies the past. It falsifies the present, and it falsifies the future. It falsifies statistics. It pretends not to possess an omnipotent and unprincipled police apparatus. It pretends to respect human rights. It pretends to persecute no one. It pretends to fear nothing. It pretends to pretend nothing.[12]

How could one survive, and resist, in this "vast ocean . . . of manipulated life"? Politics, understood as the contest for power, would not suffice; indeed, as previous efforts at resistance had shown, it would be entirely futile, if not lethal. A new kind of politics had to be developed on the basis of a reconstituted culture, a revivified civil society. The source of that revitalization would be the conscientious decisions of individuals determined to act as persons, as subjects rather than objects of power. The only form of resistance capable of challenging Communism at its root, which was its most vulnerable point, was what Havel called "living in the truth," or what John Paul II would describe in Poland in 1983 as "calling good and evil by name."[13] Communist tyranny could be resisted only through the affirmation that there was, in fact, an objective moral order that transcended and stood in judgment on the Communist culture of the lie. The fact of that transcendent moral order summoned forth from individuals the courage to live in the truth, to call good and evil by their right names.

"Living in the truth," living according to real moral norms rather than the false norms of the Communist "world of appearances," meant living responsibly rather than simply reactively. Havel, not often given to putting things in overt religious terms, did so at one point in "The Power of the Powerless," where, addressing the sense of hopelessness that often overwhelmed those who wanted to resist, he simply affirmed that "the Lord has set us down" here, and that there was no way to "lie our way" out of the situation by avoiding it.[14] One could not live responsibly in some hoped-for future if one could not bring oneself to live responsibly now.

The Czech philosopher Václav Benda, a Catholic colleague of Havel's in the human-rights movement Charter 77, took the argument one step further. The objective moral truth that was to be lived in resistance to the culture of the lie, said Benda, must not be reduced to an alternative ideology, especially if one believed that all moral truth was a reflection of the Truth made manifest in the incarnate Son of God:

> It is . . . not enough merely to look out for one's soul and believe that Truth—the Truth which in a particular place and time took on human form and walked among people and assumed their suffering—is no more than a *position* which has to be *maintained*. . . .
>
> If . . . the chief form of the present political evil is a restrictive heaviness that all citizens carry on their shoulders and at the same time *within* them, then the only possibility is to shake that evil off, escape its power, and to seek truth. Under such circumstances, every genuine struggle for one's soul becomes an openly political act, and a creative act at that, because it is no longer merely "defining oneself" against something else . . . but rather a jettisoning of ballast and opening oneself up to what is new and unknown. . . . Christians can and should become one of the means by which this potential is released and made manifest.[15]

Benda's concluding line is particularly important. To assert that the democratic experiment has to engage the question of moral truth neither forecloses moral argument nor precludes the development of moral insight. On the contrary, a democracy conducting its affairs against a transcendent horizon of moral truth—the truth about the human person and human community—will find itself "opening . . .

up to what is new and unknown." And the Church can and should be of assistance to society in that effort to conduct public life against a horizon that is wide enough to include the moral aspirations of the citizenry.

Skeptical relativism discloses a narrow, cramped universe. It knows chiefly what it cannot know, and it cannot seriously defend the freedom that it proclaims to be the principal value of public life. If a climate of skeptical relativism becomes dominant in the public discourse of a democracy, that democracy is in grave danger: for it will be unable to give a compelling account of its commitment to persuasion rather than raw coercion as the medium of public exchange. In such circumstances, civil society dissolves; and, as we have seen, there can be no democracy without the foundation of civil society. Forty years ago, John Courtney Murray, concerned that Americans were insufficiently attentive to the moral principles on which their democratic experiment had been founded, warned against the dissolution of a morally grounded civil society in these ominous terms: "Perhaps the dissolution . . . may one day be consummated. Perhaps one day the noble many-storeyed mansion of democracy will be dismantled, levelled to the dimensions of a flat majoritarianism, which is no mansion but a barn, perhaps even a tool shed in which the weapons of tyranny may be forged."[16]

On the other hand, and according to the testimony of Havel and Benda, the world of the truth is far more open and capacious, and far more congenial to the democratic project. Affirming the fact of the truth and then living in that truth empowers citizens to take control of their own lives and to resist the suffocating "heaviness" of tyranny. A democracy conscious of its accountability to the truth will be open to the future, open to critique, open to genuine reform, and open to the participation of all.

TRUTH AND FREEDOM: FIVE IMPLICATIONS FOR DEMOCRACY

Between the recondite speculations of moral philosophy and theology and the rough hurly-burly of democratic politics there is sometimes thought to be a great gulf fixed—to borrow an image from Luke—that no one may cross. The nature of the "moral act," the possibility of defining certain acts as "intrinsically evil," the capacity of the human person to act on some instinct for the good—what in the world do these arcane topics have to do with *politics?*

As it happens, a lot.

Every democracy today, established or new, is faced with certain unavoidable moral questions. For instance, what is *equality before the law?* It is clear that in many ways human beings are not equal: in intelligence, energy, beauty, willpower, creativity. What do we mean, then, when we say that the equality of all persons before the law is a building block of democracy? On what principled basis do we ascribe equality to persons in the legal order? Does that equality prevent the state's acknowledging, through certain benefits, the importance of traditional communities like the heterosexual family of father, mother, and children? What is the relation between the legal equality of individual citizens before the law and the socio-cultural fact that those individuals are also members of racial, ethnic, and/or religious groups?

Then there is the question of *the boundaries of democratic political community.* Who is in it? What sustains it? Why should we give it our allegiance? Given all the other claims on my loyalty—family, ethnic group or tribe, religious community, profession, union, party—what is the nature and scope of my loyalty to the democratic *polis,* to my city, state, or country? And how does that political community contribute to genuine human flourishing? Does it simply set the legal framework for the pursuit of personal goals and desires, or must that framework itself be built upon a concept of the goods of human life? What are our responsibilities as a political community to those forms of human life that we find inconvenient or heavily burdensome: the ethnically or racially "other," the unplanned and unborn child, the adherent to an "alien" religion, the terminally ill patient in the nursing home?

And what about *passions and interests?* Whatever else we can say about men and women at the end of the twentieth century, we can certainly say that they have not become perfected creatures, incapable of selfishness, cruelty, or greed. What is it, in individuals and societies, that harnesses our passions and channels our interests so that they destroy neither us nor our communities, but in fact contribute to our well-being? Is that harnessing and channeling primarily a function of the structures of public life? Are there other, perhaps prior, factors in play?

How do we maintain *integrity in public life* and in government? During the past three decades in the United States we have invested considerable energy in devising ever more elaborate "codes of ethics" for public officials. Yet the problem of corruption in office seems worse than before. No one expects those in public life to be perfect. But democracy cannot flourish, and may not be able to survive, amid vast public cynicism about corruption. Is there no remedy for declining integrity besides the inadequate one of thickening the "ethics manuals" at every level of government?

Finally, what about *the problem of decadence?* Can democracies endure if they become what Zbigniew Brzezinski has termed "permissive cornucopias"?[17] Does unparalleled material abundance inevitably lead to a culture in which *having* more is taken as the sole index of *being* more? What happens to democracy when the culture treats human sexuality as just another contact sport? What happens to a democracy in which rates of out-of-wedlock births reach historically unparalleled altitudes in all social classes and approach 75 per cent in some of society's most fragile neighborhoods? Do forms of "entertainment" that appeal solely to what used to be called our "baser instincts" have anything to do with the survival of the institutions of self-governance? Having defeated the idols of race and class that informed the totalitarian theories of Nazism and Communism, do the developed democracies risk being subverted by another idol: the pleasure principle, understood as the chief motive driving the "autonomous self"?

To be sure, these questions present themselves differently in different democratic societies. But news reports make it apparent that virtually all democracies, old or new, are struggling with the moral issues posed by the sexual revolution, the rapid development of medical technology, and the passions embodied in resurgent ethnic, tribal, and/or religious identity. Whether the issue is the status of guest workers in Germany, the availability of "adult entertainment" on Polish television, physician-assisted suicide in the Netherlands, Muslim religious practice in France, business ethics in the Czech Republic, the rights of linguistic and religious minorities in Slovakia, the corruption of public life in Italy, the relations among religious communities in India, or the abortion license in the United States, democracies around the world are confronting the hard fact that, for all the academic chatter about democracy as a "thin" Republic of

Procedures, the procedures themselves break down when they are not sustained by the kind of civil society that can be built only upon shared moral convictions.

In sum, what may seem, at first blush, to be impossibly stratospheric disputes among the moral philosophers and theologians turn out to have enormous public consequences.

Veritatis Splendor ("The Splendor of the Truth"), Pope John Paul II's 1993 encyclical on the basic structure of Christian morality, was issued primarily to address certain serious problems in Catholic moral theology. But John Paul's discussion of the nature of the moral life touches on questions of the democratic prospect both directly and indirectly, and in ways that challenge the moral understandings of all those who believe that built into every human life is an aspiration to goodness. Five points in *Veritatis Splendor* may help bring the debate down to where these passionately contested political issues can be most fruitfully deliberated: the level of first principles.

1. Equality Before the Law

The bedrock democratic principle of the equality of persons before the law is constantly threatened by racial, ethnic, and religious prejudice, as well as by the palpable inequality of individuals in their physical, intellectual, and aesthetic capabilities. And yet a democracy that does not acknowledge the equality of persons before the law is an oxymoron. How can the commitment to that equality be sustained among diverse peoples of different religious and philosophical perspectives?

In a bold intellectual move, John Paul II suggests that democratic equality is directly related to the moral-philosophical question of whether certain acts are intrinsically wrong, always and everywhere, irrespective of intentions or possible consequences. "Genuine democracy," the Pope writes, can exist only

> on the basis of the equality of all its members, who possess common rights and duties. *When it is a matter of the moral norms prohibiting intrinsic evil, there are no privileges or exceptions for anyone.* It makes no difference whether one is the master of the world or the "poorest of the poor" on the face of the earth. Before the demands of morality we are all absolutely equal.[18]

Democratic equality before the law, then, is an embodiment in public life of the fundamental moral equality of all persons. That moral equality means we are all accountable to certain basic and exceptionless moral norms. And what are these exceptionless norms? What acts do they prohibit? To illustrate the theoretical point, *Veritatis Splendor* turns to what is generally regarded as the most "liberal" of the Second Vatican Council's documents, the Pastoral Constitution on the Church in the Modern World *(Gaudium et Spes)*. There, the Council Fathers identified acts that are always and everywhere seriously wrong, in and of themselves and regardless of circumstances, because they are "hostile to life itself": acts such as homicide, genocide, mutilation, torture, "attempts to coerce the spirit," slavery, and "prostitution and trafficking in women and children."[19] The prohibition of these acts is absolute and binding; no one may appeal to wealth, position, political power, or anything else to justify participating in them.

The moral fact of intrinsic evil has consequences for society as well as for individuals, for it sets the foundation on which equality of persons may be most securely asserted. Why? Because that foundation is unchanging. Acts that are intrinsically evil always do grave damage to the humanity of the person committing them as well as to their victims. The reality of intrinsically evil acts is therefore not merely a *proscription* of certain behaviors: it constitutes a personalist *affirmation* of the goods necessary for human flourishing, individually and in a civil society. That personalism, which stresses our essential and unbreakable relationship to other human beings in a community of moral equality, is far more likely to strengthen a democratic citizenry's commitment to equality before the law than notions of "autonomy" that reduce the citizen to an atomized individual with, at best, a very tenuous moral connection to others.

2. The Boundaries of Democratic Political Community

If "democracy" is more than a formal institutional admixture of political procedures—if it involves the sustaining and nurturing of Maritain's community of "civic friendship," or what Havel, Benda, and their colleagues called "civil society"—then the character of the relationships within a democracy cannot be sufficiently described in legal terms alone. Something else, something *more,* is required of a democratic citizenry. That something more might be described as a morally based sense of mutual obligation and responsibility.

Throughout human history, political communities have formed around many modes of obligation: tribal, ethnic, racial, "national" (in the modern sense). But while the democratic political community cannot be Platonically abstracted from these enduring realities of the human condition, it cannot be reduced to them, either. For if the democratic experiment is an expression in public life of certain fundamental truths about the human person, then true democrats must acknowledge that the boundaries of their political community cannot be ultimately defined in tribal, ethnic, confessional, or racial terms.

To be sure, in some democracies, one racial or ethnic group, one tribe, or one religious community may predominate; it seems likely that there will be more Christians than Jews in America, more Poles than Ukrainians in Poland, and more Caucasian Frenchmen than North African Muslims in France, at least for the foreseeable future. But the fact of minority communities (which is an unavoidable aspect of modernity) does not preclude the formation of democratic political community *if,* as John Paul puts it in *Veritatis Splendor,* "social coexistence" is based on "a morality which acknowledges certain norms as valid always and for everyone, with no exception."[20]

The reality of an objective moral order that can be discerned from a careful reflection on human nature and human action thus provides a crucial layer of the moral-cultural foundation on which pluralistic democratic political community can be built. The moral obligations of others—including racially, ethnically, and/or religiously different "others"—are a mirror in which I can discern my own moral obligations, and indeed my own humanity. And that sense of common moral obligation is the basis of democratic community in a civil society, a society in which the chasms of racial, ethnic, and religious difference are bridged for purposes of achieving the common good.

There is an old truth here, of course. The "second tablet" of the Decalogue has, for millennia, been understood to constitute what John Paul II calls "the indispensable rules of all social life."[21] But the old truth bears repeating, given the pressures that plurality—the sheer facts of racial, ethnic, and confessional difference—puts on virtually all democracies today. And it is a truth that reminds us to be very careful not to draw the boundaries of democratic political community too narrowly.

This matter of boundary-setting touches questions far beyond the problems of racial, ethnic, and religious discrimination that roil all human societies. There is, for example, and especially in the developed democracies, the question of lives that place special burdens on the democratic community and on individual citizens. Unplanned and unborn children, burdensome old people, the severely handicapped —are these lives inside or outside the boundaries of mutual obligation and legal protection that define civil society in a law-governed democracy? What happens to its moral texture if a democratic political community declares burdensome life "outside" those boundaries of obligation and protection? Or, to sharpen the point considerably: on what principled grounds would we distinguish such an exclusion from the loathsome concept of *lebensunwertes Leben,* "life not worth living," that was used to justify the Holocaust and the Nazi euthanasia program?

References to the Nazi period are always fraught with dangers, not least the danger of trivializing the horror of those times by comparison with lesser evils. And yet the questions must be pressed. For it was not fevered Nazi ideologues but an eminent German jurist (Karl Binding) and a distinguished psychiatrist (Alfred Hoche) who published a book on the elimination of the mentally ill entitled *The Permit to Destroy Life Not Worth Living.* Thirteen years before Hitler's rise to power, Binding and Hoche gave the sanction of law and medical science to the claim that a political community could legitimately declare certain of its members who "required extended custodial care without any prospect of advantage to the state" to be so far beyond the boundaries of mutual obligation and protection as to be entirely disposable. And once that moral boundary was breached on behalf of burdensome or "inconvenient life," it became ever easier for the maniacs and the great haters to rationalize the elimination of other lives that they classified as "parasitic": those of Jews, gypsies, and homosexuals.[22]

This is not to suggest that any contemporary democracy is about to follow the path of Nazi Germany. But it is to be reminded, with James T. Burchaell, that "the flesh-hungry barbarity which enjoyed, then, its freedom to stalk the land cannot be killed. It can only be caged. It creeps abroad in other guises, at other times, on other errands."[23] Decisions about, say, the continued medical treatment of a terminally ill patient with little hope of recovering any significant brain function will never be easy or straightforward. Christians will understand that, in these cases especially, "now we see in a mirror dimly" (I Cor. 13:12). But it is precisely that lack of clarity, plus the reality of the social-ethical slippery slope (amply and brutally demonstrated in the twentieth century), that should raise cautions about "solving" the problems of burdensome life by the simple legal expedient of narrowing the communal boundaries of obligation and protection. In addition to the grave injustices that this may entail against individuals, the democratic experiment itself may be severely compromised by such acts of exclusion.[24]

3. Passions and Interests

Getting along with one's neighbors is a problem as old as Cain and Abel. That ancient problem can be severely exacerbated in modern commercial societies. The market can direct energies and interests into productive and profitable enterprise. But at the same time the market can feed passions and promote self-interest in ways that can be destructive of both individuals and communities—*if* those passions and interests are not disciplined by a public moral culture that tempers the fevers of acquisitiveness and pleasure-seeking. For, left unchecked, those fevers can result in new forms of tyranny in both personal and public life.[25]

We do not find it hard to understand that the depredations of Nazi and Communist totalitarians were rooted in their denial of certain truths about the human person. The Nazi ideology of race strikes us as crude, vulgar, irrational, while the Communist defense of murder in the name of revolutionary justice executed on class enemies cuts uncomfortably close to the bone for middle-class people in the West. But we may have trouble applying a parallel diagnosis to the moral-cultural situation of democracies.

Yet why should democracies be immune from the threat of tyranny, if of a different sort? Unbridled passions and the unrestrained pursuit of personal interest are not conducive to a civilized social life, or to a country's taking seriously its international responsibilities.[26] Thus democracies have long understood that personal and commercial passions and interests have to be constrained by both law and moral-cultural habit. But what justifies legal regulation of the market and sustains the moral-cultural habits of self-command that can restrain personal passions? John Paul II does not believe that these justifications can be merely instrumental (i.e., deemed appropriate because they "work"). Rather, they must be grounded, once again, in certain truths about the human person:

> If there is no transcendent truth, in obedience to which man achieves his full identity, then there is no sure principle for guaranteeing just relations between people. Their self-interest as a class, group, or nation would inevitably set them in opposition to one another. If one does not acknowledge transcendent truth, then the force of power takes over, and each person tends to make full use of the means at his disposal in order to impose his own interests or his own opinion, with no regard for the rights of others. People are then respected only to the extent that they can be exploited for selfish ends.[27]

The habits of even a virtuous citizenry are not enough to guarantee the maintenance of a civil society capable of sustaining democracy and a well-functioning market. Legal and regulatory structures are essential for channeling the explosive energies of free people into enterprises that support genuine human flourishing and that advance the common good. But like the moral habits of individuals, those structures will endure over time only if they are grounded, not simply in expedience, but in publicly acknowledged convictions about the nature and goods of human beings, as individuals and as members of the community.

4. Integrity in Public Life

"Good government" is a perennial problem for democracies, as for most other states throughout recorded history. The goal is clear: democracies want public servants and public officials of whom the citizenry can say what Frederick the Great said of his Prussian officers: "They will not lie, and they cannot be bought." But how are we to achieve that?

Not by circulating hefty "ethics manuals," or by subjecting public officials to hours of ethics lectures. American public life is filled with scandals at a time when "ethics" has become something of a cottage industry, inside and outside government. Why? Because rules and regulations work only insofar as they express the settled convictions of the community, internalized by individual public officials, about the obligations of public life.

"Integrity in government" cannot be achieved on the cheap. As John Paul II noted in *Veritatis Splendor:*

> . . . [T]ruthfulness in the relations between those governing and those governed, openness in public administration, impartiality in the service of the body politic, respect for the rights of political adversaries, safeguarding the rights of the accused against summary trials and convictions, the just and honest use of public funds, the rejection of equivocal or illicit means in order to gain, preserve, or increase power at any cost—all these are principles which are primarily rooted in, and in fact derive their singular urgency from, the transcendent value of the person and the objective moral demands of the functioning of states.[28]

In short, it is the "truth about man," about the human person and human relationships in community, that provides the most secure foundation for the integrity of public life. And here we may also find another defect in skeptical relativism as a philosophical foundation for the democratic experiment. Not only does skeptical relativism insufficiently defend the freedom that democracy is intended to serve; it also erodes the moral culture of civil society by making it ever more difficult to explain to one another, and especially to the young, the necessity of honesty in public life. We cannot remove the moral reference points from many other aspects of our common life (on the grounds that a democracy cannot adjudicate between competing moral systems) without calling into question the very notion of a "moral life" that could inform our efforts to insure "ethics in government." For there is a protean quality to skepticism and relativity in morals: justified in one sphere of life, it will soon colonize other spheres as well.

Truth serves freedom; it does not negate freedom. As John Paul II noted, history has taught us that "a democracy without values easily turns into open or thinly disguised totalitarianism."[29] Thus recent agitations about "integrity in government" or "ethics in public life" remind us that the attempt to sever morality from politics inevitably ends up destroying politics and reducing public life to the raw quest for power, understood as my capacity to inflict my will-to-power on you. The totalitarian temptation is the result of the exile of morality from the public square.

5. The Problem of Decadence

In recent years intellectual and political leaders of the newly industrialized countries of East Asia have been openly critical of "decaying" Western societies. To be sure, some of this criticism has smacked of the hypocritical, as certain tyrannies seek to justify their defiance of the "third wave" of democratization.[30] But it would be a grave mistake for the West to dismiss the entire critique from the East as the self-serving rhetoric of politicians clinging to power.

Writing in the Spring 1994 issue of The Washington Quarterly, for example, Kishore Mahbubani, former representative of Singapore to the United Nations, argues that "most East Asians have no desire to see the United States fall off a cliff." Nonetheless, according to Ambassador Mahbubani, that is precisely what is at stake these days, for "the United States . . . is approaching a cliff of which it seems as yet blissfully ignorant." And the fall, should it happen, will be the result, not of military disempowerment, but rather of profound "social decay."

Mahbubani then laid out a stern empirical indictment:

Since 1960, the U.S. population has grown by 41 percent. In the same period, there has been a 560 percent increase in violent crimes, a 419 percent increase in illegitimate births, a 400 percent increase in divorce rates, a 300 percent increase of children living in single-parent homes, a more than 200 percent increase in teenage suicide rates, and a drop of almost 80 points in Scholastic Aptitude Test scores. A recent report by the United Nations Development Program also ranks the United States number one among industrialized countries in intentional homicides, reported rapes, and percentage of prisoners. The number of prison inmates has gone up from 329,821 in 1980 to 883,593 in 1992. Hunger in the United States has increased by 50 percent since 1985. The American elite think they understand this phenomenon because they see it on TV.

The reality is that they are still not conscious of this social decay, mainly because most of them have retreated into distant suburbs, enclaves, and townships to shut themselves out and away from it.[31]

At least some members of the "American elite" are aware of the new problem of decadence in American life. Analyzing the same indices of social decay and the social policies concocted in response to them, Daniel Patrick Moynihan writes of "defining deviancy down." On this analysis, the social breakdown has become so severe, indeed so incomprehensible, that Americans have tried to cope with it through a form of psychological denial. In Charles Krauthammer's phrase, we have responded to an epidemic by "defining away most of the disease." That is, "we lower the threshold for what we are prepared to call normal in order to keep the volume of deviancy—redefined deviancy—within manageable proportions."[32]

Moreover, neither Moynihan nor Krauthammer is reluctant to identify the cause of this "explosion of deviancy in family life, criminal behavior, and public displays of psychosis." The cause is, says Krauthammer, the "moral deregulation of the 1960s." But those who cannot admit that a moral crisis preceded and made possible the social crisis must come up with some other explanation for the behaviors we see all around us, and the strategy they have chosen is "redefining deviancy down so as to explain away and make 'normal' what a more civilized, ordered, and healthy society long ago would have labeled—and long ago did label—deviant." Krauthammer believes that the problem is even worse, for while "defining deviancy down" we have also been "defining deviancy up," so that what was once regarded as "normal" (e.g., the traditional family) is now considered a cauldron of pathology.

Redefining deviancy is not simply a matter of manipulating data and definitions. It is, at bottom, a matter of moral philosophy and of public moral culture. Over the past several generations, and throughout the Western democratic world, the demands of classical Western morality—which means, primarily, biblical morality—have been systematically weakened. The weakening is unmistakable in the law, in the teaching of many churches, and in the general expectations that people have of themselves and of one another. This "moral deregulation," as Krauthammer styles it, has several sources. Some of them are honorable, if misguided: thus the tendency of churches to "lower the bar" of sexual morality out of pastoral concern for Christians who find classic Christian sexual morality too demanding. In other instances, as we have seen, the "moral deregulation" of Western democracies has followed hard on the heels of the intellectuals' claim that we cannot know moral norms with any certainty. Either way, the net result—"moral deregulation"—seems clear. To deny that there is a causal relationship between this moral deregulation and the social decay deplored by Ambassador Mahbubani, Senator Moynihan, and Dr. Krauthammer requires a willful act of self-deception.

Ambassador Mahbubani's solution to the crisis of decadence in the West is to constrain, rather dramatically, the exercise of what most democracies would regard as basic civil rights. No doubt those are too often understood, today, in terms of the will-to-pleasure of the imperial autonomous Self and the litigiousness of the Republic of Procedures. But many Americans will be understandably reluctant to take instruction on the reform of their society from the representative of an authoritarian government that decrees what kinds of haircuts are acceptable for its citizens and what newspapers they may read.

The better solution lies in a reform of our understanding of morality and its relation to truth and democracy. This renovation of our democratic moral culture can draw on, even as it extends, the religious and civic traditions of public virtue that once informed the democratic experiment in the United States. And here, too, *Veritatis Splendor* can be of considerable help. Although John Paul's language on this point is explicitly theological, the implications of his analysis of "defining deviancy down" are quite public, and carry far beyond the boundaries of Roman Catholicism:

> *Christ has redeemed us!* This means that he has given us the possibility of realizing the *entire* truth of our being; he has set our freedom free from the *domination* of concupiscence. And if redeemed man still sins, this is not due to an imperfection of Christ's redemptive act, but to man's will not to avail himself of the grace which flows from that act. . . .
>
> In this context, appropriate allowance is made both for *God's mercy* towards the sin of the man who experiences conversion and for the *understanding of human weakness*. Such understanding never means compromising and falsifying the standard of good and evil

in order to adapt it to particular circumstances. It is quite human for the sinner to acknowledge his weakness and to ask mercy for his failings; what is unacceptable is the attitude of one who makes his own weakness the criterion of the truth about the good, so that he can feel self-justified, without even the need to have recourse to God and his mercy. An attitude of this sort corrupts the morality of society as a whole, since it encourages doubt about the objectivity of the moral law in general and a rejection of the absoluteness of moral prohibitions regarding specific human acts, and it ends up confusing all judgments about values.[33]

Freedom is not license. When the public understanding of freedom deteriorates into a general license to pursue one's personal "needs" and gratifications so long as no one else gets hurt, democracy has ceased to become a noble moral experiment in the possibility of self-governance ordered to the common good. The individual who is shackled by his or her desires is no less chained than were Václav Havel and Václav Benda when they were arrested for challenging the Communist culture of the lie. Indeed, Havel and Benda, imprisoned, were freer than the man who is held captive by the walls of his cupidity. For Havel and Benda retained the true human freedom of moral initiative, and by acting on that freedom, they could break the power of the tyranny that bound them.

In Christian terms, Christ redeems our liberty from our desires, and that redemption serves the cause of a true human freedom. But whether one thinks about the democratic prospect in explicitly Christian categories or not, it has become imperative to distinguish genuine freedom from decadent license. The experiment in "moral deregulation" that has been conducted throughout the West for the better part of two generations has borne its fruits, and they are bitter, even poisonous. Lowering the bar of public morality does not lead to personal happiness, nor does it contribute to a deepening of democratic civility. And the ones who suffer the most dreadful consequences of the breakdown of public moral order are the most vulnerable members of community, especially the poor and the dispossessed. For they have the least margin of error, and the narrowest margin of safety.

The alternative to the debasement of freedom into license is not the denial of freedom but its fulfillment in goodness, in human flourishing. Freedom fulfilled in goodness is freedom completed and magnified in adherence to the truth: that is the challenge that has to be raised in the face of the social crisis of Western societies today. To be sure, those who would reconnect freedom and truth ought to avoid becoming scolds or nags; as John Paul writes, "a clear and forceful presentation of moral truth can never be separated from a heartfelt respect, born of that patient and trusting love which man always needs along his moral journey, a journey frequently wearisome on account of difficulties, weakness, and painful situations."[34]

But a genuinely transforming love embraces the hard arguments, avoids moral smugness, and takes up the long and difficult task of moral persuasion. It speaks truth to the power of what an earlier generation called "concupiscence": to the allure of "doing it my way." Because, for the Christian, truth is liberating. And an authentic, liberating love of others "does not result . . . from concealing or weakening moral truth, but rather from proposing it in its most profound meaning as an outpouring of God's eternal Wisdom . . . and as a service to man, to the growth of his freedom and to the attainment of his happiness."[35]

An Impossible Dream?

The way we think about the relation between truth and freedom, and the way those concepts are embodied in law and in our public culture, turns out, then, to have a lot to do with the functioning of democratic society. The weaker the link between freedom and truth, the greater the danger that the democratic experiment will implode.

So it may be agreed, as an abstract *desideratum,* that we ought to try to reconnect freedom and truth in the democratic experiment. But can it be done? Is it really possible to re-create public moral argument, based on the notion of an objective and transcendent moral order, in late-twentieth-century America and in other democratic societies?

There is good cause to wonder. In the United States, the language of "autonomy" and "personal choice" has achieved a virtually canonical status in politics, even amidst the general "unsecularization" of society. And it is a brave, even reckless, politician who will say that Emperor Autonomy has no clothes.

College teachers of moral philosophy suggest that the rout has been even more complete among the young. A distinguished American political philosopher complained to a colleague in late 1993 that students came to his elite university already saturated in moral skepticism and relativism. The colleague, a resourceful soul, replied, "Ask them whether it's ever right to commit rape, discriminate on the basis of sexual orientation, or park in spaces reserved for the handicapped." One professor at a Catholic college claims that his students, asked to name a "virtue," could at best come up with "cleanliness." A frequent lecturer on campuses (an exponent of orthodox Judaism, as it happens) often asks his young audiences which they would rescue if they had to choose between saving their pet dog or a drowning stranger; the dog invariably wins.

Openings to Renewal

None of this is, to put it gently, reassuring. And yet, in the debates in the mid-1990s on welfare reform, crime, and the crisis of the American urban underclass, one began to hear hints of a new openness to the possibility that the decline of "character" and "the virtues" has had something to do with the problems of social pathology that have turned many American inner cities into free-fire zones. Similar rumblings are being heard in the new debate over school choice and the reform of American public education.

Three further examples suggest that perhaps we can be cautiously optimistic about the possibility of reconnecting freedom and truth in public moral discourse. For the first we must look back several decades to the civil-rights movement during its classic period, between the Montgomery bus boycott of 1955-56 and congressional passage of the Voting Rights Act in 1965. For ten years, black Americans pressed their claims for profound social and legal change in explicitly moral terms: legal segregation contradicted the American promise of liberty and justice for all; legal segregation violated the human dignity and the inalienable human rights that were the "self-evident truths" on which the American claim to independent nationhood rested. But, above all, and in a word, legal segregation was morally *wrong*. And the power of that claim was great enough that, in the brief period of a decade, it overturned the legal structure of a pattern of social relationships between the races that had endured for over three hundred years.

Perhaps even more impressively, the moral claim of the movement was instrumental in changing majority attitudes about the rights of minority peoples.

Less successful politically, but no less impressive in its staying power, has been the right-to-life movement. In the face of entrenched and often bitter opposition from the main opinion-making centers of American society, a grassroots movement with millions of adherents has insisted for over twenty years that the Supreme Court's jurisprudence on this question is mistaken; that its effects on our society have been pernicious; and, above all, that abortion-on-demand is *wrong*. Moreover, the right-to-life movement has acted on its convictions by creating, from entirely voluntary contributions, an extensive network of facilities to care for women caught in the dilemma of unwanted pregnancy. In January 1973, the country's most influential newspaper, the *New York Times,* claimed that the Supreme Court, by declaring unrestricted abortion-on-demand a basic constitutional right in *Roe v. Wade,* had settled the abortion debate in America. That has most emphatically not been the case. The ongoing turmoil over the abortion license testifies to the continuing power of public moral argument to shape American public life.

Finally, there was, as we have seen, the debate in late 1990 and early 1991 over the possible use of U.S. military force to reverse Iraq's invasion and occupation of Kuwait. That public debate was conducted in explicitly moral terms, drawn from the natural-law logic of the classic just-war tradition. "Just cause," "right intention," "legitimate authority," "reasonable chance of success," "last resort," "proportionality," and "discrimination" were all contested in a months-long argument that was loud, raucous, occasionally incoherent, frequently sharp-edged: in a word, democratic. But it powerfully demonstrated that Americans could still conduct a serious public moral argument on a matter of grave national importance, even in the rather forbidding arena of foreign and military policy.

In sum, while there is ample evidence to support Alasdair MacIntyre's claim that the barbarians have been in charge for quite a while, the final verdict is not in. For there is significant, if not overwhelming, counterevidence to suggest the possibility of the revival of public moral argument in America, despite the extraordinary cultural power of "autonomy" and "choice."

The new democracies of the post-Communist world have experienced the problem of freedom-and-truth in different ways than the United States. Decades of totalitarian repression have frequently led to a public psychology in which any discussion of "public moral culture" risks being tarred with the brush of the repressive past. Then there is the moral-ecological damage left by the Communist culture of the lie: habits formed over forty years, whether they involve cheating on taxes or beggaring one's neighbor, are not easily broken. Intellectuals in the new democracies have also been affected, perhaps more than they realize, by the notion that the "autonomy project" is the *sine qua non* of democratic freedom and the necessary correlate of the "normal society" for which they had hoped during their underground days of dissent.

And yet one would like to think that the experience of 1989, and of the decade that made 1989 possible, has not been so quickly forgotten. These new democracies, after all, were born out of a witness to the truth that was powerful enough to bring down the world's worst tyranny, and to do so without violence. Surely that experience can be drawn upon today as the new democracies work to consolidate their transition to democracy and the free economy.

The Witness of an Open Church

To preach and teach publicly the link between truth and freedom, the Church must bear witness within itself to the connection between Christian liberty and the truth about the human person, human community, human history, and human destiny. An "open Church" will best give effective witness to its belief that freedom is fulfilled in a free adherence to the truth.[36]

An "open Church" is ecumenical in both ecclesiastical and political terms. It engages the social-ethical insights of Christians from various theological traditions, and from various streams of political philosophy. An "open Church" cherishes diversity. It does not simply *tolerate* differences of opinion about the full meaning of social justice: it welcomes and encourages them, in the conviction that, as God has given us no single blueprint for the right ordering of society, the frank engagement of different visions of the just society strengthens the quest for truth and helps to correct our inevitable errors.

An "open Church" promotes consultation, discussion, and debate among its members about the *oughts* of our public life. Its ordained leaders will be eager to engage in the fullest possible consultation with their lay brothers and sisters in Christ. The social witness of the Church will not, in other words, be the private preserve of a clerical or bureaucratic elite.

An "open Church" will enable its people to be good citizens and effective public servants. It will take positions on public-policy questions, not so much to advance its own particular judgment as to empower its people to make their own decisions responsibly and effectively. An "open Church" will understand that it speaks most persuasively when the people who are the Church are doing the speaking; its leaders will understand that they speak more credibly when they speak with the informed agreement of those whom they would lead. Sometimes leaders of the Church will have to challenge the people of God to discern more carefully their public moral responsibilities; that challenge can even take the form, under grave circumstances, of serious confrontation. But even these confrontations will take place according to the ancient maxim *In necessariis unitas, in dubiis libertas, in omnibus caritas:* "In necessary things, unity; in disputed things, freedom; in all things, charity."

An "open Church" can be receptive to a wide variety of proposals for the right ordering of social, political, and economic life precisely because its reflection on public affairs is firmly grounded in its convictions about religious and moral truth. Christians have pursued their mission to be salt and light in the world for almost two thousand years, and within an extraordinarily wide variety of public circumstances. During those two millennia, Christians have not infrequently disagreed about the most appropriate ways to pursue peace, freedom, justice, civil order, and prosperity. Such disagreements should not be surprising, nor need they be destructive. For the Church's unity in Christ is greater than any contingent judgment about public affairs on which Christians may be divided.

In all these ways, then, the "open Church" becomes, in Richard John Neuhaus's memorable phrase, a zone of truth-telling in a world of mendacity. Not the least of those worldly lies are lies about the meaning and ends of freedom. Precisely because its defining mission is the proclamation of the truth that sets men free in the deepest meaning of human freedom, the "open Church" can confront the many cultures of the lie that threaten freedom. And in so doing, the "open Church" will deepen the moral-cultural foundations of the democratic experiment, enhancing its capacity to contribute to the flourishing of human beings in all their dimensions—including their openness to the God who gave us life and liberty, at the same time.

Notes

In the notes that follow, the numbers after ecclesiastical documents (e.g., *Dignitatis Humanae, Evangelium Vitae*) refer to the section of the document being cited, rather than to page numbers. Italics in the cited documents, here in the notes and in the text above, are in the originals unless otherwise indicated.

PROLOGUE

1. John Courtney Murray, "The Construction of a Christian Culture," in J. Leon Hooper, S.J., ed., *Bridging the Sacred and the Secular: Selected Writings of John Courtney Murray, S.J.* (Washington: Georgetown University Press, 1994), 118-23.

2. Hans Urs von Balthasar, *Credo: Meditations on the Apostles' Creed* (New York: Crossroad, 1990), 54.

3. Hans Urs von Balthasar, *The Threefold Garland: The World's Salvation in Mary's Prayer* (San Francisco: Ignatius Press, 1982), 99.

4. Charles Krauthammer, "A Social Conservative Credo," *The Public Interest,* Fall 1995, 17.

5. Irving Kristol, "American Conservatism 1945-1995," *The Public Interest,* Fall 1995, 90.

6. John Paul II, Address to the General Assembly of the United Nations Organization, October 5, 1995; the citation is from *Gaudium et Spes,* 16.

7. Ibid.

8. Ibid.

CHAPTER ONE

1. *Redemptor Hominis,* 21, 2.

2. On "deification," see two volumes by Jaroslav Pelikan: *The Emergence of the*

Catholic Tradition, 100-600 (Chicago: University of Chicago Press, 1971), 155, 233-34, and *The Spirit of Eastern Christendom, 600-1700* (Chicago: University of Chicago Press, 1974), 10-12, 14, 34-35, 46, 227, 247, 259-60, 267-68, 290.

3. Dorothy L. Sayers, Introduction to *Dante: The Divine Comedy, Purgatory* (London: Penguin Books, 1955), 37.

4. Office of Readings, December 30; from the treatise "On the Refutation of All Heresies."

5. See Luke 9:28-36 and parallels.

6. Hans Urs von Balthasar, *The Glory of the Lord,* vol. 3: *Studies in Theological Styles —Lay Styles* (San Francisco: Ignatius Press, 1986), 100.

7. See Robin Lane Fox, *Pagans and Christians* (New York: Knopf, 1986).

8. See my study, *The Final Revolution: The Resistance Church and the Collapse of Communism* (New York: Oxford University Press, 1992). For an anecdotal, ecumenical review of this phenomenon, see Barbara von der Heydt, *Candles Behind the Wall* (Grand Rapids, Mich.: Eerdmans, 1993).

9. For a journalistic account of this moral revolution, see Timothy Garton Ash, *The Uses of Adversity* (New York: Vintage Books, 1990).

10. See Acts 2.

11. The Catechism of the Catholic Church discusses this aspect of the basic Christian confession of faith in paragraphs 748-975. The Nicene-Constantinopolitan Creed, which is widely used in the liturgy, includes unity and apostolicity among the distinguishing "marks" of the Church *(". . . unam, sanctam, catholicam, et apostolican Ecclesiam")*.

12. See Ephesians 4:4-6.

13. Charles W. Colson, *The Body* (Dallas: Word, 1992), 68. Questions of ecclesiology are among the most urgent in the new evangelical-Catholic theological dialogue in America. See, for example, Richard John Neuhaus, "The Catholic Difference," in Neuhaus and Charles Colson, eds., *Evangelicals and Catholics Together: Toward a Common Mission* (Dallas: Word, 1995), 175-227.

14. *Gaudium et Spes,* 40:

Proceeding from the love of the eternal Father, the Church was founded by Christ in time and gathered into one by the Holy Spirit. It has a saving and eschatological purpose which can only be fully attained in the next life. But it is now present here on earth and is composed of men; they, the members of the earthly city, are called to form the family of the children of God even in this present history of mankind and to increase it continually until the Lord comes. Made one in view of heavenly benefits and enriched by them, this family has been "constituted and organized as a society in the present world" by Christ, and "provided with means adapted to its visible and social union." Thus the Church, at once "a visible organization and a spiritual community," travels the same journey as all mankind and shares the same earthly lot with the world: it is to be a leaven and, as it were, the soul of human society in its renewal by Christ and transformation into the family of God.

That the earthly city and the heavenly city penetrate one another is a fact open only to the eyes of faith; moreover, it will remain the mystery of human history, which will be harassed by sin until the perfect revelation of the splendor of the sons of God. In pursuing its own salvific purposes not only does the Church communicate divine life to men but in a certain sense it casts the reflected light of that divine life over all the earth, notably in the way it heals and elevates the dignity of the human person, in the way it consoles society, and endows the daily activity of men with a deeper sense and meaning.

15. On this, see Pope John Paul II, Homily at Camden Yards, Baltimore, October 8, 1995.

16. Richard John Neuhaus, Foreword to George Weigel and Robert Royal, eds., *Building the Free Society* (Grand Rapids, Mich.: Eerdmans, 1993), xvi.

17. See Acts 2:13-41.

18. See *Gaudium et Spes,* 16, and the discussion of this point in chapter six below.

19. See William Lee Miller, *The First Liberty: Religion and the American Republic* (New York: Knopf, 1986).

20. Fyodor Dostoevsky, *The Brothers Karamazov,* trans. Richard Pevear and Larissa Volokhonsky (New York: Vintage Books, 1991), 254-55, 256-57.

21. See Dumas Malone, *Jefferson the Virginian* (Boston: Little, Brown, 1948), 188.

22. Instruction on Christian Freedom and Liberation, 44.

23. Richard John Neuhaus, *The Naked Public Square: Religion and Democracy in America* (Grand Rapids, Mich.: Eerdmans, 1984).

24. Robert Bellah, "Civil Religion in America," in *Beyond Belief: Religion in a Post-Traditional World* (New York: Harper and Row, 1970), 168-89.

25. *Redemptoris Missio,* 39.

26. On Nietzsche's analysis of the spiritual crisis of European civilization, see Frederick Copleston, S.J., *A History of Philosophy,* vol. 7 (Westminster, Md: Newman Press, 1963), 390-420.

27. *Gaudium et Spes,* 76.

28. *Gaudium et Spes,* 1.

CHAPTER TWO

1. The phrase, though not the time-frame, is from Raymond E. Brown, *The Churches the Apostles Left Behind* (New York: Paulist Press, 1984).

2. For the text of the letter, see *The Apostolic Fathers,* 2d ed., trans. J. B. Lightfoot and J. R. Hammer, ed. and rev. by Michael W. Holmes (Grand Rapids, Mich.: Baker, 1989), 296-306. To provide patristic warrant for their teaching that "each individual layman must be a witness before the world to the resurrection and life of the Lord Jesus, and a sign of the living God" (*Lumen Gentium,* 38), the Fathers of the Second Vatican Council cited *Diognetus* 6.1. The *Letter to Diognetus* is also referenced three times in the new Catechism of the Catholic Church: on the duties of Christian citizens (2240); on the right to life of the unborn (2271); and on the "public" meaning of the Lord's Prayer as directed to the One who is "in heaven" (2796).

3. *Letter to Diognetus,* 6.1.

4. Ibid., 5.1-10. The author of *Diognetus* goes on to make clear that the "unusual character" of their citizenship had some unusual consequences for Christians:

They love everyone and by everyone they are persecuted. They are unknown, yet they are condemned; they are put to death, yet they are brought to life. They are poor, yet they make many rich; they are in need of everything, yet they abound in everything. They are dishonored, yet they are glorified in their dishonor; they are slandered, yet they are vindicated. They are cursed, yet they bless; they are insulted, yet they offer respect. When they do good, they are punished as evildoers; when they are punished, they rejoice as though brought to life. . . . Those who hate them are unable to give a reason for their hostility. [Ibid.]

5. Catechism of the Catholic Church, 1818, 1817.

6. Hans Urs von Balthasar, "Church and World," in *Truth Is Symphonic: Aspects of Christian Pluralism* (San Francisco: Ignatius Press, 1987), 98.

7. *Letter to Diognetus,* 6.7.

8. See Francis Fukuyama, "The End of History?" *The National Interest* 16 (Summer 1989): 1-18.

9. A temptation that goes back, on some readings of the New Testament evidence, to the original apostolic band. See, for example, Dorothy L. Sayers's portrait of Judas in *The Man Born to Be King* (San Francisco: Ignatius Press, 1990).

10. See Balthasar, "Church and World," 98.

11. Hans Urs von Balthasar, "The Three Forms of Hope," in *Truth is Symphonic,* 190-92.

12. Hans Urs von Balthasar, *The Glory of the Lord,* vol. 1: *Seeing the Form* (San Francisco: Ignatius Press, 1982), 36.

13. Contemplation and action are thus not antinomies. "Contemplation melds into action, or it is not contemplation," according to Balthasar. Cited in Edward T. Oakes, *Pattern of Redemption: The Theology of Hans Urs von Balthasar* (New York: Crossroad, 1994), 147.

14. Thus John Paul II, in the 1991 social encyclical *Centesimus Annus,* asserts that the social doctrine of the Church "is not an ideology" (46) and has been developed "not in order to recover former privileges or to impose [the Church's] own vision" of the right-ordering of politics (53), but as an "indispensable and ideal orientation" (43), a horizon of reflection radiating from the "care and responsibility for man" entrusted to the Church by Christ (53), and thus constituting a "valid instrument for evangelization" (54).

15. Balthasar, "Church and World," 96.

16. Vatican II, *Lumen Gentium,* 1.

17. Cited in Christoph Schönborn, "The Hope of Heaven, the Hope of Earth," *First Things* 52 (April 1995): 32-38.

18. See John Courtney Murray, *We Hold These Truths: Catholic Reflections on the American Proposition* (Garden City, N.J.: Doubleday Image Books, 1964), 43. This point will be developed further in chapter seven below.

19. John Paul II, *Tertio Millennio Adveniente,* 37; on the next century as a "springtime for the Gospel," see *Redemptoris Missio,* 86.

20. John Paul II developed this point further in his 1995 encyclical on ecumenism, *Ut Unum Sint:*

In a theocentric vision, we Christians already have a common martyrology. This also includes the martyrs of our own century, more numerous than one might think, and it shows how, at a profound level, God preserves communion among the baptized in the supreme demand of faith, manifested in the sacrifice of life itself. The fact that one can die for the faith shows that other demands of the faith can also be met. I have already remarked, and with deep joy, how an imperfect but real communion is preserved and is growing at many levels of ecclesial life. I now add that this communion is *already* perfect in what we all consider the highest point of the life of grace, *martyria* unto death, the truest communion possible with Christ who shed his blood, and by that sacrifice brings near those who once were far off (cf. Ephesians 2:13). [*Ut Unum Sint*, 84, emphasis added]

21. On martyrdom as the "form" of discipleship, see John Paul II, *Veritatis Splendor*, 90-94.

22. Vatican Council II, *Gaudium et Spes*, 22.

23. John Paul II, Homily at Camden Yards, Baltimore, October 8, 1995.

24. See Richard John Neuhaus, "Joshing Richard Rorty," *First Things* 8 (December 1990): 14-24.

25. The Deists among the Founding Fathers were not, for example, overly concerned about the world's redemption. But as the bishops of the United States argued at the Third Plenary Council of Baltimore in 1884, the American Founders built better than they knew. Or, as John Courtney Murray put it three-quarters of a century later, the success of the American democratic experiment rested, not on the thin epistemological and anthropological foundations of "eighteenth century individualistic rationalism," but on the moral culture of a people who had "learned [their] own personal dignity in the school of Christian faith," whether they recognized that patrimony or not. (See Murray, *We Hold These Truths*, 45, 50.)

The American democratic experiment, like every other one, depends for its legitimation on warrants it cannot produce in and of itself. For all the inadequacies of their philosophical position, the Founders still knew that they had to give an account of their actions, before "nature's God" and in honor of "a decent respect to the opinions of mankind" (as they put it in the Declaration of Independence). The peculiar danger of our present circumstance is the denial, by philosophers and political theorists, of the very possibility of such warrants and such an account. This point will be pursued further in the next chapter.

26. On this point, see Richard John Neuhaus, "Can Atheists Be Good Citizens?" *First Things* 15 (August/September 1991): 17-21. (Reprinted in Richard John Neuhaus and George Weigel, eds., *Being Christian Today: An American Conversation* [Washington: Ethics and Public Policy Center, 1992].)

27. See Balthasar, "Church and World," 96.

28. Ibid.

29. See ibid.

30. See John Paul II, Address to the General Assembly of the United Nations, October 5, 1995. See also my essay, "Are Human Rights Still Universal?" *Commentary*, February 1995, 41-45. For a reflection on how this problem asserts itself in U.N. fora today, see Mary Ann Glendon, "What Happened at Beijing," *First Things* 59 (January 1996), 30-36.

31. *Letter to Diognetus*, 7.4.

32. The defense of religious freedom, viewed from this angle, is thus an expression of the Church's commitment to what in Roman Catholic terms has come to be understood as the core social-ethical principle of *subsidiarity*.

33. In his homily at Camden Yards, Baltimore, on October 8, 1995, Pope John Paul II cited this as "the basic question before a democratic society."

34. Thus the Church's contesting for genuine pluralism becomes, in these circumstances, an expression of the Church's commitment to what in Roman Catholic terms has become known as the core social-ethical principle of *solidarity*.

35. Catechism of the Catholic Church, 1913.

36. This was empirically demonstrated at the 1994 Cairo World Conference on Population and the 1995 Beijing World Conference on Women, where a populist Church challenged the plans of an international cultural-bureaucratic elite to impose a certain construal of human sexuality on the entire world in the name of feminist ideologies that have little or nothing to do with how 95 per cent of the world's women actually live.

37. See, for example, section five of *Centesimus Annus*, "State and Culture."

38. Francis Fukuyama, *Trust: The Social Virtues and the Creation of Prosperity* (New York: The Free Press, 1995), 11. For a fuller discussion of this proposal, see my essay, "Capitalism for Humans," *Commentary*, October 1995, 34-38.

CHAPTER THREE

1. Robert L. Wilken, *The Christians as the Romans Saw Them* (New Haven: Yale University Press, 1984).

2. Cited in Christoph Schönborn, "The Hope of Heaven, the Hope of Earth," *First Things* 52 (April 1995): 32-38.

3. See Russell Hittinger, "The Supreme Court v. Religion," *Crisis*, May 1993, 22-30, and Nathan Lewin, "The Church-State Game: A Symposium on *Kiryas Joel*," *First Things* 47 (November 1994): 39-40.

4. H. L. Mencken, no orthodox Christian, assayed another withering critique of liberal theology in his obituary column in praise of the intellectual consistency of the Presbyterian fundamentalist J. Gresham Machen:

[Machen] fell out with the reformers who, in late years, have been trying to convert the Presbyterian Church into a kind of literary and social club, devoted vaguely to good works. . . .

It is my belief, as a friendly neutral in all such high and ghostly matters, that the body of doctrine known as Modernism is completely incompatible, not only with anything rationally describable as Christianity, but also with anything deserving to pass as religion in general. Religion, if it is to retain any genuine significance, can never be reduced to a series of sweet attitudes, possible to anyone not actually in jail for felony. It is, on the contrary, a corpus of powerful and profound convictions, many of them not open to logical analysis. . . .

What the Modernists have done . . . [is] to get rid of all the logical difficulties of religion, and yet preserve a generally pious cast of mind. It is a vain enterprise. What they have left, once they have achieved their imprudent scavenging, is hardly more than a row of hollow platitudes, as empty [of] psychological force and effect as so many nursery rhymes. [H. L. Mencken, "Dr. Fundamentalis," Baltimore *Evening Sun*, January 18, 1937]

5. See Jacques Maritain, *Christianity and Democracy* (San Francisco: Ignatius Press, 1986).

6. Cited in Richard Wightman Fox, *Reinhold Niebuhr: A Biography* (New York: Pantheon Books, 1985), 219.

7. See the essay "John Courtney Murray and the Catholic Human Rights Revolution," in my *Catholicism and the Renewal of American Democracy* (New York: Paulist Press, 1989).

8. On this point, see John Courtney Murray, *We Hold These Truths: Catholic Reflections on the American Proposition* (Garden City, N.J.: Doubleday Image Books, 1964), 39-85.

9. See my study *The Final Revolution* (New York: Oxford University Press, 1992), chapter five, for a detailed examination of this process.

10. See Schönborn, "The Hope of Heaven," 34.

11. C. S. Lewis, "The Weight of Glory," in *The Weight of Glory and Other Addresses* (New York: Macmillan, 1990), 19.

12. See chapter two of my book *The Final Revolution*.

13. See Richard John Neuhaus, "What the Fundamentalists Want," *Commentary*, May 1985, 43.

14. Murray, *We Hold These Truths*, 34.

15. For more on plurality/pluralism, with special reference to church/state questions, see my essay "Achieving Disagreement: From Indifference to Pluralism," *This World* 24 (Winter 1989): 54-63.

16. Richard John Neuhaus, "Can Atheists Be Good Citizens?" *First Things* 15 (August/September 1991): 21. (Reprinted in Richard John Neuhaus and George Weigel, eds., *Being Christian Today: An American Conversation* [Washington: Ethics and Public Policy Center, 1992].)

17. Ibid., 20.

18. Ibid.

19. Richard John Neuhaus, "The Public Square," *First Things* 42 (April 1994): 67.

20. See Alasdair MacIntyre, *After Virtue* (Notre Dame: University of Notre Dame Press, 1981).

21. On this point, see Richard John Neuhaus, "The Truth About Freedom," *Wall Street Journal*, October 8, 1993.

22. See ibid.

23. James Madison, "To the Honorable the General Assembly of the Commonwealth of Virginia: A Memorial and Remonstrance," in William Lee Miller, *The First Liberty: Religion and the American Republic*, appendix 2 (New York: Knopf, 1986), 359-64.

24. As John Paul II put it in *Tertio Millennio Adveniente*:

Another painful chapter of history to which the sons and daughters of the Church must return with a spirit of repentance is that of the acquiescence given, especially in certain centuries, to intolerance and even the use of violence in the service of truth.

It is true than an accurate historical judgment cannot prescind from careful study of the cultural conditioning of the times, as a result of which many people may have held in good faith that an authentic witness to truth could include suppressing the opinions of others or at least paying no attention to them. Many factors frequently converged to create assumptions which justified intolerance and fostered an emotional climate from which only great spirits, truly free and filled with God, were in some way able to break free. Yet the consideration of mitigating factors does not exonerate the Church from the obligation to express profound regret for the weaknesses of so many of her sons and daughters who sullied her face, preventing her from fully mirroring the image of her crucified Lord, the supreme witness of patient love and humble meekness. From these painful moments of the past a lesson can be drawn for the future, leading all Christians to adhere fully to the sublime principle stated by the [Second Vatican] Council [in *Dignitatis Humanae,* 1]: "The truth cannot impose itself except by virtue of its own truth, as it wins over the mind with both gentleness and power." [35]

25. Justices Kennedy, O'Connor, and Souter, in *Casey* v. *Planned Parenthood of Southeastern Pennsylvania,* 112 Sup. Ct. 2791 (1992), at 2807.

26. On this point, see the editorial "Abortion and a Nation at War," *First Things* 26 (October 1992): 9-13.

CHAPTER FOUR

1. On the origins of the religious new right, see Michael Cromartie, ed., *No Longer Exiles* (Washington: Ethics and Public Policy Center, 1993). On the concept of a "defensive offensive," see Nathan Glazer, "Fundamentalists: A Defensive Offensive," in Richard John Neuhaus and Michael Cromartie, eds., *Piety and Politics* (Washington: Ethics and Public Policy Center, 1987).

2. On this and other examples of the battering of Catholicism and its representatives in recent years, see my essay "The New Anti-Catholicism," *Commentary,* June 1992, 25-31.

3. On the question of the academy and religion, see Robert L. Wilken, "Who Will Speak *for* the Religious Traditions?" in Wilken, *Remembering the Christian Past* (Grand Rapids, Mich.: Eerdmans, 1995), 1-23.

4. See Stephen L. Carter, *The Culture of Disbelief* (New York: Basic Books, 1993), and Richard John Neuhaus, *The Naked Public Square: Religion and Democracy in America.* (Grand Rapids, Mich.: Eerdmans, 1984).

5. The White House, Office of the Press Secretary, "Remarks by the President at Signing Ceremony for the Religious Freedom Restoration Act," November 16, 1993.

6. President Clinton's comments at the signing of RFRA and on other occasions were in sharp contrast to the discomforts that President Bush experienced in publicly acknowledging religious faith. Some will attribute this, and not without reason, to the cultural differences between Kennebunkport Episcopalians and Little Rock Baptists. But even Bush's most ardent admirers would have to concede that he was, to put it bluntly, terrified by the "religion issue," which he seemed to regard as an expression of the "right-wing agenda stuff" he reportedly deplored. Most memorably, during the 1988 primaries, Bush, asked to recall what he was thinking about when he was floating alone in the Pacific after his plane had been shot down by the Japanese, replied that he had thought about "Mom and Dad, about our country, about God . . . and about the separation of church and state."

At the 1995 Christian Coalition "Road to Victory Conference," held in Washington, D.C., Ralph Reed characterized President Clinton's appeal to religious language and imagery as less a matter of the bully pulpit than of "the pulpit of bull." (See the *New York Times,* September 9, 1995, p. A9.) There is an element of (obvious) truth here, although the protestations of piety from many Republican presidential aspirants at the Christian Coalition consistory in September 1995 were surely susceptible to a similar criticism. In the case of President Clinton, I think that the religious language and imagery used is genuine but sorely lacking in follow-through at the level of policy and personnel.

7. See John Courtney Murray, *We Hold These Truths: Catholic Reflections on the American Proposition* (Garden City, N.J.: Doubleday Image Books, 1964), 126.

8. See John Paul II, *Veritatis Splendor,* 38-53.

9. See ibid., 6-27, in which John Paul reflects on the gospel story of Jesus and the rich young man who wants to know what he must do to be saved.

10. See John Paul II, *Evangelium Vitae,* 62. As we saw above in chapter two, the *Letter to Diognetus* witnesses to the ancient character of this Christian conviction.

11. See "The Homosexual Movement: A Statement by the Ramsey Colloquium," in *First Things* 41 (March 1994): 15-20.

12. See my essay " 'Rights' Are Not Always Trumps," *Los Angeles Times,* September 15, 1992.

13. This schema will be explored in more detail in chapter seven.

14. See Terry Eastland, ed., *Religious Liberty in the Supreme Court* (Grand Rapids, Mich.: Ethics and Public Policy Center/Eerdmans, 1995), 213-33.

15. See Mary Ann Glendon and Raul F. Yanas, "Structural Free Exercise," *Michigan Law Review* 90 (December 1991): 477-550.

16. See Richard John Neuhaus, "A New Order of Religious Freedom," *First Things* 20 (February 1992): 13-17.

17. See Irving Kristol, "The Coming Conservative Century," *Wall Street Journal,* February 1, 1993; reprinted in Michael Cromartie, ed., *Disciples and Democracy: Religious Conservatives and the Future of American Politics* (Grand Rapids, Mich.: Ethics and Public Policy Center/Eerdmans, 1994).

18. See Mary Ann Glendon, *Rights-Talk* (New York: Free Press, 1991).

Chapter Five

1. On the Rhapsodic Theater, see Bolesław Taborski, Introduction to Karol Wojtyła, *The Collected Plays and Writings on Theater* (Berkeley: University of California Press, 1987), 1-16.

2. On the Pope's role in the Cairo affair, see my essay "What Really Happened at Cairo, and Why," in Michael Cromartie, ed., *The Nine Lives of Population Control* (Grand Rapids, Mich.: Ethics and Public Policy Center/Eerdmans, 1995).

3. *Redemptor Hominis,* 8, citing *Gaudium et Spes,* 22.

4. Tad Szulc, *John Paul II: The Biography* (New York: Simon and Schuster, 1995).

5. See George Huntston Williams, *The Mind of John Paul II: Origins of His Thought and Action* (New York: Seabury, 1981), 7.

6. Aleksandr Solzhenitsyn, "Men Have Forgotten God," *National Review,* July 22, 1983.

7. *Tertio Millennio Adveniente,* 4; the citation is from *Gaudium et Spes,* 22.

8. See Kenneth L. Schmitz, *At the Center of the Human Drama* (Washington: Catholic University of America Press, 1993).

9. See Richard John Neuhaus, *The Catholic Moment* (San Francisco: Harper & Row, 1987), 284.

10. *Tertio Millennio Adveniente,* 36.

11. Ibid., 37.

12. Ibid., 24.

13. Ibid., 55.

14. The universality of basic human rights was a key theme in the Pope's address to the United Nations General Assembly on October 5, 1995.

15. Richard John Neuhaus, "That They May Be One," *First Things* 56 (October 1995): 74.

16. Cited in *L'Osservatore Romano,* English weekly edition, June 28, 1995, 11.

CHAPTER SIX

1. From *Mirari Vos,* as cited and discussed in Roger Aubert et al., *History of the Church,* vol. 8: *The Church Between Revolution and Restoration* (New York: Crossroad, 1981), 286-92. The historical and sociological context of Gregory XVI's condemnation is well summarized by Rodger Charles, S.J.:

> Gregory XVI was a temporal ruler faced with a revolt in his own dominions, a revolt which was in the name of a liberalism which . . . was in practice anti-clerical and anti-Christian. . . . The Pope could not accept state indifferentism in matters of religion, nor grant liberty of conscience while these implied positive anti-clerical and anti-Christian attitudes. Liberty of the press and separation of the Church and the state were likewise rejected absolutely because of their secularist implications. *This was the essence of the papal dilemma: popes, as vicars of Christ, could hardly recommend policies which, if put into practice in their own states, would link them [i.e., the popes] with men and ideas both anti-clerical and anti-religious.* Only when the question of temporal power of the papacy had been solved . . . could the situation satisfactorily be resolved. [*The Social Teaching of Vatican II* (San Francisco: Ignatius Press, 1982), 239, emphasis added]

2. For a portrait of Pius IX that usefully complexifies many of the regnant stereotypes, see E. E. Y. Hales, *Pio Nono: A Study in European Politics and Religion in the Nineteenth Century* (London: Eyre & Spottiswoode, 1954).

3. The Holy See was not alone in this judgment, though the logic of concern varied from institution to institution. See Henry A. Kissinger, *A World Restored: Metternich, Castlereagh and the Problems of Peace, 1812-1822* (Boston: Houghton Mifflin, 1973).

4. For a discussion of this point, see John Courtney Murray, *We Hold These Truths: Catholic Reflections on the American Proposition* (Garden City, N.J.: Doubleday Image Books, 1964), 40 ff.

The danger in question was encapsulated in the Abbe Sieyes's defense of the replacement of the old States-General by the revolutionary National Assembly: "The nation exists before all, it is the origin of everything, it is the law itself." Cited by Conor Cruise O'Brien in "A Lost Chance to Save the Jews?" (*New York Review of Books,* April 27, 1989, 27). O'Brien correctly identifies the Jacobin current as the forerunner of twentieth-century totalitarianism, and chillingly cites the German theologian Gerhard Kittel (a "moderate"), who wrote in 1933, in *Die Jüdenfrage,* that "'Justice' is not an abstraction but something which grows out of the blood and soil and history of a *Volk."* O'Brien could, of course, have cited any number of Leninist *mots* to this effect, too.

Murray was not inclined to back off this hard judgment on the Jacobin tradition in the wake of the new "spirit of Vatican II." Thus, in a 1966 commentary on the evolution of the Declaration on Religious Freedom *(Dignitatis Humanae),* he condemned

> ... that desire to deny and destroy the past which was the very essence of Enlightenment rationalism (whereby it aroused the bitter antipathy, for instance, of Edmund Burke). What appeared on the surface . . . was not progress but simply revolution. Society as civil was not simply being differentiated from society as religious; the two societies were being violently separated, and civil society was being stripped of all religious substance. The order of civil law and political jurisdiction was not simply being differentiated from the order of moral law and ecclesiastical jurisdiction; a complete rupture was made between the two orders of law and the two authorities, and they were set at hostile variance, each with the other. Society and the state were not invested with their due secularity; they were roughly clothed in the alien garments of continental laicism. [John Courtney Murray, "The Declaration on Religious Freedom," in J. Leon Hooper, S.J., ed., *Bridging the Sacred and the Secular* (Washington: Georgetown University Press, 1994), 191]

5. Pope Pius VII (1800-23) was something of a countercase. Despite his personal suffering at the hands of Napoleon, Pius VII was not so thoroughly soured on the liberal political project as his successors Leo XII, Gregory XVI, and Pius IX. As Cardinal Luigi Barnaba Chiaramonti, Pius VII was a compromise candidate at the conclave of 1800, but one who had shown his moderate colors at Christmas 1797, when he shocked his conservative congregants with a sermon in which he declared there was no necessary conflict between Christianity and democracy. As pope, Pius VII and his secretary of state, the brilliant Cardinal Ercole Consalvi, tried to "blend administrative, judicial, and financial reforms on the liberal French model with the antiquated papal system"—an effort at cross-breeding that "exasperated reactionaries and progressives alike, and led to serious revolts" (J. N. D. Kelly, *The Oxford Dictionary of Popes* [Oxford: Oxford University Press, 1986], 302-4). Pius VII's modest reforms were rolled back by his successor Leo XII (1823-29), who also took up again the rhetorical cudgels against liberalism. Thus ended what might be called the Chiaramonti/Consalvi experiment in rapprochement between Roman Catholicism and the liberalizing political reforms of the day. For the next fifty years, retrenchment would dominate Vatican policy, and the notion of conservative reform pioneered by Pius VII and Consalvi would fall by the wayside.

6. See Owen Chadwick, *The Secularization of the European Mind in the 19th Century* (Cambridge: Cambridge University Press, 1975).

7. It is worth noting that these were the two conciliar documents on which the archbishop of Kraków, Karol Wojtyła, worked most intensively during the third and fourth periods of Vatican II.

8. Arthur Schlesinger, Sr., once told the dean of American Catholic historians, John Tracy Ellis, that "I regard the prejudice against your Church as the deepest bias in the history of the American people." Cited in John Tracy Ellis, *American Catholicism*, 2d ed., rev. (Chicago: University of Chicago Press, 1969), 151. Some Mormons might contest the claim that the U.S. government had never conducted an overt program of religious persecution.

9. "Cardinal Gibbons on Church and State," in John Tracy Ellis, ed., *Documents of American Catholic History*, vol. 2 (Wilmington: Michael Glazier, 1987), 462-63 (emphasis added).

10. Gerald P. Fogarty, S.J., *The Vatican and the American Hierarchy from 1870 to 1965* (Wilmington: Michael Glazier, 1985), 41.

11. *Longinqua Oceani*, in Ellis, *Documents of American Catholic History*, vol. 2, 502.

12. See Anthony Rhodes, *The Vatican in the Age of the Dictators, 1922-1945* (New York: Holt, Rinehart and Winston, 1973), 14-15.

13. See Jacques Maritain, *Christianity and Democracy* (San Francisco: Ignatius Press, 1986). Maritain had an interesting historical perspective on the events through which he was living, in exile in the United States:

> We are looking on at the liquidation of what is known as the "modern world" which ceased to be modern a quarter of a century ago when the First World War marked its entry into the past. The question is: in what will this liquidation result? . . . [T]he tremendous historical fund of energy and truth accumulated for centuries is still available to human freedom, the forces of renewal are on the alert and it is still up to us to make sure that this catastrophe of the modern world is not a regression to a perverted aping of the Ancient Regime or of the Middle Ages and that it does not wind up in the totalitarian putrefaction of the German New Order. It is up to us rather to see that it emerges in a new and truly creative age, where man, in suffering and hope, will resume his journey toward the conquest of freedom. [Pp. 11, 17]

14. The divisions in pre-war French society are well captured, in fictional form, in Piers Paul Read, *The Free Frenchman* (New York: Ivy Books, 1986).

15. Note also the connection between these national Christian Democratic movements and the movement for West European integration that eventually led to the Common Market and the European Parliament. This raises an interesting question in terms of the debate, in the 1990s, over the future of European integration. Post–World War II Christian Democratic parties in western Europe have traditionally been "pro-European." Will this position be sustainable as the institutions of the European Community show themselves as susceptible to gross bureaucratization and ideological manipulation as the institutions of the United Nations? The new democracies of east central Europe are also raising interesting questions about the use of "Christian" in the name of a political party or faction.

16. Cited in Joseph A. Komonchak, "Subsidiarity in the Church: The State of the Question," *The Jurist* 48 (1988): 299.

17. Is there a connection between the principle of subsidiarity and the American

concept of federalism here? It would be going considerably out of bounds to suggest that Madison's concept of federalism, as suggested in *Federalist 10* and *Federalist 51,* was informed by the classic Catholic social theory that eventually evolved the principle of subsidiarity; Madison should not be taken as a kind of proto–Pius XI. Indeed, *Federalist 10* and *Federalist 51* endorse decentralized decision-making not as an expression of human possibility, but as a remedy for human defects (the defect of faction). On the other hand, one can argue that federal arrangements (irrespective of their political-philosophical rationale) are one possible expression, in history, of the principle of subsidiarity. One could possibly go further and suggest that the principle of subsidiarity establishes a firmer moral-cultural and indeed philosophical foundation for federal arrangements than Madison's "let a thousand factions bloom" (so to speak) so that no one of them may become oppressively dominant. Grounded as it is in an ontology of the person that links *being* and *acting,* and that regards human community as rooted in the social nature of the human person, the principle of subsidiarity might provide a more satisfactory basis for federalism than the voluntarism with which Madison is (wrongfully, in my view) often charged, but of which some of his successors in American political theory (principally the "progressivist" historians of the Parrington/Beard school) are surely guilty.

18. These definitions, as well as the schema above, are adapted from Komonchak, "Subsidiarity in the Church."

19. On the Königswinter Circle, see Franz H. Mueller, *The Church and the Social Question* (Washington: American Enterprise Institute, 1984), 116-17.

20. On this distinction between the two encyclicals, cf. Mueller, *The Church and the Social Question,* 114.

21. See George Weigel, "John Courtney Murray and the Catholic Human Rights Revolution," *This World* 15 (Fall 1986): 14-27.

22. For a detailed examination of the Murray/Fenton/Connell controversy, see Donald Pelotte, *John Courtney Murray: Theologian in Conflict* (New York: Paulist Press, 1975).

23. *Dignitatis Humanae,* 2.

24. *Gaudium et Spes,* 16.

25. *Veritatis Splendor,* 58.

26. Thus *Dignitatis Humanae:*

It is in accordance with their dignity that all men, because they are persons, that is, beings endowed with reason and free will and therefore bearing personal responsibility, are both impelled by their nature and bound by a moral obligation to seek the truth, especially religious truth. They are also bound to adhere to the truth once they come to know it and [to] direct their whole lives in accordance with the demands of truth. But men cannot satisfy this obligation in a way that is in keeping with their own nature unless they enjoy both psychological freedom and immunity from external coercion. Therefore *the right of religious freedom has its foundation not in the subjective attitude of the individual but in his very nature.* For this reason the right to this immunity continues to exist even in those who do not live up to their obligation of seeking the truth and adhering to it. The exercise of this right cannot be interfered with as long as the just requirements of public order are observed. [2, emphasis added]

27. Ibid.

28. Chief among these "prior" social institutions and the fundamental values they incarnate are what Murray called the *res sacrae in temporalibus,* those "sacred things in man's secular life" of which the Church had been the traditional guardian:

> . . . man's relation to God and to the Church, the inner unity of human personality as citizen and Christian but one man, the integrity of the human body, the husband-wife relationship, the political obligation, the moral values inherent in economic and cultural activity as aspects of human life, the works of justice and charity which are the necessary expressions of the Christian and human spirit, and finally that patrimony of ideas which are the basis of civilized life—the ideas of law and right, of political power and the obligations of citizenship, of property, etc. [John Courtney Murray, "Paul Blanshard and the New Nativism," *The Month* [new series] 5, no. 4 (April 1951): 224]

29. And in the further sense that, should a democracy "subtract" such basic human rights as religious freedom from its roster of essential constitutional and/or legal protections for the human person, that state would cease to be a democracy in any morally meaningful sense of the term: as was made manifest by the spurious "people's democracies" of the late Warsaw Pact.

30. Murray summed up the personal/public connection in *Dignitatis Humanae* in these words:

> The foundation of the [human and civil right to free exercise of religion] . . . is the truth of human dignity. The object of the right—freedom from coercion in religious matters—is the first debt due in justice to the human person. The final motive for respect of the right is a love [or] appreciation of the personal dignity of man. Religious freedom itself is [thus] the first of all freedoms in a well-organized society, without which no other human and civil freedoms can be safe. [Murray, "The Declaration on Religious Freedom," 199]

31. John Courtney Murray, S.J., "The Issue of Church and State at Vatican Council II," *Theological Studies* 27, no. 4 (December 1966): 586.

32. For a fuller discussion of the Instruction, and references, see my *Tranquillitas Ordinis: The Present Failure and Future Promise of American Catholic Thought on War and Peace* (New York: Oxford University Press, 1987), 291ff.

33. Instruction on Certain Aspects of the "Theology of Liberation," 17.

34. Instruction on Christian Freedom and Liberation, 95.

35. *Sollicitudo Rei Socialis,* 16.

36. Ibid., 44.

37. Ibid. (emphasis added).

38. Ibid.

39. Cited in *New York Times,* April 6, 1987.

40. Cited in *Origins* 17, no. 15 (25 September 1987).

41. John Paul returned to this Actonian theme in his 1995 pastoral pilgrimage to the United States; see his homily at the papal Mass at Camden Yards and his remarks at the Cathedral of Mary Our Queen in Baltimore, October 8, 1995.

42. See John Paul II, *Centesimus Annus,* chapter three, "The Year 1989."

43. *Centesimus Annus,* 46.

44. *Evangelium Vitae,* 18.
45. Ibid.
46. *Evangelium Vitae,* 20.
47. I am indebted for this analysis to Russell Hittinger.

CHAPTER SEVEN

1. Francis Fukuyama, "The End of History?" *The National Interest* 16 (Summer 1989): 16. Fukuyama has refined his position and now argues that the replenishment of "social capital" is essential to the survival of democracy and the market. See his 1995 book *Trust: The Social Virtues and the Creation of Prosperity* (Free Press).

2. A brief interpolation: I do not mean to argue here, in the manner of the unrepentant left and the isolationist/libertarian right, that since Communism would eventually have failed anyway, containment (and its revivification by Ronald Reagan, Margaret Thatcher, and Helmut Kohl) was unnecessary and wasteful. The grave "anthropological" errors of Communism would ultimately have led to the failure of the Communist experiment in social engineering. But absent containment, the immense human suffering that Communism caused would have been extended even further, and the demise of the Communist system would have been delayed long into the future. Communism collapsed when it did, and the way it did, because of the intersection (and interaction) of Western foreign and military policies with a moral-cultural revolution that made possible the re-creation of civil society in central and eastern Europe.

3. Rocco Buttiglione, "The Free Economy and the Free Man," in George Weigel, ed., *A New Worldly Order: John Paul II and Human Freedom* (Washington: Ethics and Public Policy Center, 1992), 70.

4. *Casey v. Planned Parenthood of Southeastern Pennsylvania,* 112 Sup. Ct. 2791, at 2807.

5. Ibid.

6. The concept of a "narrow infinity" is a variant on G. K. Chesterton's description of the "madman":

> His mind moves in a perfect but narrow circle. A small circle is quite as infinite as a large circle; but, though it is quite as infinite, it is not so large. . . . There is such a thing as a narrow universality; there is such a thing as a small and cramped eternity; you may see it in many modern religions. [*Orthodoxy* (New York: Doubleday Image Books, 1959), 20]

Including, I might add, the religion that worships the imperial autonomous Self.

7. Hans Urs von Balthasar, *A Theology of History* (San Francisco: Ignatius Press, 1994), 133. And here, too, in this matter of the interior structure of freedom, we may be reminded that Christians are a people "ahead of time":

> . . . for the Christian [the] freedom [brought about by the messianic intervention in history] is already present. It is present in a fullness that can never be improved upon, and human progress can proceed now only in reference to this being-at-hand *(parousia)* of the Last, the Absolute, the *eschaton* of history. No upward advance can ever even draw near to that, let alone catch it up and pass it. . . . There can,

therefore, be no question of a convergence or harmonizing of the history of the world and the history of the Kingdom; but as the parable says, the wheat and the tares grow *together,* because the increasing responsibility toward himself of historical, cultural man, and the increasing responsibility toward God of the believers who administer the inheritance of Christ both equally lead to ever-sharper alternatives and decisions. [139-40]

John Paul and Balthasar seem agreed that the eschatological horizon of Christian faith creates a singular Christian optic on history (and thus on politics and economics). But while Balthasar stresses the parallel growth of "wheat and tares," John Paul's emphasis in *Centesimus Annus* and elsewhere seems to be on the post-Christendom Church as a leaven in the world, witnessing to the relationship between the "truth about man" and the exercise of freedom, and thus helping build a culture of freedom and a civilization of love.

8. *Centesimus Annus,* 4. John Paul refers here to the "new conception of society and of the State, and consequently of authority itself" that emerged in the French Revolution. One of the intriguing aspects of *Centesimus Annus,* however, is the way in which the Pope's reflection on the free society at the end of the twentieth century tacitly brings the American revolutionary experience of 1776—which was, as we have seen, a different expression of the eighteenth-century quest for freedom—into the dialogue.

9. Ibid.

10. Ibid.

11. Ibid., 6.

12. Ibid., 8.

13. Ibid., 11.

14. Ibid., 29.

15. Ibid.

16. Ibid.

17. Ibid., 43.

18. Ibid.

19. Ibid., 13.

20. Ibid., 19.

21. See my book *The Final Revolution* (New York: Oxford University Press, 1992), chapters three and four, for the dramatic (and yet subtly executed) difference John Paul II made in the *Ostpolitik* of the Holy See.

22. *Centesimus Annus,* 22.

23. Ibid., 23.

24. Ibid., 24.

25. Ibid.

26. Ibid.

27. On the role of these various factors in 1989, see my book *The Final Revolution,* chapter one.

28. *Centesimus Annus,* 25.

29. Ibid., 42.

30. As, for example, Michael Novak has argued in *The Spirit of Democratic Capitalism* (New York: Simon and Schuster, 1982) and *The Catholic Ethic and the Spirit of Capitalism* (New York: Free Press, 1993).

31. *Centesimus Annus,* 32.

32. Ibid.

33. Ibid., 48.

34. Ibid., 32. The Pope continues:

Man's intelligence enables him to discover the earth's productive potential and the many different ways in which human needs can be satisfied. It is his disciplined work in close collaboration with others that makes possible the creation of ever more extensive *working communities* which can be relied upon to transform natural and human environments. Important virtues are involved in this process, such as diligence, industriousness, prudence in undertaking reasonable risks, reliability and fidelity in interpersonal relationships, as well as courage in carrying out decisions which are difficult and painful but necessary, both for the overall working of a business and in meeting possible setbacks.

35. Ibid., 26.

36. See Richard John Neuhaus, *Doing Well and Doing Good: The Challenge to the Christian Capitalist* (New York: Doubleday, 1992).

37. *Centesimus Annus,* 24. This section of the encyclical follows the Pope's dissection of the failures of Marxist economics, and thus constitutes another challenge to the "materialistic" interpretation of 1989.

38. Ibid., 36.

39. Ibid., 39.

40. Ibid., 36.

41. Ibid., 48. It would not offend against charity to suggest that this critique has not been seriously engaged by the major Catholic social-welfare agencies in the United States.

42. Ibid.

43. See Alexis de Tocqueville, *Democracy in America,* trans. George Lawrence, ed. J. P. Mayer (New York: Harper & Row, 1966), 513-24.

44. *Centesimus Annus,* 36.

45. Ibid.

46. Ibid., 46.

47. Ibid.

48. Ibid., 47.

49. John Courtney Murray, *We Hold These Truths: Catholic Reflections on the American Proposition* (New York: Doubleday Image Books, 1964), 47.

50. Ibid., 25.

51. Ibid., 40.

52. Ibid., 43.

53. See ibid., 45.

54. Ibid.

55. Ibid.

56. Ibid., 46.

57. Ibid., 47.

58. Ibid.

59. Ibid., 48.

CHAPTER EIGHT

1. Václav Havel, "A Call for Sacrifice," *Foreign Affairs* 73:2, 4.

2. *Centesimus Annus,* 41.

3. Milton Friedman, "Goods in Conflict?" in George Weigel, ed., *A New Worldly Order* (Washington: Ethics and Public Policy Center, 1992), 75-77.

4. *Centesimus Annus,* 41.

5. The same question is asked, of course, though rarely so politely, about the religious new right in American politics.

6. *Centesimus Annus,* 46.

7. *Redemptoris Missio,* 39.

8. Alasdair MacIntyre, *After Virtue* (Notre Dame: University of Notre Dame Press, 1984), 1.

9. Ibid., 245.

10. Ibid.

11. Václav Havel, "The Power of the Powerless," in Havel et al., *The Power of the Powerless: Citizens Against the State in Central Eastern Europe* (Armonk, N.Y.: M. E. Sharpe, 1990), 30.

12. Ibid., 31.

13. Timothy Garton Ash, *The Uses of Adversity: Essays on the Fate of Central Europe* (New York: Random, 1989), 48.

14. Havel, "The Power of the Powerless," 81.

15. Václav Benda, "Catholicism and Politics," in Havel et al., *The Power of the Powerless,* 117.

16. John Courtney Murray, *We Hold These Truths: Catholic Reflections on the American Proposition* (Garden City, N.J.: Doubleday Image Books, 1964), 53.

17. See Zbigniew Brzezinski, *Out of Control: Global Turmoil on the Eve of the 21st Century* (New York: Scribner's, 1993).

18. *Veritatis Splendor,* 96.

19. *Gaudium et Spes,* 27.

20. *Veritatis Splendor,* 97.

21. Ibid.

22. See James T. Burtchaell, *Rachel Weeping* (San Franciso: Harper & Row, 1982), 151, 153.

23. Ibid., 236.

24. The author of the article on "Ethics" in the *Encyclopaedia Britannica,* the Australian philosopher Peter Singer, makes plain his disagreement with John Paul's "sanctity of life" ethic and proposes substituting a "quality of life" ethic in *Re-thinking Life and Death: The Collapse of Our Traditional Ethics* (New York: St. Martin's Press, 1994). But Singer's analysis never begins to grapple with the implications for a law-governed democracy of a private right to lethal violence, exercised in a license to abortion and/or euthanasia. Nor does Singer address the question of what it means for the culture of democracy when one group within society claims the right to determine whether another (individual or group) enjoys a "quality of life" sufficient to warrant its being "counted" within the community of the commonly protected. In the 1920s, the proponents of this view were at least more honest about calling their project by its rightful name: eugenics.

25. "Creative destruction" was one of the chief dynamics of capitalism analyzed by Joseph Schumpeter. The issue here is how to prevent creative destruction from becoming destructive destruction.

26. See Brzezinski, *Out of Control,* for an analysis of the link between decadence at home and irresponsibility abroad.

27. *Centesimus Annus,* 44.

28. *Veritatis Splendor,* 101.

29. *Centesimus Annus,* 46.

30. See Samuel Huntington, "Democracy's Third Wave," *Journal of Democracy* 2, no. 2 (April 1994): 12-34.

31. Kishore Mahbubani, "The United States: 'Go East, Young Man,'" *The Washington Quarterly* 17, no. 2 (Spring 1994): 6.

32. Charles Krauthammer, "Defining Deviancy Up," *The New Republic,* November 22, 1993, 20.

33. *Veritatis Splendor,* 103-4.

34. *Veritatis Splendor,* 95.

35. Ibid.

36. The following description of the "open Church" draws on concepts first articulated in "Religion and Democracy," the foundational document of the Institute on Religion and Democracy. "Religion and Democracy" was drafted by Richard John Neuhaus in 1981 and revised by me in 1991, in both instances prior to being approved by the Institute board.

Index of Names

NOTE: *In addition to proper names, the following topics are included in this index: abortion, culture war, euthanasia, homosexuality, human rights, just-war tradition, liberation theology, natural law, pro-life movement, religious freedom, subsidiarity.*